ISBN 978-1-331-81826-7
PIBN 10238804

THE
WHITE SLAVE
MARKET

BY

MRS. ARCHIBALD MACKIRDY
(OLIVE CHRISTIAN MALVERY)

AND

W. N. WILLIS

WITH A FRONTISPIECE IN HALF-TONE

ELEVENTH EDITION

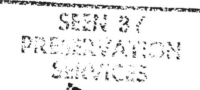
LONDON
STANLEY PAUL & CO
31 ESSEX STREET, STRAND, W.C.

FIRST PUBLISHED IN THE YEAR 1912

Dedication

With all respectful duty this book is dedicated to THE HONOURABLE THE SPEAKER AND THE HONOURABLE MEMBERS OF THE HOUSE OF COMMONS OF GREAT BRITAIN IN PARLIAMENT ASSEMBLED, *with the fervent hope that the truths it unfolds may awaken their sympathy and engage their support for an Act to protect the mothers and the daughters of the nation.*

CONTENTS

IGNORANCE

Ignorance is the curse of God,
Knowledge the wing wherewith we fly to heaven.

Henry VII.

Ignorance is the devil's best asset.
But for ignorance half the dungeons in hell must perforce
be closed.

Old Proverb.

THE WHITE SLAVE MARKET

CHAPTER I

SLAVES

No one to whom Fate or Providence has been kind cares to step from pleasant everyday ways of life into treacherous and dangerous paths which lead to suffering and unpopularity. No man or woman who has within grasp means of following a pleasant way in life would accept a grievous charge and painful labour, save for conscience' sake, and with the hope of waking public opinion to its duty in a matter of national importance.

To-day I see outside my window the first flowers of spring making lovely my beautiful garden. The sky is very blue—all flecked with snowy clouds—and only to see the snowdrops and the primroses and the crocuses makes me want to be out, forgetting everything that is cruel and hard. I would like to cast all unhappy thoughts aside, and forget that there are such things in the world as pain and injustice and cruelty and misery.

My little children are very sweet. They laugh and play, and when I look at them and hear them I feel that the normal, quiet, simple life that a woman in fairly easy circumstances can lead is the natural and wholesome one to have; and that a perfect home with beautiful, happy children, loyal people to serve one, loving friends, opportunities of pleasant social service, and a possibility of forgetting all ugly things are apt to make one want to hold them so dearly as to resent disagreeable duties outside. And surely these are precious and satisfying gifts! One would be inclined to think that only fools would hold them lightly. I hold them very dear. For many years my life has not been easy, and I have knowledge—the very memory of which wakes old pains and terrible unhappiness—not for myself, for I have in many ways been blessed, but for others long passed out of my sight and lost, with whom I travelled a little while in poverty and pain, some of whom were kind to me, and to some of whom, thank God, I was able to hold out a helping hand. And I often feel now that I would like to forget all those pains of poverty and injustice I suffered for others, and be happy and quiet and at peace watching my flowers grow and my children unfold their lovely minds, progressing each towards what I pray God may be a glorious consummation of life.

Into the quietude and peace of this little sheltered, lovely place has come a horrid messenger of pain. A little time ago a letter reached me from the publisher who is now issuing this book, begging that I would join Mr. Willis in the production of it. The publisher put before me the social duty, and the flattering but inconvenient reminder that the British public know me well and respect me, and that thousands in this country love me for some small service which it has been my happy fortune to render to my fellow-creatures who have been less happily placed than I am. He said, "There is no one in this country who could present these terrible facts to the public as you could without offending them—without antagonising them; yet so truthfully and strongly that *they would want to do something to help.*" I replied that I did not feel inclined to embark upon this work. The subject with which he wished me to deal is one that I have tried to avoid, because what I know of it is so terrible, and so agonising, and so far-reaching that I have really felt impotent to do anything. All that is sweet and clean and lovely, all that is hopeful and tender and gracious appeals to me, as it does to all women who are natural. I had not hitherto been able to see that it was my duty to touch a horrible thing which I cannot kill or eliminate; therefore, I refused to have anything to do with this work.

But by some strange fatality, or perhaps

I should say by one of those hard-to-understand coincidences which we who have had a large experience of life learn to recognise as the working of God, having in our minds the words of the old hymn, "God moves in a mysterious way"—by some such agency there came to me within a week three other letters of application from different sources, absolutely unconnected with the publisher of this book or the co-writer of it, entreating my influence and service in this very field. Not caring to harden my heart and close my ears to that severe yet insistent command which enjoins upon all of us who try humbly to walk the heavenly way that we are to take up those burdens that it is our duty to bear, I faced the matter, and set about making investigations and inquiries as to the possible results of publishing such a book as this. I wanted to be assured that such a publication would be for the public good and the good of the victims of the white slave traffic.

To begin with, it is a horrible thing that people should exploit crime and sin, the miseries and foibles of their fellow-creatures, with the sordid purpose of making money. We do not wish to be too hard upon those who write unpleasant books—their circumstances may be difficult—but those who are not driven by need commit a crime against society, which if justice were allied to law would be punished with extreme severity, when they traffic in nasty, unclean literature.

Finally I agreed, in the public interest, to write this book with Mr. Willis, from facts gathered by him in the East.

The white slave traffic, which forms the subject of this book, has already been partially written about, but the part of it relating to the East has not been previously dealt with in a volume of this kind. Even in this country the fearful trade has not much diminished. It is quite true that some very notorious houses or rendezvous have been closed, and that one restaurant which was haunted by the unhappy women who have no means of getting a living but by selling themselves to men, has been raided and shut up. But this was chiefly done by the work of the Salvation Army, as I know, for I went out with the midnight workers and saw what was happening.

To give you three concrete cases from my own knowledge, let me tell you first of a young German woman who wrote to the Salvation Army begging for help and protection. It appears she had been in service in Hamburg with a woman whom she thought was married, but who she afterwards discovered was only living with the man. After a quarrel one day the woman left Hamburg with her servant and came to London, expecting that the man would send for her and pay her expenses back; but as he did not do so the woman was urged by two men friends to go on Piccadilly. They took an expensive flat in a central part, which was visited by bad men. The mistress urged the girl to go wrong with one of the visitors, and because she refused she was treated badly and shut up. However, the girl managed to send a letter to the Salvation Army asking for help, and describing the position she was in. One of the officers was sent to the flat, and after some trouble with the mistress managed to take the girl away in a cab to the Salvation Army quarters in Mare Street. Here she was kept a little while and then sent back to Hamburg to a respectable place. The Army has received many grateful letters from the girl expressing her thanks for the help and protection she received in time of danger. She has also sent a small sum of money to help towards the expense that was entailed on her account.

The second story, which follows, is from the records of Major Hillyer, Matron of Mackirdy House: A captain of the Salvation Army in Holland wrote to Major Hillyer informing her that a young girl aged sixteen was being sent to a situation in London. Before the girl arrived an officer called on the future mistress, but was treated with scant courtesy, and, the interview being so unsatisfactory, it was thought advisable that the girl should not go to the place. The girl was met at Liverpool Street Station and taken to the mid-night quarters of the Salvation Army, instead of to the situation. Later that night two men arrived asking for the girl, whom they said they had gone to the station to meet, but she had been taken away by a Salvationist. Inquiries were made, and it was discovered that the girl had obtained the situation through a Registry Office at The Hague, at £25 a year. When the woman in charge of the office heard inquiries were being made, she at once offered to pay the girl's return fare to Holland, although she had already paid for her to come to England. The girl was eventually sent back to Holland, whence she has written several times expressing her thanks for all that had been done for her. We are all very pleased with these results. But unfortunately the next little history came to our notice too late to save the girl.

A young German girl wrote from her home to a Registry Office in London inquiring if she could get a situation as servant. The woman in charge of the office wrote and told her to come to England and she would get a place at once. On the girl's arrival she found that the house was a house of infamy, and straightway went wrong. She was rescued, but too late to save her honour, by two gentlemen whom she happened to hear speaking German at a railway station, and whom she told of her trouble. They went to the Salvation Army Depot at Regent Street and reported the matter. After a great deal of difficulty some officers got the girl away from the bad house into a Home, but she would not stay, " the life " having taken too great a hold of her. This is a case of a quite good girl falling on coming to London.

It was not long ago that a magistrate dealing with a case of a man touting for patrons for a fearful, low house, said that it seemed almost a worse thing for unhappy women to be driven into hideous secret dens than for them to be situated where they could be watched by the police. We agree with this entirely. It cannot serve the purpose of morality, health, or cleanliness, nor advance the ideals of Christianity one jot, to drive away numbers of diseased, unhappy, deplorable women from positions where society could, as it were, keep a guard over them, to by-ways and slums where they can entice perhaps ignorant and undefended men, rob them, blackmail them, invest them with disease, and let them go forth to taint others with whom they come in contact. No logical person could imagine that there is anything to congratulate ourselves about in having done things of this sort. There is, of course, a very marvellous work being prosecuted among unnamed thousands who go to recruit and keep up the strength of the army of the oldest profession in the world. But the *source of the supply* is not watched sufficiently, nor stemmed. If this book can—in a measure at least—stop the supply of girls to the fatal sisterhood, and save innocent and ignorant girls from being decoyed abroad, surely something will have been accomplished !

We are going to tell you part of the story of this Christian slave traffic. It is carried on by the inhabitants of Christian nations, by people who would be extremely angry if you were to call them heathens. There is not one single moment of pleasure that we can anticipate in telling this story. It is not to have any literary embellishments; it is to be divested of all attempts at ornamentation or " dishing up." We have determined to write it in simple, straightforward, unadorned language. One does not trim the remains of a plague-diseased patient, nor decorate dust-heaps. But one owes something to one's self and to the great majority of society in demanding, rightly we think, that we should not be offended unduly with matters over which we have no control, and *with which we are unable to deal.* The *only* reason that I have consented to join Mr. Willis in writing this book is that we, as a people, *are* able to deal with this matter, and we could, if we had the courage to do what is decent and right, stop *absolutely* this slave trade, which for iniquity and un-nameable cruelty, indecency, and danger has no parallel in the history of that other and dead trade which a spirit like Wilberforce, in spite of popular opinion and vested interests, went forth in the strength of God and killed. To an onlooker, before slavery in America was abolished, no more hopeless task could have been imagined than for any man or woman to set out to wake public opinion to a sense of abhorrence and duty so strong that it would demand to have slavery abolished. There were thousands upon thousands of decent, charming, cultured, and very good

2

people living upon the produce of slavery. Thousands of excellent Christians held slaves and thought it no harm—indeed in many cases the slaves were extremely well treated. The effect of slavery upon the slaveholders was in many cases as bad as the effect of slavery upon the slaves. Both classes suffered immeasurably. So it is with this fearful traffic. It is not only that a few women and girls and a few men are sacrificed, but because we have persistently closed our eyes to a thing which we have chosen to consider as improper, and which, without question, is exceedingly indecent, the whole of society is paying the debt of these slaves whose tears from unknown corners of the earth have been counted by God.

The late deeply lamented King Edward VII. advocated the organisation of a wonderful system for the elimination of consumption from our midst. Now, consumption claims only one-seventh of the victims that the diseases incident to the white slave traffic do. I have been to something like a dozen conferences within the last eighteen months— conferences on National Morals, on Eugenics, Mutual Reform Societies, and Degeneration of the Race conferences, and as I have sat there and listened to the speeches made, largely by doctors and ministers, I have wondered how it is that not a single one of them has ever mentioned the one—I may say the universal cause of disease and of degeneration which threatens, unless dealt with immediately, to wreck the future of our nation, and not our nation only but other nations which have not had the sense to study the matter and take preventive measures. In Germany a soldier who contracts a certain disease or transmits it to another suffers at the hands of the law three years' rigorous imprisonment. Sensible Germany! In England soldiers back from Eastern countries drift about our towns, marry quite decent girls, and launch upon the nation scores of children who ought not to live —and often do not live. Poor innocent victims of their parents' crimes! Not this only, but rich and well-to-do men contract the awful disease and give it to their wives and children. The results—blindness, weak eyes, throat and other diseases—are apparent in thousands of homes. We need not dilate upon this point. Consumption is child's play to the evils under which we are suffering. But, for some inscrutable reason, consumption is considered rather a romantic disease, and people are quite pleased to fuss about trying to eliminate it.

But, alas! The terrible disease this book attempts to lay bare is more deadly than the worst form of consumption, for not only does it kill the body but it destroys the souls of thousands of innocents. For what ? For money. Yes, whilst it kills our young girls it keeps in almost affluence thousands, and many thousands, despicable perverts of manhood—wretches whom the law and the false modesty of some well-disposed persons shield by refusing to believe the unfolded truths and facts of this fearful trade in all its revolting ugliness. Our one hope is that once the truth is laid bare before an astonished and ashamed public, something will be done to check or kill the evil right out.

The one redeeming feature of this book is that we are able to present to you a *cure* for this traffic, and to show you how, if you wish it, the slave trade can be killed. It can within five years be absolutely, entirely, and completely destroyed. It is, I believe, a battle that will have to be fought as much by women as by men, and it will have to be fought by *good* women—by refined, gentle, happily placed, and fortunate women, because they have most power and most influence. But the carrying out of the campaign must be undertaken largely by men; and there are men who are willing to help—great men, who love their country, and who serve God through loss as well as gain—men who are willing to risk unpopularity and hardness to set free "the souls in prison"—the unfortunate girls in the bondage of the traffickers.

When some of the facts that are in this book were sent to me to read, I could not sleep for days. They made me ill. I would like to have thrown the manuscript into the fire to get rid of it—to forget, if possible, the whole thing; but that was not possible. At last I wrote to the head of the police in London, whom I know, and I told him about this book. We are not aiming at anything so foolish as the abolition of prostitution, for as long

as the world lasts prostitution will last also.
That we can quite make up our minds to.
But it will be prostitution modified as soon as
we have the sense to recognise that we must
organise and arrange that particular trade; and
we must protect our young, and see that no
woman becomes a prostitute because she has
no friends, and because she is poor or ill-used
and homeless, and that no man must become
a victim because he is taken unawares and
led into a trap at some weak moment. I
wrote to others also. There must be knowledge of this thing, and the knowledge must
be common. Every lad and girl who comes
into our charge must have that knowledge.
Knowledge is not evil; it is power, protection,
and righteousness if it is sanctified. Knowledge is the power and the strength of God;
ignorance, the devil's best asset.

I also saw the editor of *Truth*, and had
a long talk with him; and I said to him,
"You know there is no need for me to
touch this thing." But if I do help to get
these facts made public, shall we be able to
kill this traffic? The opinion is that we
shall, if the country helps us, kill the awful
thing. It is the general belief that education
on these matters is needed.

Only a short time ago a girl wrote to me.
She came from the North and belonged to a
decent, well-to-do, middle-class family. She
was one of those unhappy children who have
never been given any trade or profession or
any interests outside her home, and she

wanted what every normal girl ought to want—a husband. Unfortunately she did not know how to get one. She had not the knowledge which would have protected her. There was in this same town a man who had come from Egypt and was taking his finals in medicine, finishing with a special course at a hospital for tropical diseases. The girl met him and fell in love with him—it was as much her fault as his—hers through ignorance, his through design. He persuaded her that he could not say anything about marriage because his father would not furnish him with money to finish his course; and so she left her home and went with him to another city. He promptly deserted her when she was expecting a child, and though she had been left with money she was placed in the house of a bad old woman, who would have eventually enslaved her and forced her out to earn money on the streets when there was nothing else for her. She did not tell me the truth when she wrote to me, nor did she in the subsequent interviews; but gradually we got at some of the facts, and when she had been cared for and nursed through her trouble and an immense amount of love and care lavished upon her, she broke down utterly and gave us the whole case as it was. We were able to compel the man to marry her. I told him if he did not do so, or if he left her unprovided for, I would make it quite impossible for him to earn a living in any place, as I knew the officials in many of these

countries, and my husband had been for
nearly thirty years Consul in the East. I
said we would not for a single moment allow
him to destroy this girl and go away happy.
As a matter of fact he was not really a bad
fellow. I asked the good people who were
working with me in the case if they thought
marriage was the only solution in a case like
that, as I did not feel sure that the girl
would be happy if the man was compelled to
marry her. But this was thought extremely
wicked on my part. I thought he should
have been made to provide for her and not
compelled to marry her, unless she very
much wished it and there was a likelihood of
their settling down happily. However, they
were married, and it seems to have turned
out all right. The man's people were very
good and sent money.

Another case was of a poor girl who was led
astray by a German. One has to remember
that in these cases men do not find it extremely difficult to lead these girls astray,
and it always rouses a storm of anger in me
when I find that girls, partly through ignorance, partly through dulness and hard circumstances, have persuaded themselves to
believe obvious lies. The trouble is that in
all the warnings they get nobody ever tells
them the price they will have to pay for a
temporary pleasure. It is a quarrel that
some of us have against the good people who
have constituted themselves teachers and
guardians of the young that they deal with

these matters from rather a sentimental and hyper-religious point of view. The girl found herself in a hopeless condition. The man left her £20 and went to Germany: as far as he was concerned, if that girl had not chanced upon powerful friends she also would have been obliged to go on the streets, as her people to this day will have nothing to do with her. They have repudiated her and have forbidden her to use their name. The man has not married her, and I can hardly see how he could, considering he was not independent; but money has been provided for her and her child to supplement her scanty earnings. She is not a skilled worker, but she is now in training and likes her work, and will, we hope, do extremely well. These are two cases *out of scores*. There are many more: the majority of them are far more unhappy than these. These are the good specimens. Alas, for the bad cases! They can be counted by hundreds in their awful ugliness.

The reason this fearful trade exists and flourishes in the midst and under the very noses of good, proper-living people is, primarily, because of the existence of the despicable creatures known as " pimps " and " bludgers." Thousands of men known as " bludgers " live upon the tainted earnings of unfortunate women; and there are hundreds—aye, thousands—of procuresses who make large sums by decoying girls to sin. The law deals very lightly with these three classes of individuals, who keep the trade flourishing so that they themselves may flourish. In this book we deal with the " pimp," the " bludger," and the procuress.

Now, this book has not been written for careless and selfish people, and it has not been written for nasty-minded people. It has been written for the best men and women that our country contains—for those men and women who have the light which all of us have who have chosen to ask for it, and who are seeking it—for those men and women who have received in their daily walk in life, being Christians, wisdom because they are always in the hands of the Source of Wisdom—for those men and women who are pure, because no one who has been touched by the grace of the Divine can be anything but pure, seeing that the very source of our existence, the breath of our breath, the Giver of our life is pure. It is written for true and conscientious men and women who are willing to go out from the sanctified home which is so infinitely precious to us, so beautiful, so rare, and so exquisite : to go out from these into the thorny, stony way and to learn what manner of service it is that is required of us at this critical instant. I have no fear that this book being placed in the hands of the public can do harm ; those to whom it might do harm have already been harmed. It will stir rage in many hearts who take pleasure in evil things, for the truth is not welcome to those who are walking crookedly, and the light is hid always from those whose ways of life demand the dark lanes. And so we send out this book, hoping that it will kill the traffic. Men do not light a candle and put it under a bushel, and in sending out this book we are obeying the Divine command to "let your light shine before men." The book has been written with no other object than just to do one definitely-described and studied piece of work; and that is, to *kill absolutely* and speedily the slave trade in girls and women that is being carried on between this country and Europe, and our Eastern possessions, and South America. The editors of some of the most powerful newspapers and magazines of this country have very kindly promised to give their interest for this object. They also know of the facts because of the various reports they have had from time to time, and from independent sources they have learned of these things.

As for the police, they are only too willing to do what they can to stop this traffic. With the help of various societies who are interested in this work, various ministers, and editors of papers, we have thought out several ways by which it can be made so difficult for any man or woman to carry on this trade that they would have to give it up. These methods we shall relate when we have finished our story. But first of all it is necessary—and you will see the reasonableness of this—that you should really know what is going on, and have facts given to you.

Many of the cases given here are reported in the Police Courts of the different countries, where they can be traced and verified if necessary. But others are tragedies which have for their victims nameless creatures, unknown and uncared for. It is not at all impossible, nor is it a difficult matter for us to take up this question and deal with it effectually and for ever, and then we can drop it; so that there should be no more necessity for placing books like this before the public. Neither you nor I wish to spend our lives sorrowing over and troubling about these things. We want to do our part and then to be set free. But we cannot claim freedom until our duty is done.

CHAPTER II

MR. WILLIS, writing of this trade in Egypt, says :

The plague of the "pimp" and his co-partner, the procuress, in Egypt is bad enough, in all conscience, but, from a European standpoint, it does not assume the awful seriousness of the aspect of the traffic in the Middle East and the Far East as regards the literal slaughter of white women and girls. Egypt is comparatively close at hand, and is, so to speak, under stricter observation than the Middle East or Far East. Unfortunate white girls decoyed to Egypt have some chance of escaping the hellish bonds of the "pimp," or those who conduct houses of ill-fame, but in the Middle East and Far East such opportunities do not exist. The strong, vigilant societies established in England give special attention to the cities of Alexandria, Cairo, Port Said, etc. On the active committees of such societies we find the Earl of Aberdeen and his philanthropic Countess, Mrs. Fawcett, and other enthusiastic workers who are not

28

ashamed to come down from their high stations to help, with unsparing hand, to protect the daughters of the poor. The late Mr. W. T. Stead also gave special attention to the Near East in his life's work against the traffic in white women. But, unfortunately, these splendid hunters-down of the white slave dealers in the Near East have totally neglected the fearful ravages of the monstrous "pimp" in the Middle East or the Far East. In Egypt, meetings are held, committees formed, and time and money expended in attempts to eradicate the plague so far as British women are concerned. In this way splendid results are achieved; indeed, hundreds, perhaps thousands, of young, innocent, and ignorant European girls are saved from a life of shame, and from disease and untimely death in the Near East, by the keen vigilance of the societies formed for their protection. These good results are only accomplished by the societies publishing broadcast the dangers that surround young girls who ignorantly play with the fires of sensuality in Egypt. Few girls—certainly no innocent girl—would venture abroad to Egypt once she knew what is expected of her. This the vigilance committees should well advertise. Publicity soon destroys ignorance.

The astute trafficker in white women is fully cognisant of the risk he runs in taking young European girls to Egypt. There are, of course, great numbers of European women of ill-fame in Cairo, Alexandria, and Port

Said, but many of these are soiled or diseased harlots of Europe. They go on tour during the season to "do" the various towns. They generally travel in batches of three or four, in charge of a "missus." Some of them open houses for the season; others put up at second-class hotels. In either case they usually engage what we should call "runners"—young Egyptian youths who slink around the mean ways of Eastern life in search of "customers" for the harlots who have come to town. With the work of these women we are not at present dealing, beyond venturing an opinion that the traffic they pursue should be controlled so as to prevent, among other things, diseased prostitutes of Europe taking plague germs into Egypt. Many of these women earn "big money," and their trips during the season are a source of revenue for the quack doctors of Egypt.

The "pimp," as we know him, generally descends on Egypt with his wife, or assumed wife, who, of course, must be good-looking and thoroughly know her business. In many cases the woman is an expert thief, and robs and helps her "pimp" husband to blackmail an old gentleman or two to cover the expenses account. The "pimp" and his wife generally stay at the best hotels, patronised by young Englishmen with a superabundance of money and a poverty of brains. These young bloods are usually sent out by their parents to "do" the Continent and wind up with Egypt—a big percentage get "done" and wind up in the hospital. The "pimp" and his "missus" play for these young fools, and nearly always catch them. When the "pimp" and his "missus" have finished "doing" Egypt, the "missus," in a motherly sort of way, chooses a good-looking Greek maiden or two, sometimes a Greek girl with a plentiful dash of Arab blood in her veins, large lustrous eyes, and well-formed limbs. Such girls are engaged as handmaids to the "missus," and are taken abroad in the most open manner—sometimes to the Far East, sometimes even to the Argentine. Once away from their own dreamy land of romance and idleness, these wretched children of a wretched country become slaves ; indeed, as soon as they are out at sea, on the high waterway to disease and death, the children of Egypt or of Greece are "broken in" to the plague of immorality, and are generally forced to earn their expenses *en route* to the home of their complete destruction. On landing in the Far East or the Argentine they are sold, as a rule, outright to brothel-keepers. Sometimes the girls are merely rented on the hire system, so much of their wages being allocated to provide their board, so much to the "missus" of the house of ill-fame, and so much to the "pimp." They get nothing at all for themselves beyond scanty clothing, meagre food, and a good "hiding" occasionally to "knock the nonsense out of them."

Excepting pure white Greeks, very few of these girls find their way to the Far East.

If they are pure white, pretty, and well developed, there is a market for them at Shanghai, Hong-Kong, Siam, Singapore, and Rangoon. But they must be pure white, for the Eastern potentate with affluence to gratify his sensual pleasures requires a real white woman. The Eastern Asiatic draws the colour line pretty firmly when he is trading for harlotry. For such purposes he wants the white girl; but when he marries to get heirs to his goods and chattels he always takes for that purpose a woman of his own nationality.

In the East, especially the Near East, woman has never had a high status. From time immemorial she has been looked upon merely as a necessary adjunct to the needs and affairs of man, or nature. For centuries past—aye, far away back into the first twilight of fable—the mothers of the nation have always been kept in the secluded suburbs of the nation's affairs. They have always been subject to their master's will or whim; and even to the present day their position is little better than that of well-fed and scantily clothed slaves, with no hope of salvation or prospect beyond the " romance " of marrying to please their masters and bear them children. In the middle classes in the East a girl is doomed as soon as she is born.

Most of the Middle and Far Eastern countries possess no industrial enterprise and no manufactures. Education is neglected, and advancement—at least for women—is put back almost to the stage where Jesus of Nazareth found it. Now, as in His time, the woman in the East lolls about in secluded idleness, dreaming of legends and, perhaps, hoping against hope for a brighter future, until, poor wretch, she is caught, and used, and cast aside to fight the fearful battle of her sex in a country where a horse or a dog is better loved and better cared for than a woman. It was the Christ, to Whom all Christians pray, Who first publicly recognised the awfulness of the position of woman in the East. The Divine Master picked up wretched women from the roadside, absolved the harlot, and took women into the administration of His religion and His law. But when He died, the voices of that pious band of women who followed Him, even to the foot of the Cross, with an inspired and lasting love, were hushed, and for years remained silent. When Jesus died women were thrust back into obscurity and disappeared completely from the affairs of the Church and from the public affairs of Christianity.

Women in the East had, until Jesus lived, been neglected and despised, they were without hope and without order, rights, or recognition. The disciples whom Jesus left to preach His religion to mankind formed the first Christian Order for women— it was the Order of the Deaconesses. Into this Order were gathered deserted mothers, deserted wives, widows, and young girls;

3

thus were women first brought within the pale and protection of the Church and of Christianity, when the Church had been in existence scarcely one decade. The women Deaconesses thus created became pious souls who ministered to the poor, the sick, and the lonely, their noble Samaritan work commencing in Jerusalem, extending afterwards under the direction of the first great woman of the Order—Tabitha, the rich widow— throughout Asia, and penetrating even within the palace walls of Rome.

But alas for the efforts of the Divine Master and the efforts of His followers in those days, when Christianity was "an association in charity of the poor," little has since been accomplished in raising the status of women in Asia, even at the present day. At the moment of writing these lines native raiders, traders in girls' flesh, and procurers are busy scouring Upper Egypt, Arabia, the small islands washed by the Ægean Sea, and Greece—scouring and ravishing and herding together young, innocent, and totally ignorant girls to maintain the supply of human flesh to meet the fearful demand that exists in houses of ill-fame in Cairo, Alexandria, Port Said, and minor seaport towns in the Near East.

Most of these abominable raiders and traders are half Egyptian, half Arabian; some are half Turk, half Arabian. Their helpless victims are taken in consignments to the horrible sacrifice. Generally they are

" rested " outside Cairo, or off Alexandria, or Port Said, where purchasers of the living human flesh arrive in ones or twos and take their pick.

" Feed My lambs "—was the beautiful injunction of Jesus.

" Kill Christ's lambs "—is the fearful oath of the white slave raider—and this in the face of Christendom!

At first I thought it absolutely impossible that a country occupied and garrisoned by a nation professing Christianity would tolerate such dealings in the open. I did not believe what I heard; it seemed too incredible. One day I had a chat on the subject with an hotel clerk at Cairo, an intelligent young Hebrew, born in Turkey. When I opened my eyes in horror at what he told me, he laughed outright and exclaimed :

" The British have already made themselves unpopular by interfering with the customs of the country and attempting to protect the poor, and they dare not interfere with a highly lucrative traffic in women. Many of the most powerful men in Cairo and in Alexandria are directly or indirectly interested in the traffic; some of them finance the traders, others are actual partners with traders. To keep themselves ' good ' with influential and powerful men the traders occasionally select a comely young girl—generally a Greek maiden—as a present for an influential ' friend.' They are, of course, afraid of Lord Kitchener, but no one seriously bothers about the maids who are bought and sold, especially if they are Greek maids."

"It is all very difficult to believe," I replied, "and I should like to see some of these traffickers when they arrive here with a batch of girls. You give me an opportunity to see for myself, and I will pay you."

Quick as lightning the hotel clerk asked, "How much—English money?"

"Two sovereigns," I replied; "but I must actually see them when they land, and I must have an opportunity of speaking to the trader."

The clerk agreed, and the bargain was sealed. Most of the fellows one meets in hotels in the East would venture almost to murder for £2 in gold.

Some days afterwards the clerk told me that a batch of young Greek and Rhodes Island girls had come to town and I had better see them that night, as they might be distributed the following day.

I fixed a time in the afternoon, and at the appointed hour I pocketed my revolver—as a precautionary measure—filled my pocket with Burma cigars, and, accompanied by the clerk, drove off in a ramshackle trap to one of the suburbs of Cairo. On the journey I explained to my companion the killing power of a Colt six-shooter. This was another precautionary measure, to disabuse his mind of any possible idea of having "a cheap proposition" to face if treachery were in the air.

In due course we arrived at an Egyptian two-story building abutting on to the street. After knocking several times, we were ushered into a dark, musty, dusty sitting-room on the right. Having sat there for a few minutes staring at each other, a young Egyptian man, in native costume and with slippered feet, came along the passage from the back of the building. An animated conversation, punctuated with full-stops and full stares at me, followed between the Egyptian and my clerk friend. The young Egyptian appeared to have been taken by surprise, and I deemed it prudent to be on the qui vive to avoid such a contingency happening to me.

After further debate the clerk intimated to me that " cash down " was the point at issue. I handed him a sovereign, showed him another sovereign, and when fumbling for the coins " accidentally " exposed the revolver in my vest pocket.

The first sovereign having again changed hands, the interesting individual in the native costume led the way to the back of the house and down eight or ten rickety wooden steps into a small square-paved yard, enclosed, prison-like, by high brick walls. Crossing this yard we went through a one-story building, where cooking and washing-up operations were in full swing. Passing out of this building we entered another yard paved with smooth stones. At the extreme end of this yard was a big, shed-like building, towards which the gentleman in the native attire led the way, unlocked a large door, and bade us enter.

My clerk friend went first; I cautiously followed.

"There they are!" exclaimed the clerk. "They have not long arrived. They are tired and not brushed up yet."

I shall never forget the sight. Up to that moment I had suspected that the whole thing was a mere ruse or a conspiracy of some kind that would end in an argument and in my losing at least a sovereign. But no. There, sure enough, resting in different postures on mats on the stone floor, were eleven young girls. Poor little youngsters! Poor little children—offsprings of the poor, the beloved of the Founder of Christianity. What a spectacle!—those tender, crouching young things, half clothed, perhaps half fed, with tear-scalded eyes and matted and tousled hair. I never wish to see such a sight again. I have often wished I had never seen it. It first made me melancholy; then it made my blood boil. If the Kingdom of God truly be the inheritance of the poor, surely these poor little kidnapped youngsters from Greece, Asia Minor, Rhodes Island, and other islands washed by the Ægean Sea will receive from God the pity savage man and brutalised Christianity deny them. They were, indeed, "His lambs," prepared for the "butcher trafficker." It was enough to make one curse the country that permitted such brutality to be perpetrated upon the young and the innocent. The sight brought back to my memory the touching verses—sacred recollections of childhood's happy days—in which Coleridge depicts the " weeping eye " of the holy monk when, twelve hundred years ago, he saw in the Roman Forum a band of English fair-haired child slaves, and how the good priest, moved by pity, straightway sent St. Augustine to England—

> To tell of God's glad tidings
> Of joy, beyond the grave—
> To tell how Jesus came to earth
> The souls of men to save.
> So truly did the old man cry,
> " *Non Angli sunt, sed Angeli.*" [1]

I was informed that the eleven little maidens had been secured by a noted raider principally at Tripoli, and the poor island of Rhodes, and other small islands, and brought to Cairo for sale—for sale and purchase as openly as a butcher buys grass-fed lambs and drives them to the shambles to be slaughtered, devoured, and forgotten. Such was the fate of those eleven children.

Strong man though I am—and I have seen a good deal of the rough ways and places of life—I turned from that shed sick at heart and with a sense of shame and horror. The click of the lock that kept the youngsters prisoners echoed in my mind for days, and re-echoes still.

[1] "They are not Angles, but Angels."

But what could I do ?   I, a stranger in a
strange land !   Indeed, what can that master
of men, Lord Kitchener, do to avert such fearful trafficking amongst the young in a strange,
mystic land, whose people cling tenaciously
to the customs of the country, no matter how
hideous or inhuman those customs may be ?
The work of saving the young in those regions
belongs to Christianised Europe.   Christ's
ministers on earth must take the fearful
matter in hand, and, with energy and funds,
help to beat the monster of the white slave
traffic down until killed outright.

At Cairo a few pious Greek and Moham-
medan gentlemen have humanely established
a " Ligue de Prophylaxie Sanitaire et contre
la Traite des Blanches," to aid girl victims
of the white slave traffic.   If necessary, the
girls are medically treated, and the adminis-
trators of the worthy institution afterwards
communicate with the police, who, in turn,
communicate with the country or community
to which the victims belong.   But, alas ! in
Cairo the religious line is drawn very tightly
and, in consequence, some of the residents
decline to co-operate with those holding a
faith or creed different from their own.   So the
hideous trade flourishes, and, of course, the
traffickers flourish with it.   Divided religion,
divided counsels, divided nationalities—all
these help the trafficker and keep him
flourishing.

For the protection of Greek maidens a Bill
has been passed by the Greek Parliament, at

the instance of Mr. Bernaki, an estimable
Minister with a full knowledge of Egypt and
its affairs. The Bill—now, of course, an Act
—prohibits any girl from leaving her country
without a permit from the Mayor of the
municipality in which her parents live.
Application for such permit must be made
by the girl's parents or lawful guardians, who
are required to supply full particulars as to
the girl's name, age, and reason for desiring
to leave the country. If any one is accom-
panying her the name of the person must be
supplied. In the event of a certificate being
granted, it has to be produced on the girl's
arrival at Port Said or Alexandria. Without
such a certificate she is not permitted to
remain in Egypt, but is immediately repa-
triated. This useful piece of legislation
does much to minimise the traffic in young
girls, but without the co-operation of the
Egyptian Government it is almost futile to
hope to kill the atrocious trade.

The unspeakable creatures in this traffic
will, it is hoped, says the *Westminster Gazette*,
have reason to remember the recent visit to
Egypt of Mr. W. A. Coote, inasmuch as the
interest of Lord Kitchener has been aroused.
In a timely article on the subject, in its issue
of April 11th this year, the journal quoted
said that Mr. Coote went to Egypt at the
request of the International Bureau, of which
the Bishop of Westminster is president and
the Dean of Westminster is chairman; and
he also took with him a mandate from the

National Committees of Europe to investigate the state of things so far as the white slave traffic is concerned and to organise and extend the work of the committees for its suppression.

"Egypt," said Mr. Coote, "is a flourishing market for these traffickers. It is the gateway to the Near East; and, owing to the cosmopolitan character of the people, suppression work encounters many and serious difficulties. Indeed, criminals of all kinds are favoured by the Capitulations and the circumlocution of trial by the Mixed Tribunals; and in the case of the white slave traders, who can only be tried by their respective Consuls, justice is particularly slow and uncertain. *If the Egyptian police have evidence that a certain man is not only a trader, but is in actual possession of foreign girls, no steps can be taken without first submitting the evidence to the Consul of the country to which the man claims to belong*, and from this official a warrant for arrest must be obtained. The trial then takes place at the Consular Court. Lord Cromer, who took a keen interest in the efforts to suppress this traffic, called the attention of the British Government to the legal difficulties; and his successor, the late Sir Eldon Gorst, went so far in his annual report as to say that while the Capitulations were allowed to deal with this question successful legal action against the traffickers was almost impossible."

Mr. Coote is of opinion that the evils of

the Capitulations must be left for the British Government and the European Powers to deal with. Speaking of his object in visiting Egypt, he said it was to arouse the public conscience and to organise national committees similar to those formed in every European country, with the object of dealing with the problem of the white slave traffic by international co-operation. From the leaders of the various foreign communities he received a sympathetic welcome, and on all hands a disposition to help was strikingly indicated. A considerable number of the most influential Mohammedans associated themselves with his mission, and to their efforts he is much indebted. In Cairo and Port Said the Mohammedans displayed similar friendliness, and differences of nationality and creed were overcome in the formation of the committees.

The white slave traffic in Egypt is now mainly recruited from the women of Russia, Austria, and France; but until a year ago the young women of Greece were the principal victims.

Mr. Coote had a long conversation with Lord Kitchener on the subject, and found him most sympathetic. Lord Kitchener expressed great interest in the question as it affects Egypt, and impressed Mr. Coote with confidence that he is to be relied upon for practical support whenever occasion arises to exert his official position. He has a real live interest in the question, and discussed it from many points of view. All his suggestions were in the direction of more effective action against the traffickers, and Mr. Coote is convinced that if Lord Kitchener could have his way, independently of the Capitulations, Egypt would soon be cleared of the white slave trader.

This conviction of Mr. Coote's touches the nerve-spring of the subject. There can be no doubt that if Lord Kitchener had the power, the trade would speedily be killed. Any one who knows the great master mind of Kitchener —whom poor Steevens alluded to as "a human machine," who levelled all opposing forces—knows full well that if he had the power, the trading in the bodies and lives of young innocent children would have a very short career. He would, in fact, kill the traffic in three months, if he had the power. But he has not the power. The mixed courts, the different nationalities, are impediments that stop the hand of the greatest of all modern generals from striking down the loathsome mongrels who live and thrive and batten on the bodies and souls of helpless juvenile humanity. And God help us, for even this matter is made a *political* bone of contention!

PORT SAID: THE GERM INCUBATOR

Beyond all quibble Port Said, for its size, is the deadliest spot on earth. As legend has it that Damascus, in the old days of Asia, was the original site of the Garden of Eden, or the "Paradise of God," so the bare and hideous facts in our day proclaim Port Said to be the devil's resting-ground.

It is a seaport, with a highly cosmopolitan population of Arabs, Turks, Roumanians, Afrikanders, Greeks, bloodthirsty islanders from the Ægean Sea, French, Germans, Poles, Egyptians, and Italians, with a slight sprinkling of English, intermixed in an unhealthy conglomerate of lazy lawlessness. Situated at the mouth of the Suez Canal, it is a gate of the water highways to the East, the Middle East, the Dutch Indies, the Malay Archipelago, and south to Australia and New Zealand.

The trade is of course considerable, and much allowance must be made for the class and character of people who travel through and use the port as they travel; but there can be no possible excuse for keeping the place in a filthy, unspeakable, germ-breeding condition. It is now an absolute danger-spot for every man who rests an hour or more in it. When an important passenger-boat arrives at Port Said, the steamer is fairly besieged by an army of guides with registered badges on their arms, whose sole affair in life seems to be guiding the innocent and the ignorant to the exhibition of revolting sights such as would have done credit to Nero's best entertainment manager. When the guide, who is generally half Egyptian and half Greek, gains your confidence by producing sundry registration papers as to his guideship, none of which you understand, he gathers together half a dozen sightseers and leads the way, after begging you to be careful of false guides. Once in his charge in the streets of Port Said, after having successfully beaten off about half a dozen other guides, he whispers to you assiduously, "Gentlemen, liker see nicer picture, very good picture?"

If you're out for information, you say "Certainly." He then successfully elbows you into a respectable-looking shop, whispers something to a good-looking Greek behind the counter, who beckons you to follow him to a secluded room at the back. Here he produces a box with most filthy faked pictures, many of which are printed in Japan. They are disgusting and clumsy fakes, the cost of which would be about ten a penny. The "modest" Turk asks you 1s. each. You decline post-cards; then obscene literature is produced, and for an obscene book which would cost about 2d. to print, 2s. 6d. is requested, and if the customer be a little foolish, and more than a little drunk, 5s. is considered a fair price.

Then the guide, in dread of losing you, hurries you off to a squatty, one-story building with a red lamp projecting over the door. He knocks with authority and demands admittance. Your sane traveller hesitates to enter this ill-looking place, but the guide vehemently protests—and they are adepts at protesting. A young man, or an unsophisticated youth, or a young fool who considers himself clever, would have small chance of withstanding the "protests" of these guides, whose business it is to get your money.

Once inside these dens of iniquity, licentiousness runs riot. About twelve or fourteen young girls are sheltered in such dens, and they are brought in by the "missus" of the house to entertain the boat visitors; and, beyond question, the entertainment is appalling. Poor little wretched girls!—some of them little more than children, some of course old and a bit brazen—they are all made to dance in the nude and carry on obscene antics for the amusement of the passengers with money to lose.

The Government-registered guide is a sort of master of the ceremonies; whilst a huge, evil-looking African nigger, dressed in the garb of a waiter, takes up a position in the corner, ready to knock a noisy visitor senseless. More drink, more dancing, the bills paid, and the guide then assures you that there are dozens of *better* houses with *better* girls, and he proceeds to take you the round—if, of course, you are fool enough to follow; and as a percentage of men are born fools, and die fools, it is fair to conclude that lots of fools follow this registered guide.

As I was on my way from the Far East to England, to submit my notes to that great journalist whose life the insatiable sea has claimed, Mr. W. T. Stead, I determined, at some risk and cost, to get first-hand information at Port Said. I spoke to this woman

who kept the house with the old "red lamp."
She is, I think, a Roumanian half-breed;
she was certainly bred in Southern Europe.
I asked her plainly if many English or
American girls found their way to her suburb
of hell.

She replied: "No, no. The life is too
rough; besides, it's dangerous here to have
much to do with English girls. French
prostitutes and Belgian women come here in
great numbers, but, unless they are diseased,
they are very expensive. We could not afford
to live at all if we employed the better
women."

"Where, then," I asked, "do you draw your
supplies from—Cairo and Alexandria?"

"Oh no," she laughed. "The 'missuses'
in Alexandria and Cairo get in their girls just
as I get mine—sometimes from Greece, but
principally from the Islands. The Greek folk
have been kicking up a noise over losing so
many girls that they have tried to stop it;
but they'll never stop it. Girls come away
from wretched, poverty-stricken homes and
enjoy life here. I have three Greek girls
with me at present, and very good girls they
are. Did you notice that little dark girl—
the one who would not dance? Well, she
came from Corsica. She came here with
about fifteen others. I picked her out, and
made a bad bargain, for she is always crying or sulking. The two tall girls came
from Rhodes Island. We get plenty of good-
looking girls. I know all the dealers, and

they know me as an honest woman, and they trust me."

I asked her what she paid for these girls, but she either grew tired or suspicious of my questions. The great, burly African nigger kept dodging in and out of the room; but I had got sufficient information, and it is the broad, undeniable fact that the white slave traffic is carried on to-day in the Near East by organised gangs, who flourish in defiance of all Christian principles in a country garrisoned by the soldiers of a Christian King. It was ever so. The importance accorded to vital questions relating to the redressing of social evils has from the early days been secondary to political considerations; and as political considerations rule Egypt, and as expediency takes the place of right and truth, the hand is *shackled* that could, and gladly would, strike the "white slavers" down without compunction. That hand is Lord Kitchener's.

It is only fair to say that there are several committees at Port Said attempting to do good. The Greek committee for the care of Greek girls is doing good work, Madame Koenig is also an enthusiastic worker; but without the fear and dread of Lord Kitchener a "slaver" goes his way unheeding committees and societies, being assured that if he cannot get the "white slaves" into Egypt by one door he can by another. The sighs of the philanthropic, the sobs, the tears, nay,

4

the blood of his victims, are to him as folly which he regards not.

Some day the people of England will wake up, and, through their Parliament, tell Lord Kitchener to stop the traffic, to kill the inhuman monster who deals in the flesh of the piteously weeping children of the poor.   Then the traffic will be stopped—stopped with a fearful, heavy, and swift hand.   Not before.

CHAPTER III

HAUNTS OF THE WHITE SLAVE TRADER

WE are fully conscious of the responsibility we undertake in making the truths in this book known.

We are also fully convinced that the revelations will stir the hearts and minds of all the people of this country, and we hope and believe that the Press—a great, if not the greatest, weapon against darkness —will enlighten the nation regarding this work, and that the Government will be urged to initiate much-needed reforms, and pass new laws relating to the white slave traffic, especially in the East.

It is not unlikely the Government will give the stereotyped reply kept in stock for such occasions, this being that :

"The Government of India, of Burma, of the Straits Settlements, of the Federated Malay States (including Singapore), of Hong-Kong and the Eastern Treaty Ports, enforce a strict prohibition against British women of ill-fame plying their trade in these Asiatic dependencies; the law is rigidly enforced in Calcutta, Madras, Bombay, Poona, Burma, Penang, Singapore, Hong-Kong, and British Borneo, that no *British* woman is allowed under the law to live a life of infamy, either in the houses of ill-fame or with coloured Asiatics.

" British women living in open or secret adultery with Indian potentates or Indian merchants have been deported when found out."

An instance may be given of the powerful Rajah of ——, who kept a British woman, brought to him by a " pimp," in his palace under his protection. News of this woman came to the Government, and the Government promptly deported the woman and reprimanded the Rajah. The reply would of course be true—we admit it; and we will go further and say that the authorities, stationed at some of the resting grounds in the East we have named, are very vigilant, and are horrified at the traffic in British women. But, alas! some of the best Britishers in authority in our possessions in the East are powerless to act against the traffic in white women, being fearful of the conscientious ignorance of many well-disposed persons in England. Even Lord Roberts quailed before a monster meeting at Exeter Hall over his letter *re* a supply of women being brought within the cantonment.

The officials in the countries we have named are British. They are men of honour, who loathe, as they would a deadly plague, the despicable " pimp." It will also be averred by the authorities at Whitehall that the judges and magistrates in our Eastern possessions are quite capable of dealing with cases arising from the traffic in women as they occur. We agree with this also. We also know that all good men are not dead in the East; we admit that the judges and magistrates of the superior courts of India, Burma, of Singapore, Penang, and Hong-Kong, are a splendid reflex of all the highest traditional probity that has, for the last couple of centuries at least, surrounded British justice and British judges from the Law Courts at Temple Bar right to the farthest portion of the earth, where the British flag flies.

To some persons who are ignorant of the greatness of Britain's Eastern possessions, and who consider the affairs and the life in the East to be one topsy-turvy conglomeration of all that is unwholesome, it would come as an intellectual revelation, and as a cause for pride and thankfulness in their British heritage, if they could seat themselves in the superior court at Penang or Singapore and minutely observe the great judges dispensing justice between all manner of men, all castes, colours, and creeds, and of every tongue, in the name of and on behalf of the British nation. Further, it is safe to say that, but for the purity of justice, but for the unimpeachable probity of the judges of the superior and indeed the lower courts, in the East and Middle East, Britain could not hold these possessions a clear month. It is the judges and justice, and the innate knowledge that justice will be done without fear or without favour, that binds with ties of steel every caste, colour, and tongue to the British Empire and the British flag.

Now we hope to show that this pure justice under the present law is the " despicable pimp's " greatest asset. The " pimp," who is clever, sober, and cold-blooded in his calculations, knows the law and how to break it without breaking his skin. He knows the judges are in their places to administer the law—not to strain it or to practise an unwritten code; therefore, with ordinary care and the use of his brains he sails along uninterrupted, bringing girls to disease and death unmolested by the authorities who cannot break the law, even to punish such a vile wretch! Under the present system, if a " pimp " arrives at, say, Singapore with an English girl, he can take her where he likes and do what he likes *provided the girl does not complain*, and no one dare under the law interfere with him. If any questions are asked, the " pimp " readily asserts that the lady is his wife; if there are two women, the other lady is said to be her sister. By our law and usage a woman takes *her husband's nationality*, and this is quite as it ought to be;

but it is a point in favour of the "pimp." He claims to be an American or an Austrian or a German or a Russian, and he stands on his dignity against interference. If the girl is questioned she, poor fool, claims the "pimp" as her husband. She is new to the business, in a strange country, and her only safety seems to be to cling to the human boa-constrictor, the "pimp," who later on will slime her over and destroy her. She soon finds herself in Malay Street, disgraced, dishonoured, and diseased, while the "pimp" —sheltered, if not protected, by British justice—sails off looking for fresh recruits.

At the Treaty Port of Shanghai, the Hon. John Goodnow fought hard a few years ago to prevent the daughters of America being brought to the East to lead fearful lives. He worked in close union with a British Consul at Shanghai, and he tried honestly to break down all mouldy forms of convention and get authority from Washington to deport from the Treaty Port all American women of ill-fame. But his efforts were futile. I think he did deport several, but one American "missus," who keeps a gorgeous palace of infamy and about twenty young American girls, overcame the Consul's worrying by marrying off the girls, as they arrived, to young or old Italian degenerates— worthless fellows hanging about—who married these girls for a trifle and drew monthly stipends for the use of their names only! The girls then plied their trade as the wives of Italians, which abolished the American Consul's jurisdiction over them.

The Hon. John Goodnow, baffled in his good work at every point, unsupported by Washington, abandoned his office as though to shut out from his mind the fearful traffic in the East of the daughters of the most civilised nation of modern times. Mr. John Davidson succeeded him and did not try to go beyond his routine duties, so the trade grew and flourished, and stands to-day as a monument of mocking iniquity. In the Far East—that is Hong-Kong, Shanghai, etc.—the poorer and meaner "pimp" does not flourish so conspicuously nor thrive at his nefarious business as he does at Singapore, Siam, and other places. The traffic at Hong-Kong and Shanghai is principally in the hands of American "missuses"—that is, the big traffic in white girls is in the hands of these women. In Hong-Kong Gage Street, and other streets running off Gage Street, are full of bad houses. In Lyndhurst Terrace too are houses occupied by American "missuses." Hundreds of American girls pass through Gage Street and Lyndhurst Terrace during the year, and, if they live, eventually find themselves, when their bloom is gone, and they become addicted to drink and drugs, in the Chinese quarter in Takkn Road, where nearly three hundred brothels exist, each house containing from a dozen to twenty unfortunates of all colours, creeds, and castes.

One of the leading "missuses" of Lyndhurst

Terrace actually told me that she draws her supplies from New York and San Francisco, generally *by cable code*. She explained that she has a private cable code, and if her agents in New York or San Francisco are in trouble with two or three young girls, about whom inquiries are being made, they cable to her and arrangements are made to have the young Americans shipped off in charge of an old and retired " pro," who dresses in the garb of a nurse and watches the girls until she delivers the " goods " at Hong-Kong. The girls pass through into Gage Street or Lyndhurst Terrace and, of course, that is all that can be known of them under the present inglorious system. This American " missus " rarely trades for the " pimps." She declares they are not only dangerous but they are too avaricious and they want all the girls' money; so she conducts her own business, principally by cable. This American " missus " is very notorious in the East: she is known to the inner circle of the trade as " Madame Chloral." She earned this name through her predilection for placing a grain of chloral in the beer or whisky or wine of the principal frequenters of her gorgeously furnished house off Gage Street. The chloral sends the men to sleep, when robbing them is made easy. If they have nothing worth stealing, " Madame Chloral " considers they are better asleep than fooling around breaking up her crockery.

Occasionally this woman takes trips abroad to " do " Siam or Sigon, the French colony.

She always takes two, three, or perhaps four young girls with her. At Bangkok she rents a furnished house, engages a brougham and servants, and sets up business. Her stock-in-trade consists of three or four fair young American girls and a full supply of chloral. She is a very well spoken woman, takes the greatest care of her own health, does not drink or smoke, and will not, if she can help it, have diseased girls about her. She has no lover or protector. She speculates in rubber, in tin, and in rice, and it is said that it takes three or four cranys (clerks) to keep her books in order. The saddest feature of this fearful woman's excursions is her return to Hong-Kong to her place of infamy. She nearly always *returns alone*. The daughters of America are left behind—God only knows where, and God only knows their end. And this is what they call triumphant civilisation !

There will be found further on in this book a pathetic story related by an unhappy woman called Madame V., which throws some light on the methods of procuresses and "pimps." Sad as is the story, Madame V.'s is in reality one of the brighter cases in all the dreadful list one comes across when inquiring into this subject. In the nature of things only a very few of the girls who are trapped and taken to these houses in the East attain to the position of becoming mistress of one. In their trade, to become a "missus" is a much-desired but seldom-attained end. If they are not actually killed in the houses to which they are taken, they are simply thrust out to die somewhere else, having lost their bloom and passed their period of usefulness. So, there must be no confusion in the minds of the public between the "missuses" who are keepers of the bad houses, and in league with the "pimps"—women who by a stroke of good fortune in their own line of work have attained to some sort of independence—and the unhappy girls who are trapped and taken out for actual use by men in these places. The "missus" and the "pimps" can share the spoils, and do, but the girls themselves never make any profit out of their vocation. They have food and of course plenty of drink, but the clothes with which they are provided are of the scantiest and flimsiest description, and not such as they could escape in. They are not allowed out— so have no need of money, and what is paid to them by the men who come in is simply confiscated by the "missus" and the "pimp," under one excuse or another.

Even in London and in various other British cities, prostitutes seldom make much money for themselves. What they earn is taken away from them, and they are blackmailed on every side. They have to pay six times the rent which is ordinarily demanded for any place where they live, and the women in whose houses they take rooms always black- mail them. In many cases the landladies hold them perpetually in debt and terrorise them, so that they are afraid to make any attempt to get away.

In France the condition of these unhappy women is somewhat different. In Paris they are kept to a certain quarter, and we have been told by people who have lived in France many years, and who know conditions very well, that many of the women are thrifty and saving, and they often put by enough money to retire upon, living quietly in the country when they are too old to follow their " profession." There, too, the women are safer and less liable to the terrible diseases which ravage them in this country, where there is no supervision, and nobody cares how they suffer, or with what poison they infect others. The public has not yet realised the virulence of the dreadful diseases which desolate the ranks of prostitutes. It has never been realised that the most innocent and harmless person might be infected, and that indeed many thousands of innocent and harmless young girls and youths are infected yearly without knowing what is the real complaint from which they suffer. If three cases of cholera were heard of in England, the whole country would be in a state of panic; and yet here we have something just as virulent and perhaps more horrible than cholera, because it causes a more lingering death and more prolonged sufferings.

We have been told by people who know the East very well that the women in India —that is, the native women—who follow this trade are often quite decent creatures of their sort. They do not rob or attempt to blackmail men who consort with them, and the occupation is followed often from generation to generation. The women in this class dress in a peculiar manner, and can always be distinguished. They look indeed pretty in their clean, gay garments. It is a common thing for women to go from Persia to Bombay, Calcutta, Poona, and Burma, from very poor districts, and to stay there in the city for purposes of prostitution, having set before them the task of collecting twenty thousand rupees; and when this sum is saved out of their earnings they return to their villages, and marry and settle down. These women avoid disease, and do not realise the sin or shame, or both, of their occupation. They are not Christians. They go out into the field far from their own country, earn money in the way described, and return rich to their poor people. Of course, these are the women who escape the plagues which usually follow prostitution.

The worst horror which the victims of the white slave traffic have to face when they are taken out to the East is that they are sold, not to European men exclusively—only the very attractive ones and those who keep a healthy look have that fate—but to any of the natives who pay for them, and if they are unattractive or troublesome they are actually sold to the vilest opium dens and to shame. How can we possibly suppose that we can attract to Christianity the heathen people who live in these countries when they see with their own eyes that Christian women are brought to their lands and sold for evil purposes ? The natives know all about these things; they are not secrets to them. The dishonour that we suffer by these deeds is unthinkable. The British Government, of course, has not complete control over all the islands in the Eastern Archipelago. The Dutch own Java; Sumatra, Siam, and Borneo are divided up, but still the British are predominant, and it lies with our Government to adjust these matters. It becomes amusing in the face of these revelations to think of the fuss that was made about the " Chinese Slavery." I suppose it will be very offensive to many good people if we remark that the " Chinese Slavery " only became intolerable when it could be made to serve the political purposes of a party. But the unhappy victims of a white slave trader can never serve any one's political purpose, nobody can use them for any purpose but the unfortunate one to which they seem doomed. There is nothing to be got out of them—no " kudos," no gain, no praise, nothing but unpopularity; and so why on earth should any party politicians concern themselves about the matter ? All they have done so far, if the subject has been broached, is to pooh-pooh the whole thing and shelve the question because it is not profitable to themselves to pursue these inquiries further. Now we hope to present this evil as a *national disgrace* and danger, and Members of Parliament, be their party what it may, can join issue here and act together for the defence of our womanhood and Christian womanhood the world over. We do not make our appeal to party politicians, but we are making it on behalf of these poor slaves to the people of this country, and to all just *men* irrespective of party or creed.

Even America, democratic though she may perhaps be, is in many ways a less free country than this country is. Germany is police-ridden and aristocracy-ridden; Russia has hardly emerged out of barbarity as yet. But here the voice of the people is the only thing that really counts, when all is said and done. It is the people who send men to Parliament, it is the people who decide what salary the King shall receive, and it is as well that the nation should keep before it its ideals of freedom, and insist upon justice for the humble and great alike. Therefore, we ask the representatives of the people to enlighten the people, and ask their support for new laws to be enacted to meet present and future conditions.

In dealing with these profoundly pathetic tragedies which affect the poor and obscure, the unknown, and the ignorant and the weak, we would like to give the people the story of their woes, and we ask them to shelter and protect the innocent and the helpless. We put this case before the nation, not before

sects and classes and societies or "parties."
It was quite recently that a case was
told to me of a man and woman who were
taking away a young girl from Liverpool to
the Argentine. By what specious lies they
got hold of this girl no one knows. The
police were very suspicious of these people,
but they had nothing definite to go on, and
the girl was well primed with her tale. She
said she was the niece of the man and woman,
and was going out to a millinery business.
Hearing of this case makes one wonder
whether that girl will meet the fate of many
other girls of whom we have been told in
such books as have been mentioned here.
Now there *is* a way in which these cases can
be dealt with, and we will propose in a
separate chapter methods by which the traffic
may be killed.

The Argentine is a very happy hunting-
ground for the "pimp." To begin with, it
is a very rich country, and the men there
have a great deal of money to spend on their
pleasures. Ordinary prostitution, of course,
is carried on in all these rich cities; and that
being an occupation which has existed almost
since the foundation of the world, we have
no reason to hope that we can ever entirely
abolish it. If women of that class who are
already lost to virtue choose to go out to
these strange countries to prosecute a trade
with which they have made themselves
familiar, they must take the risks. I do not
see how we can prevent them going; but we

ought to be able to prevent virtuous and innocent women and young girls from being *trapped* for houses of ill-fame in these places. A case was tried in the courts of this country about three years ago, respecting a young English girl who had been taken to the Argentine by a so-called theatrical agent. When she got there she found that she was simply to display herself in a place where men came to look on whatever women were provided for their sensual excitement, and that she was expected to lead a bad life. She managed to escape, and the case came into the courts. But how very rarely does one hear of creatures of the " pimp's " class being brought to justice !

The officers of the Salvation Army have been engaged for the last five or six years in trying to combat the " pimp " who takes our girls to France, and it is a work which has interested me very much indeed, as I have personally known cases of girls being cajoled into going to so-called " theatrical engagements " in Paris. This work of dealing with the white slave traffic between this country and France especially is one into which the Salvation Army organisation has been putting its whole strength and influence. There can be no possible reason for people to doubt the exactness of their statements; yet they have not been able to get sufficient legal support for the work they are trying to do, which is to prevent the exportation of young girls from this country to Paris and Marseilles

5

and other French towns for immoral purposes.
The cases where girls are offered music-hall
and theatrical engagements, and are taken
over to the Continent only to find themselves
recruited for prostitution, are so common as
to excite hardly any interest at all.

The National Council of Public Morals,
and all those of us who are interested in the
welfare of girls, are trying to get the age of
consent raised, but even this seems impossible
to manage. As the law now stands, it is not
the *exact* age which matters; it is merely
necessary for a bad man or woman to say
a girl victim *looked sixteen*. They are not
required to *prove* that she is sixteen before
they ruin her.

There must be some secret reason why the
Parliaments of this country have heretofore
been so loath to deal with any matters
relating to the protection of women. They
have occupied themselves frantically with all
sorts of trivial matters, but when asked to
deal with any question that concerns the
protection of the young women of this
country there have always been difficulties in
the way of proceeding with the work. But
now, in this age of reform, we hope and pray
that the attitude of Parliament may be strongly
in favour of the abolition of the white slave
traffic to the East and abroad especially.

The excessive sentences passed on the
women window - smashers make us hope
that men who injure and wrong women
will now be severely dealt with also. The

Government would not like the people to feel that women wrong-doers were penalised far more severely than men. To break a window is not comparable to selling an innocent girl into slavery. Yet for the first such offence the punishment is quite foolishly inadequate. Women are given over to the prison doctors to be tortured—the only man subjected to the torture went raving mad. Yet scores of women have been injured for life by these doctors. There are no women doctors in prisons to deal with women prisoners! And no women doctors to whom injured girls and women can be taken: I mean no official women doctors. Is this not utterly cruel and shocking?

With our Mackirdy Home we do an infinite amount of good among poor but good girls who find themselves stranded in this great, heartless London. A little gentle pity, kindly advice, and a timely word of encouragement sometimes saves a girl from perdition. Girls and women have been sent to us by all sorts of people, who have asked us to protect and help them, and thank God so far we have been able to do this. We have not opened the house to tramps and old women of the beggar type, for the simple reason that these old people can find shelter in the common lodging-houses; *they* are not in danger there. But for young respectable women the " pimp " and the procuress are ever on the hunt, and they are in constant danger. For pure, good, respectable women and girls to go into the common lodging-houses or into places where these dirty, wicked old people are living is very horrible in every way.

What we have always longed to do is to help the girl or woman who has not yet fallen, and who would like to follow a respectable life if the opportunity were given to her. We know that the ranks of prostitutes are filled to a large extent by those who have been compelled by fate to let go of virtue in order to live, to have food and shelter and clothing; and we must not allow ourselves to run away with the idea that there are very few women without friends to help them, or somebody to whom they can go for succour if they are in need. The unfortunate part of it is there are heart-breaking numbers of them who are not looked after, and by some misfortune or other they find themselves without shelter and without friends. For these there is always the wicked old woman who prowls the street searching for new victims, and the terrible men who are out nightly for the same purpose.

We must try and imagine ourselves in the position of a girl who has nothing to fall back upon, who has no friends who are well off enough or who care enough to help her—the girl who has been given no trade or profession, who has been provided with no money by her parents, but has been simply brought into the world to take her chance. Imagine such a position, and then try to think how one of us would feel if some one came to us with kind words and offered us comfort and security and plenty to eat and drink, making no mention of the price, but hinting in a vague sort of way of something very simple that would be required of us in return. Supposing that we were ignorant and sorely in need, is it difficult to imagine that we should be tempted by these good offers? Or one might even know quite well what it was that would be asked in return for present help, and yet, facing the evils—starvation and loneliness, and the terror of being without a protector or friend—how long do you suppose any one could hold out and keep on the right way? We must also consider this: the ignorance of the results of immorality is so profound that no girl knows about the diseases she is liable to until she gets them. There is another thing that I would also ask you to think about, and that is that we who have been so fortunate and so happy as to have been well trained, we who have developed intelligences, and who have many interests in life, can hardly, even by a wild stretch of imagination, put ourselves into the position of these foolish, innocent, ignorant, and silly girls, who will believe almost everything that is told to them, and who have the most extraordinary ideas of life. There is one Divine and lasting service that we can do for women and girls who need our help and protection. We can, at any rate, provide places where they in their hour

of need and temptation can go—Homes
where they can be received at any hour of
night or day without question, *their only
recommendation being their need*, and where
the questioning process will be left to an
hour when they are better fitted to give an
account of themselves, and when their confidence has been won.

At Mackirdy House the one qualification
of a girl or woman seeking admittance is
that she is in need and requires friends.
The accommodation of course is limited,
and presently I am afraid we shall find
ourselves crowded out; but there is another
house, a much larger and a better one, which
is already bought, and remains now only to
be altered and furnished. And this house,
which has been a ladies' college, is most
wonderfully suited to our purpose. It is
really two houses; so that on one side we
can receive girls who can lodge for considerable periods with us, and on the other
side we can take in temporary cases. We
have had girls who have come from Sweden
and from Denmark, from Switzerland, and
from Scotland, Wales, and Ireland. We
have of course a larger number of English
girls—London girls and girls from the
country and provincial English cities. We
have had some elderly women; and, indeed,
there are one or two at Mackirdy House
who have been a considerable time there.
They are respectable and good people, but
sadly in need of friends.

All organisations which have for their aim the uplifting and protection of girls and women demand very especially our sympathy and practical aid. It is quite within reason to suppose that some of these very girls who are now so happily working might quietly have been shipped off to some house of infamy across the seas. These things are happening every day. The men who trade in women do not go to the quarters which are inhabited by the well-to-do and the protected, they prowl about among those who are poor and those about whom least fuss would be made if they disappeared. You can see the cunningness and devilry of these creatures who try to sell human bodies and souls. Then the girls who are trapped, after drifting about from one place to another, and sinking lower and lower, are taken to those fearful hells of which we set out to tell in this book—the places where they are sold to Chinese coolies and natives of the lowest classes. The rich natives will not look at them any more, once they are old-looking and drunken and diseased.

Very few girls are taken direct to Singapore or Hong-Kong for immediate use in the native houses. They are not given over to the coolies and the riff-raff of the population until their monetary value has diminished very sadly. But that our own girls can be found in Chinese houses of infamy in Shanghai and Hong-Kong, and in native dens in the Straits Settlements, is beyond all question, though they are taken there secretly and as prisoners.

We feel it is our duty to add here a chapter on the slave traffic in Hong-Kong and Shanghai, into which Mr. Willis personally inquired, travelling to those cities on purpose to find out what was going on "behind the veil," if one may so express it.

It is horrible even to have to write of these dread things, but how much more horrible is it that they really exist to be written of! But let us pray God this may be the last time a book has to be written of the slave traffic of European Christian girls in the East. We believe the people of this country will kill the trade as soon as they know of it. The thing is to let them know of it once and for all.

CHAPTER IV

CHINA AND THE WHITE SLAVE TRAFFIC

MR. WILLIS's investigations show Hong-Kong to be a terrible place, for besides Gage Street, Lyndhurst Terrace, and the Chinese quarter in Takkn Road, the place is simply alive with continental bars and open brothels, principally kept by foreign prostitutes—Roumanians, Polish and Russian Jewesses, and different Southern European races.

These women are generally in charge of their Russian, Polish, or Roumanian masters — men of the lowest and most brutal type of "pimp"—many of them escaped criminals, who are "wanted" in their own countries. At such continental bars you may buy drinks and refreshments and take in disease at the same time. There is no possible excuse for these cesspools of iniquity, and no reason why they should be allowed to exist. If Great Britain and America, instead of turning a blind eye to them, and denying the existence of the curse, would face the matter decently and attack the traffic, it would not be difficult to kill the slave trade in the East.

At Shanghai the American element is very pronounced. A place called the " Harem " is gorgeously furnished, and the most strict forms are observed. A liveried footman opens the door, and the visitor is shown into a drawing-room with which any fine lady might well be satisfied. About twenty American girls are kept in the " Harem," but they do not remain there long, as this woman's charges are so fearfully high she must of necessity keep fresh supplies almost continuously en route. She works together with a notorious gang in San Francisco. Where the American girls disappear to, once they leave the " Harem," is a secret surrounded with much mystery, as few if any of these particular women find themselves in the Chinese dens at Scott's Road. Scott's Road is a very notorious quarter containing about three hundred Chinese dens. Each den shelters from ten to fifteen or twenty girls of every nationality. The place is as dangerous as it is loathsome. If a drunken man or licentious European reprobate enters these quarters, the chances are ten to one against his ever coming out. The place is the home of Chinese murderers and revolutionary cut-throats. Disreputable Chinese women do a large trade in bringing little Chinese girls—many of them children— into these dens of infamy. Only the other day a man and woman, both Chinese, were arrested in the act of taking six little girls from the hills into these dens.

It is on this acre of fearful iniquity that the

"pimp" likes to dump a European girl whom he has trapped, used, and beaten, taught to smoke opium and drink spirits, and who has become so degraded as to be repulsive to a white man and rejected by a decent Asiatic. The "pimp," as a climax to his dealings with the girl, dumps her, so to speak, into the dens of Scott's Road or kindred places for so much cash down—and that is the end of her. Speaking of the American women of ill-fame in the East, it is only fair to say that the American men in business in the East—or American men who travel in the East—look upon the shame of the daughters of their country with horror. One young American business man told Mr. Willis at the Hotel Astor that it was the greatest torment in the lives of decent Americans in the East, and the worst form of degradation and the greatest hindrance to business to have American women and girls used by Asiatics, who always despise the thing they use.

There is little doubt that many well-disposed persons will scorn our efforts and say these things cannot be helped; they have gone on from time immemorial, so they must go on until the Angel Gabriel sounds the last trump. This is not our view of the situation. And we reply, " Prostitution in certain forms may go on, and all human efforts may not stop it; still, if there is to be something in our midst that is, if you like to call it so, a necessary evil, why not protect the innocent? If a drain is necessary at the back of one's house to carry off the refuse of the habitation, is there **any** earthly reason why that drain should not be kept from infecting the household? Being pestiferous does not add to its usefulness, and it endangers the neighbourhood. We shall offer our remedies, and the public must judge as to their effectiveness. No useful purpose would be achieved by the recital of all the enormities of the " pimp " trade in the East without some suggestions as to their termination.

Now, in regard to what we shall propose, we have as a pattern a miniature effort by the French authorities in the great French colony of Sigon. This is a thriving colony of vast potentialities, and it is managed and controlled in a manner that reflects the greatest credit on La Belle France. In Sigon, licentiousness is not let loose to devour the young—to rot and cripple youth, and send to their graves those in the noon of life. At Sigon the traffic is in a measure at least controlled : all houses of infamy are licensed, all the women are registered, and if they are found to be diseased they are placed under restraint or deported. Soliciting in the streets is forbidden and general order in the traffic prevails. The Government was forced to take the most stringent steps to stop the riot of immorality, as the army stationed in the colony was found to be seething with disease. Men not only lost their money but their health, and numbers were returned to France with shattered constitutions, and themselves a dreadful scourge to the clean people among whom they settled. It was said their breakdown was accelerated or due to the Sigon climate, but that was a lie. It was the pestilential disease that was rampant in the East, with which many innocent youths became inoculated by having immoral relations with diseased women. The authorities on the spot recognised the truth of these matters.

The Governor-General, M. Doumier, a brave, clean-living man, set to work to purify the place. Now, the army is healthy, the citizens are not plague-stricken, and soldiers are not returned to France ruined and diseased. But there are even yet danger-spots in Sigon. There are the open continental cafés, which are being run on much the same lines as the Hong-Kong cafés. These are now, I understand, to be cleared out completely. If this is done Sigon may well be proud of her record of improvement. There is one thing very sure, and that is—the " pimp's " occupation or trade in Sigon is gone.

As we shall mention Bangkok in this book, and as Bangkok generally has a reputation it does not deserve, it is only fair and just to say that every reasonable effort is being now made in Bangkok to bring under proper control the licentious habits of the people. The present King is a very enlightened and worthy monarch. He was educated in England, finished his educational career with honours in the West, and lives up to his attainments. He is a good man, and he ascended to the throne of his ancestors with a knowledge of the world and the world's affairs which his fathers did not possess. He is surrounded by enlightened statesmen, and although the task of cleansing the country, which is his magnificent heritage, will be tremendous, there is reason to hope he will in time clear his kingdom of the worst forms of vice. The King and his ministers have undertaken the work in an earnest manner, but it must of necessity be a very gradual process, for the task is very great. We must honour and aid these fine men, and help them, when possible, in a labour which will break the back of the white slave traffic in those ports.

At the Treaty Port of Shanghai, and indeed at Hong-Kong and other Treaty Ports in that great land of mysteries and superstitions —China—the poorer and meaner "pimps" do not flourish, but the "swell" pimp is a force to be reckoned with. At Shanghai he struts about with an elastic step and an air of authority, and with a swagger which being interpreted says, "I am the only individual who can be trusted to bring a proper white girl to these parts. I do my business in a thorough, clean-cut fashion." He is proud of the fact that he fulfils orders for white girls to be sold into slavery.

The frontispiece to this volume shows the bridge leading to the Chinese dens. Once a girl crosses the "Bridge of Sighs" and of tears —aye, of blood !—no power on this earth can redeem her. The various European Consuls dare not interfere with the Chinese quarter, for fear of a general rising or general massacre. It is known that many European girls are taken at various times over this bridge into the Chinese quarter; that this is an absolute and undeniable fact no one who knows about these places will deny. Once the women enter the gates of that hell on earth, they can never retrace their steps or go back, and it is the damnable " pimps " who keep up the supply of English, French, German, and American girls for this Chinese quarter. No virtuous or untainted girl, however, is ever taken to this hell. They fetch more money elsewhere. The poor creatures have been used in Java, beaten and ill-used in Singapore, dragged about in far-off Eastern places till they are almost done for; then they are brought to Shanghai, and after living a year or two a life of degradation, they are sold into the Chinese quarter. Be it said to the credit of the British that they do try to stop British women bathing in the immoral seas of the East. If they are caught here they are deported without question. Unhappily they are not always caught, and once they pass that bridge into the Chinese quarter, they cannot be caught! No European dare enter the Chinese quarter without permission. The Americans also do their best to protect their women-folk from this unthinkable fate, as has already been stated.

As has been said, the late Hon. John Goodnow, American Consul at Shanghai, a

splendid sample of the best American manhood, struggled hard with the evil at Shanghai,
and he tried to prevent American girls coming
to live evil lives there.   He fought, poor man,
with terrible odds against him, as neither his
Government nor the American Press supported his efforts; and more than once when
he was in the act of deporting an American
girl brought to Shanghai for immoral purposes
by a German " pimp," the Consul was con-
fronted with the marriage certificate showing
that the American girl had actually been
married to the " pimp."   Thus complication
after complication followed, and the traffic
increased and multiplied, until to-day every
boat coming from the West brings its con-
signment of white flesh that must ultimately
be buried in dishonour in some dark, infamous
spot.

At Hong-Kong things were extremely bad
until the advent of Sir Frederick Lugard and
his good and clever wife, Lady Lugard, better
known as " Flora Shaw," at one time the
capable correspondent of the London *Times*.
This lady has done a great amount of good in
a quiet, unostentatious fashion by cleansing
some of the immoral dens of Hong-Kong.
Nevertheless the need for reform there is
very great still.

At Shanghai a very pretty girl was pointed
out to me, says Mr. Willis.   She had been
brought to that town by a Russian " pimp,"
and sat near my table at the Hotel Astor.

She was one of the prettiest girls I ever saw. Very refined-looking, she certainly was a woman out of the common. As she sat there, dressed in pale pink silk, and daintily toying with a morsel of food, she presented a perfect picture of womanhood beautifully modelled. Yet the most conspicuous feature about her was a pair of large, jet-black eyes which sparkled like diamonds, and seemed to tell a tale of dormant passion within her—of a hungry soul yearning for something. How came the woman there? I became interested. She caught my imagination—she was on my nerves—on my mind. When she left the dining-room I felt irritated, as I sorely wanted to speak to her—to get, if possible, her history. I went to my room. As I was going to bed a Dr. S——, an American, entered. He had just "dropped in for a chat." He took a great interest in foreign parts, and knew I had been doing some work in "hustling round." "D'ye know," he rambled on, "I'm very much taken with you. You're a good sort. I can see that as plain as daylight." I suggested a drink—the starting-point of all that is good or bad in the East. The doctor did all the talking. He came from New York, where they talk like threshing machines.

"I've just come out here," he said, "for the benefit of these yellow 'heathen Chinese.' I am carrying around with me the finest sample of charity that ever left the United States.

6

" I've invented a drug that will cure man, woman, and beast of the opium habit.   When I hit on it in the States, I knew I'd discovered the greatest glory for the Stars and Stripes. So I hastened across the pond with it ready to serve up red-hot, and I'm going to make this country realise that I'm turning their mud flats into a veritable paradise; the garden of Eden won't be in it when I've done with Shanghai.

" I don't regard myself as a benefactor of mankind," he continued, "but there's a tremendous pile of people that *do*, and they're very far off the right track. Gee! Won't this make the 'heathen Chinee' hum, some?— when he gets a sniff of my 'opium cure.' "

I quite endorsed his enterprise as a magnificent and laudable task.

"Wouldn't care to see one of the places where they smoke the drug, would you?" he queried.

I told him I certainly would, as I was desirous of learning as much of the places I visited as possible.

"All right then," said the doctor; "I'll come and have dinner with you to-night, and then I'll take you round for a squint."

Before he left he induced me to give him a donation towards a Chinese charity with an unpronounceable name, and left me—the charity richer and I poorer by ten dollars.

He turned up for dinner full of spirits— of mixed sorts I should imagine. We took a rickisha, and our "Tshia, tshia"-yelling coolies quickly perambulated his light cart through a maze of foul-smelling passages and by-streets of Shanghai. We stopped at a dimly lighted house in a side street and entered a dismal building. At the door we were assailed by a heavy, nauseating odour that filled the air. The affable head-man, the Chinese owner of the den—for den it was—received us, and invited us, with many smiles, to sit on one of the numerous dirty stools that were placed around the dingy apartment. It was a real opium den.

A basin, containing a small quantity of foul-smelling oil, fed the wick of a flickering light that only helped to heighten the sor-didness of the surroundings in this den of malignity—nay, of death.

The Chinaman, with the evil grin of one of the imps of darkness, twisted himself into many suave bows; he fawned on us, his de-praved countenance beaming with knowing smiles. He asked what the desire of his visitors was? Lady? Or opium? Or both . . . eh?

Being enlightened on the subject, and some dollars having found their way to his greasy palm, we ascended the rickety staircase, and, to the tune of the creaking boards, landed in a dark, narrow passage on the top floor.

The foul opium-smoke-charged air almost stifled us.

Opening one of the doors in the passage he led us on to a broad ledge along the side of the house, which served as a means of access to an adjoining building: the real opium den.

Cautiously we entered; the Chinaman, placing his finger warningly on his lips, motioned us to follow.

A large and comfortable room received us. Soft velvet couches and settees, heavy carpets of the softest texture suggested an atmosphere of luxury I certainly had not expected in this vile corner.

We seated ourselves on one of the couches, while the son of the Celestial Empire spoke in a subdued voice to a hard-faced hag who had entered from a side door. She immediately took her departure, returning with two young, almond-eyed creatures dressed in the flimsiest of garments.

My companion drew one of them towards him and put his arm around the slender waist of the girl—or rather child—and then invited me to follow his example and have a try at the opium pipe. He was going to smoke, he said. He told me he only did so to get to know the drug; he could then judge of its effects better and experiment with his " cure."

The sickly smell that had been so noticeable on entering the house was quite sufficient to destroy any desire on my part for such experiments.

My companion made himself comfortable on one of the settees, the girl smoothing the pillows on his couch. He, for some reason or other, seemed a favoured patron; probably he paid handsomely for his indulgences.

The pipe, lamp, and usual paraphernalia which form the opium-smoker's outfit were soon forthcoming.

The girl sat on the edge of the couch and tended the pipe, while my friend, with his arm tightly encircling her waist, soon proved by his stertorous breathing to have fallen into a heavy sleep.

The girl dried the perspiration from his heated brow and loosened his collar, while his powerful arm still held her in a firm embrace.

The old woman now shuffled from the room unobserved, and, at a sign from her, the girl, with a weary sigh, placed her head on my companion's pillow, while she threw her arms around him. A terrible picture to contemplate! A soul in the grasp of the Lord of Hells! Now I knew my companion's hypocrisy.

The horrid drug and vice had taken possession of his brain and his manhood, and my companion, a fine specimen of nature's handiwork, was now in the grip of the vice he had wooed. He was sinking into those depths where life is meaningless beyond the desires created by the drug.

While I was thus gazing at the pitiful sight before me, the old hag's hand touched me on the shoulder, and motioned me to follow her.

I left the room. She grinned and said, "He no makee go; he stop topside. Suppose to-mollow he makee go. Ha, ha, ha!" she grinned; "ha, ha, ha!"

So, I thought, this is evidently the custom—to spend the whole night under the influence of opium, and then stagger home, like a drunken man, whilst the early rays of the rising sun were dispelling the dense vapours that hovered over the waters of the Yangtze River at beautiful Shanghai!

What I had seen was sufficient to give me a good idea of the iron grip in which the cursed opium pipe holds its victims.

The old woman came to me with the information that, for "kum sia" (a present), she would show me the house and how others smoked the drug.

Though, as I said, I was really quite sated and sick with the sight before me, yet I wanted to see the *natives* indulging in their favourite vice.

I followed the old woman, and she led me through a maze of passages until we reached a carved door. She then gently tapped, and a grinning Chinese boy of some sixteen years of age opened the door.

They had a few hurried words in whispers, and then the old hag motioned me to follow her. On entering I noticed that the room was as well fitted as the one in which I had left my friend—the same display of costly furniture, except that the general arrangement plainly showed a woman's hand.

We passed into the inner room, and—almighty Heaven! on the couch, with the cursed pipe in the grasp of her slender fingers, and nude, save for a scanty *négligé*, lay my beautiful companion of the hotel table; and, to add to the horror of it, she was attended by a Chinaman!

The beautiful creature, who had been crossing my mind all day long, lay here in an opium den, open to the gaze of every Chinaman who cared to pay for the privilege of feasting his eyes on the form of a white woman, drugged and unconscious. The sight was pitiable, most pitiable.

To see her there, unconsciously one of the main attractions of the opium hell of an unscrupulous, slant-eyed heathen, fairly unnerved me. I turned round, and with a kick sent the Chinaman flying through the door. True the woman was not British, but she was a lovely, white Christian—and to see her so fallen, so near to hell! She must immediately leave this den—and yet the horror of shame, once she could realise that I had seen her under those terrible conditions, might kill her!

I drew back. I would leave her. Probably she would be carried out unconscious when the patrons of the house had left.

I turned towards the door—when a voice seemed to say to me:

"Coward! how dare you desert a white girl in such a place and with such devils around her?"

The woman's position struck me to the heart.

I lifted the poor creature in my arms, while the frightened Chinese hag assisted me to place a cloak around the drugged form and a cloth over the pallid features.

Then I carried the unconscious girl downstairs, placed her in the rickisha, and we sped rapidly away from that disgusting den.

The girl was placed in a sheltering home, away from her tempters, but whether she stayed there or not I do not know.

During next day's rambles around the city with a Chinaman who is well acquainted with the vile doings of Shanghai's nether world, I had my eyes opened still further, for he was able to point out to me quite a number of these dens of iniquity, where nightly a queue of coolies form up to feast their eyes on the limbs of a drugged, stupefied white woman.

They pay there according to a fixed scale—an embrace may be had for a dollar—they may kiss her lips for two. The unfortunate creatures in these dens are the dregs of the European houses of infamy, women who, driven to frenzy by the constant exactions of their so-called male protector, the " pimp," or who are on the verge of despair through the terrible existence forced upon them in " the house," will take to drink or opium, and they are then lured away into the lower hells, having lost their " market value " in the richer " bad houses."

Once in these dread places, they find that to revolt is to court death, and such death as may not be named—so they drink heavily or take drugs provided for them and which mercifully dull their senses.

Can nothing be done in England—in Germany—in France—in America—to stop the devil filling up the bottomless pit of hell with the victims of the white slave traffic in the East?

Surely it is time to act! In God's name let the answer be: Yea—though the heavens fall!

CHAPTER V

CHRISTIAN SLAVES IN THE EAST

THE gentleman who has supplied most of the facts regarding the white slave traffic in the East, and whose name appears with mine on the cover of this book, has been for very many years a Member of Parliament in Sydney, Australia.

All the facts that he has given in this book find their counterparts in the experiences of residents in the East—police officers and magistrates and missionaries—and where specific stories and definite cases are given, they are for the most part recorded in the annals of the police courts of the country where the incidents took place. There is nothing at all imaginary in this book. Neither Mr. Willis nor I have adorned the tale in any way. The only thing we have done is to take out some of the most gruesome incidents, and have lightened the shadows in the darkest pictures. It is not possible to put the whole of the hideous truth of the traffic in a book which will probably be on every bookstall, on sale all over the world, and on the shelves of every library, and which we write with the object of getting it into the hands of every thinking man and woman in this country. We are compelled to soften down facts and leave out the most ghastly things.

The other day I had given me a book published recently in America. If I were a rich woman I would willingly spend several thousands of pounds in placing this book where it could be read by every one concerned. People may say, "Oh, you would put ideas into the heads of perfectly innocent girls." That is not my view or experience of giving knowledge to people. Since this slave traffic exists in our midst, since London and Liverpool and almost every other city contributes its victims to the horrible trade, I think it is not only well, but our duty, to see that our girls and men know the price that has to be paid if they connect themselves with the hideous thing, either directly or indirectly.

After reading the above-named book the question of women's suffrage loomed large in the public eye. Personally I happen to be a very busy woman, and my work has lain in other directions, so I have not connected myself with this movement. But in reading this book, which lays bare the horrid corruption and the fearful results of the white slave traffic in America, it has come home to me that the mothers of men must take part in the affairs of the nation in order to protect, not only the women victims of vice and injustice, but to shield and protect their own sons and the men whom they love. This book does not deal with the question which we are now engaged upon, which is the white slave traffic in the East especially, but you will see in these pages how corrupt and how altogether horrible a Government without women's influence can be.

If you had been, as I have been, walking the midnight streets with the soldiers of the Salvation Army, night after night, hour after hour, in starlight and rain, you would be, as I have been, awakened to the horrible power and significance of prostitution. You simply do not know what it is, and even now I do not fully know what it is, though I have seen something of it. It is because we are not able to follow step by step these unhappy creatures to their ends and see what becomes of them that we do not realise the awful significance of this traffic.

I do not for a single moment think, nor does Mr. Willis—in fact, very few people do—that prostitution can ever be killed; and we are not setting out to do anything so foolish as to try to abolish prostitution. But what we are setting out to do is this: The very worst side of prostitution is that along which are ranged wretched girls and women who have been lured or forced into the life without knowledge of what they are going into; and it is these pathetic victims of the white slave traffic we wish to serve. We do not call prostitution the white slave traffic—the two things are distinct. There are many prostitutes who have chosen that life because they prefer it, strange as this may seem; and some of the women know how to look after themselves—not many, I am afraid, but some. But the girls who are picked up by the villainous rogues who are always on the prowl hunting for the innocent and the defenceless, for the poverty-stricken one, the hungry one, and the foolish one—these we must protect, and their hunters are the vile creatures we shall hound out of existence. There is a record of a girl who succeeded in escaping from a dreadful house where she was taken, in her ignorance, and kept a prisoner. Two girls befriended her, and in talking over the terrible experiences she had gone through (she, however, says very little about them) she remarks that no words have been invented to tell what this trade really is. One of the girls asked the escaped victim, "Is it as bad as they say there?" "I don't know what they say," she replied, "but it is worse than any one *can* say. There is a lot of it no one can say, because there ain't no words that have been made for it. Just you pray God that you won't ever have to find out how bad it is."

From time to time in this country a few men are arrested, convicted, and punished for living on women whom they have made their slaves. But the punishment inflicted is in reality far too trivial. It bears no comparison at all with the crime when one considers what that crime leads to, and the dreadful suffering it entails on the victims. What we want to do is to get some laws passed in England and in our colonies and our dependencies, and especially in the East—laws such as now exist in Australia, which within a year killed the traffic in women. Two men were captured in Australia with a batch of girls whom they had brought over from Europe, and whom they took to a certain mining camp and sold to a bad life. The men were captured and imprisoned for ten years, and during that period they received several floggings at intervals. There has never been a case of white slave traffic in Australia since these cases were dealt with, and there never will be as long as it is known that to traffic in a girl means a flogging as well as ten years' rigorous imprisonment. It is absolutely the only punishment—there is no other at all that is going to deter these men from pursuing their horrible trade. I feel that not until women have political power is there the slightest chance of the white slave traffic being absolutely put down. I will tell you why. Men who are returned to Parliament have to please their constituents, and their constituents are *men*, two out of every ten of whom are interested —I will not say how—in prostitution. The interest does not take the same form with all of them. Some of them amuse themselves in one quarter and some in another; but these men feel that they do not want anything done to make prostitution difficult; and the members who go to Parliament are perfectly well aware of these facts. But we want the representatives of the people to take this tale of the infamous and cruel slavery of Christian women to the just, clean men—put it to the right people, and it will be killed sooner than the "Chinese Slavery" was killed. Politicians who are presenting to the country marvellous social reforms which they wish to introduce know as well as you and I know that they are simply playing with the surface of things; they will not come down to facts—they dare not.

If six Members of Parliament were to go down into the night streets in any of the great cities and describe what they saw there, and make a public announcement that they were going to fight this evil, they would find themselves standing almost alone. Nothing will be done from inside Parliament unless the heart of the people is stirred, and the nation's sense of justice and pity aroused. We want the Members of Parliament to undertake this task.

How intolerably horrible it is that there should be men doctors only in all but one hospital where women have to go for all manner of diseases? Even the Lock Hospital is staffed entirely by men. This is quite a dreadful state of affairs. If instead of having men doctors to examine women who are the victims of this dreadful trade, women doctors were employed, it would be one of the longest steps towards social regeneration which have been taken in our day. This is a subject with which men doctors ought not to be allowed to deal *at all*; they are unfit for the work, and it is quite improper that they should have anything to do with it. We need a great staff of women doctors— experienced, wise, kind, religious women— who would be appointed by the Government to go into every house of ill-repute. A list of such houses should be kept by the police, and there these good women should interview every single inmate, talk to each poor woman, help her if possible, and do whatever they could for her. In this way many unwilling slaves would be rescued. Those women who for economic, industrial, and other reasons elect to follow their " profession " to the end could, at any rate, be prevented from harming other people, and they could also be protected against blackmailing men and women who prey on them. I am not suggesting the making of vice easy, but what I am suggesting is the protection of the defenceless public and the protection of the weak and ignorant, foolish, and helpless girls who are trapped into the horrid slavery. If the Government would appoint in London itself, say, four women doctors, and place them in communication with the police, arm them with the authority that the factory inspectors have, whereby they could go into any house used for immoral purposes they chose to enter, much could be done.   Personally I would give the whole price that I have received for this book, and give it with joy, if I could see some such reform undertaken.

It is not quite so hopeless when a girl is trapped and kept in this country, because from time to time one may hope that opportunities of escape may come to her.   They might come, alas! too late to prevent the wreck of her life and the utter destruction of her physical person; because " the life," as it is called, gets hold of these women very soon. But still there are on all sides agencies who would help the girls, if only they could get out, and if only they would come to them for help.   But for the unfortunate wretches who are trapped and taken abroad there is simply no help at all—nobody cares for them, nobody defends them.   Many of them are tortured to death, and they all die terribly. Death, indeed, is the very best thing—the most merciful and the kindest thing they can possibly hope for; there is nothing else.

An Australian Example

We will give here an example of what the Australians do when they catch a " pimp," compared with the inactivity of the Old World. A short time ago a big trade was being done in Western Australia by the Italian creatures of this fraternity, who brought in young girls from abroad to houses of ill-fame in Western

Australia. A gang of these wretches carried on the business of girl-catching in a highly scientific and up-to-date fashion. Gangs of three or four went to continental countries; they were fairly good-looking and well informed, and possessed very plausible tongues. They had money, they were sober, and were scrupulously well dressed. They met and tempted many girls, and brought them over to the gold-fields in small batches. Some of the girls were very beautiful; some quite innocent and ignorant. On landing they were generally sold outright to a bad house-keeper, to the doom that awaited them—a doom worse than death — the terms being strictly cash down and no risks. Then these gentry would take themselves off again to secure another batch of fine fresh girls. Thus the trade in human flesh, in innocent young girls, was kept flourishing.

However, the devil himself sometimes makes mistakes, and so it was with one of this nefarious gang. A batch of eighteen continental girls was landed at the city of Perth, on the Swan River, in Western Australia, under the guidance of three Italian "pimps." These girls, most of them innocent, had no sooner arrived than the "missuses" of the various houses of ill-fame had an almost open fight as to who should have the first pick of the new batch to fill the vacant places in the ranks of the army of the "sisters of the pavement" whom death and disease had claimed. Some of these girls were sent to the gold-fields—then in a flourishing condition; two remained in Perth; and Fremantle was likewise apportioned two.

Of the four, however, who went to the gold-fields, one was a beautiful girl, a child of sunny Italy, the land of song and flowers. She was the child of pious parents; she was strictly religious, and a Roman Catholic, of course. She had been engaged as a milliner to go forth to the booming colonies to make her fortune. She, however, began to get a little suspicious even on board the boat, at the conduct of those in whose charge she was; and, as she was considered "touchy," the greatest care was taken of her until she was landed in the "right" quarter, which was inside the walls of a hell in one of the big towns of the gold-fields. Once securely inside this dreadful place the "breaking-in" process was begun, and steps were speedily taken for "knocking the nonsense" out of her. Her clothes were removed, and an old and tattered garment was given to her. The scantiest morsels of food were allowed her by the "missus," who acted as her jailer during the day. At night her "pimp" would visit her, and wild scenes took place behind bolted and barred doors between the unfortunate girl and the wretch who had trapped her. She was well built and strong, and her physical fitness helped her to resist the advances and ill-treatment of the monster in human form whose business it was to ruin

her. With superhuman strength she succeeded for days in protecting her honour.

At last her owners tried a new method.
They tied the girl to the foot of the bed
and beat her unmercifully. Her screams
were stifled by a handkerchief tied over her
mouth. Exhausted, bruised, and battered,
she lay at the foot of the bed tightly bound;
still she resisted the "pimp's" overtures.
They took the handkerchief from her mouth,
and shut her up, leaving her for the space of
two days. She prayed from her pure heart
for deliverance. At last she saw the shadow
of a man on a ladder passing the back
window of the room where she was imprisoned. She shrieked to this man for help
in the Italian language, but no response
came. This is one of the most unfortunate
things for girls who are taken from foreign
countries—they do not speak the language
of the country they are taken to, and in many
cases cannot be understood. However, this
girl next screamed for help in French, and
the man outside on the ladder fortunately
knew some French. It appears he was a
plumber about to mend a disorganised drain-
pipe. He passed quickly through the window,
released the girl, gathered part of her story,
and then bolted and barred the door from the
inside to prevent the "pimp" or the "missus"
discovering that he was helping the girl,
because he knew that had they been found
there was every probability that both would
be murdered. He dressed the girl as best

he could, and carried her out down the ladder to the nearest police station. Her safety was now assured; the poor creature was very kindly treated, and immediately a warrant was issued for the arrest of the "pimp," and he received ten years' hard labour and four floggings. This sentence practically broke up the gang of inhuman traders in Western Australia. The Australian Government sent the unfortunate girl back to her people in Italy, with every comfort that a civilised and humane people could bestow. Proceedings of this case are recorded in the courts of Western Australia, and there are one or two cases in other parts, but the trade has been killed. What Australia can do England can surely do!

It should be our business to make it impossible for any man or woman to take out a girl and sell her into slavery abroad. We shall devote a chapter to our suggested reforms for this white slave traffic in the East, and I think also in South America. If we as a nation are not powerful enough to kill this traffic, then I think our day of dissolution cannot be far off; because we can in no wise suppose that we may live under the banner of Christianity, and please ourselves entirely as to what responsibilities we shall or shall not accept. There are some duties about which we have no choice at all —they are simply given us to perform; and this is one of them.

CHAPTER VI

THE "PIMPS' CLUB" AT SINGAPORE

"As armies exist to fight, so does Christ's Church exist to save, to soothe, to protect the young and innocent, and to guide the ignorant.

"It is ignorance coupled with innocence that brings so many young girls, many of them British, to destruction in the East."

From a sermon by the REV. J. MACKENZIE.

THE Right Reverend Bishop Oldham, preaching in the Cathedral of Singapore, said :

"Brothers, St. Paul says 'if we sin "wilfully after we have received know-"ledge of the truth there remaineth no "more sacrifice of sins, but a fearful "expectation of judgment.' The time "has arrived and is now when our eyes "should be opened and our voices raised "in solemn protest and warning against "the fearful traffic that is at this moment "proceeding without let or hindrance in "the East—the traffic in white women. "For the most part these women are "trapped and decoyed or induced by "other means to come to the East by "persons known as 'pimps,' and under

" the control and guidance of these
" monsters in human form women of
" European nationalities are induced to
" leave their homes, abandon their
" friends, and follow these men all over
" the East. Every boat that comes to
" Singapore brings its quota of human
" freight in the form of these unfortunate,
" misled girls, nearly all of whom go
" into Malay Street and are borne out
" again only to be buried. It is a national
" disgrace that we as sane men and
" women cannot look this fearful evil in
" the face and deal with it without fear
" and trembling, for the protection of the
" young, the innocent, and the ignorant.
" I pray that right-minded men and
" women will cast aside any false modesty
" in dealing with this monster that has
" grown up—the traffic of the white
" women and girls in the East ; and if
" necessary watch each boat and help
" to rescue the misguided girls from
" the dreadful life that awaits them
" once they enter Malay Street. It is
" ignorance — ignorance and want of
" knowledge of the accursed world of
" the 'pimp'—that brings many a good
" girl of English, American, European,
" and French parentage to destruction
" in the East. Saving the young from
" debauch should be the duty of every
" man and every woman of all nation-
" alities and all creeds before Christ."

Bishop Oldham is the first great heart to speak out on behalf of the poor wretched and entrapped white girls who are being brought to the East in hundreds yearly—there to meet their doom. He said further, " If the authorities were as careful about allowing the capture of the white girls for the Babylonian hells, or for the uses of the low-breed coloured men out here for show purposes in their dens, as they are about an important coloured man of position taking a white wife, thousands of lives would be saved yearly." The hot, burning words of the courageous follower of Christ could not be forgotten by any one who heard them. The general mass of people of Singapore were thunderstruck. Some left the church ; others asked if such things could be true. The worthy Bishop's words probably saved many girls from destruction by the fierce enemy, for they caused many " pimps " to pause and falter in their trade while the excitement lasted ; but that pause is over, and now the girl-hunt is in full swing once more. Singapore is still the headquarters of the " pimps " in the East — still the burial-ground of thousands upon thousands of unfortunate white girls. Malay Street, with its hundreds of houses of ill-fame, still flourishes, and, of course, the British flag, with all its traditional glory, still flies at Singapore.

There are decoyed to the East, there to be sold, hundreds of European girls yearly. One may well wonder how it is that these girls, who have so many of them been brought up in very decent homes, arrive at such an unspeakable pass. But when we read our daily papers, sitting comfortably in our homes, it is curious how little such very significant items of news as the following touch us or interest us: "Girl missing from her home." The general public has not yet waked to the real meaning of the notices in the "missing" paragraphs and the "missing" columns of the papers. Almost every day some paper has a notice of a girl missing from her home. "No trace can be found of her; last seen at such and such a place." Then, again, nearly every day bogus marriages come to light; but for every one that is exposed, there are hundreds that are not known at all.

While this book was being written, a few lines in a great daily paper announced the conviction of a fiend in Germany who had murdered the mother of a beautiful girl in order that the way might be cleared for him to take the daughter into slavery in the East. The dreadful cruelties perpetrated upon the innocent and helpless victims of these "pimps" can never be fully written about. Although light has been thrown on their ways in books on the white slave traffic, little has yet been said of the white slave traffic in the East—in China and in the Straits Settlements. The despicable "pimp" in the East has the whole of the Eastern Archipelago to work in, starting from India, sailing over the Indian Ocean, plying his trade in Burma and away through the Straits of Malacca, refreshing himself at Singapore, where he does some business and enjoys himself at the "Pimps' Club." He then goes through the China Sea, through the Sea of Japan, and passes even into Russia. All the way he plies his horrid trade—in Siam, India, China, where, at such cities as Hong-Kong and Shanghai, he makes large profits. He travels through many villages out of the beaten track, and when he has European girls with him he uses as resting-grounds only those places where he feels safe from interference. The trade is not altogether without its dangers, but the dangers are not insurmountable, nor are they such as would deter any of these men. A common burglar has very much more to fear than one of these unspeakable creatures. The girls they have decoyed are dragged over miles of weary journey before they are handed over finally and sold to a life of disease and an agonising death. The "pimp" hovers like a plague all over the East, booking orders for the white girls from the West, and at certain centres they make their headquarters. At Singapore, for instance, they assemble at a recognised club belonging to themselves, a herd of these human perverts and degenerates in whose hearts and minds every instinct of good and decency has died. These miserable atoms of the human family, whom all decent men and women loathe, are a well-organised and important body in their awful business as dealers in white women. Here they fore-gather, exchange views on all topics in which they are interested, transact their business, lounge, read the papers, play cards, smoke, drink coffee, and receive and answer their letters, and on some occasions even meet their women in the silent upstair rooms where they can plan their campaign against decent folk or against persons whom they are about to blackmail. One can at least thank God for this—that very few of these beasts of prey in human form are British. So far the nation is spared the hideous humiliation of having many of her sons engaged in a traffic so vile.

These creatures are almost all foreigners, and many of them have a sort of loud smartness and flashy appearance which might well appeal to ignorant and innocent girls of the poorer classes. The business of these men is to decoy into the public market, for public hire, women who are charming to look at and who are likely to please the senses of men who will pay for them. These women must ply their trade at certain given houses.

A very bitter point about the slave traffic is this, that the girls who are sold into it, and whose bodies bring in large sums of money, never receive anything to speak of themselves. The slave traders, both men and women, take all their earnings; and thus it is that the "pimps" are always well supplied with money, not one half-penny of which have they earned themselves. And so they travel back and forth to Europe as a regular business, seeking their victims in many a quiet village or in industrial towns where the economic conditions are so severe that girls, having nothing to look forward to but sordid homes and life-long toil, fall readily into the arms of a man who promises them marriage and a good time abroad. There is also another side to the trade which these slavers follow; and that is, while they have in their possession girls or women whom they are taking to the East, they are ever on the look-out for men—especially young men—who are not over-burdened with intelligence but who have money. They set themselves to trap these men, they play cards with them, and compel the women to tempt them in one way or another.

The "pimp" is, without any exception, a cur. The one thing he would dread would be a horse-whipping. Even now he avoids, with studious care, the long arm of the law. Therefore, they choose the men with whom they have to deal with great care, just as they pick their girls with consummate caution. Most of them have been criminals from boyhood, and if not degenerates physically, they are so mentally and morally. Often they have been compelled to leave their own country for their country's good, being suspects, sandbaggers, pickpockets, blackmailers, and informers in criminal circles—the followers of some disreputable occupation, mean and low, and not too dangerous. They are not of the bold burglar type, who would crack a "crib" or a skull; they do rob, but they rob drunken men and fallen women and children. Sometimes when pressed they even rob a poor-box at a church door and the ornaments from the altar. In their own countries they are often known by the police, who have their photographs and their finger-prints, and they find it more convenient not to be seen about—if they do visit their own land they do so surreptitiously. When they have made a place too hot for them they generally adopt the profession of white slave traders. They have already served an apprenticeship in bad houses, and they know most of the evil that is to be known. They know that this particular slave trade brings money to those who follow it. They have themselves lived bad lives and they know bad women, and henceforth allow themselves to use all their power to decoy, trap, and ruin the sort of girl who will be likely to fetch most money in this terrible business. Often they marry the girl-child, because that is the easiest way to get a very young and pretty girl to leave her home secretly.

There is always some plausible tale which explains why the lover is not able to face an open marriage; and the curious part of this is—a fact that is borne out by every one who knows anything at all of this sad side of life —that these men get such a hold upon the

women whom they have deceived and enslaved
that it is the very rarest thing possible for
one of them to betray a man. Some women
who follow the trade are by nature well fitted
for it. They are abnormal creatures, and seem
to need a reckless, licentious, exciting life;
but for one such there are at least a hundred
who would give their very souls to be free of
the life if there was anything else for them to
do. They will not of course face the question of going into rescue homes and putting
themselves into the hands of rescue workers,
because they have been told, and in some
cases also they know from experience of these
places, that they are hard and cruel. The
women are looked upon with suspicion and
with immense contempt. I myself visited a
Home once when I first came to this country.
I did not know quite what I was going to see,
but was invited to inspect the work of some
"sisters," and I was taken into what was
called a "Magdalenes' Home." A number
of women with close-cropped hair were at
work over wash-tubs in a semi-underground
place. They had hideous little caps tied
partly over their heads, and stiff straight
gowns of a very ugly material. They were,
in fact, branded; and the "saintly sisters"
went among them with the same sort of air
that one would have if compelled to walk
among lepers or plague-stricken people. I
have never been more surprised at anything
in my life, because even then, ignorant as I
was of the conditions of these women's lives,

I wondered how on earth any human being could stay in such a place with such truly contemptuous people for a single moment longer than was absolutely compulsory. This is, of course, an extreme case, and wiser counsels and more Christian wisdom now prevail. "Fallen women" are given a far better chance than they used to be given even ten years ago, and many of the rescue homes are quite charming places. But how are these poor women to know this?

Then, of course, there is that dreadful habit of preaching to them. What a wonderful amount of good could be done, and how much more moral and social reform could be achieved, if we could only get people to work among those who need our service so much, *without preaching* to them! It is very difficult for such women to step suddenly from their free-and-easy life to a disciplined existence where they are compelled to give an hour at least, morning and evening, to listen, perhaps, to some dreary discourses. These are, indeed, difficulties in the way of helping what are called "fallen" women—a word I dislike immensely—to a better life, when one can only offer them that sort of existence. If we could but believe that by kindness and tenderness and a holy liberty we would do more for them than by preaching at them and compelling them to attend services, and if we could but make up our minds to believe also that the Eternal Father is quite capable of speaking to His own children and doing His own work in His own way in their souls if we would do our part, very much greater and better results would be obtained by those who do what is called "rescue work."

With the unfortunate slaves of the "pimps," however, there is nothing in the world that could be worse than their fate ; but they are held so closely, and their doom is fulfilled in distant places, so there is no one who can help and rescue them. There are no less than eighty well-known "pimps" who flourish at Singapore alone, and congregate in their open club—known to all who care to know. Mr. Willis writes that in the course of his inquiries he spoke to an officer of many years' experience in the East of the fearful ravages the "pimps" are making among various girls in the West. The officer, a good man and a decent Britisher, said, "Yes, they are like a pack of hungry wolves let loose amongst a field of lambs. We know all their fearful work—and all the East knows it—but it is almost impossible to arrest these men unless the women turn informers, and to do this the law asks her in many cases to betray the man whom she imagines to be her lover. Far more easy would it be to ask her to destroy herself. These men keep very quiet here at Singapore, which might be called the key to the East, but is unfortunately really the key to perdition—the high-road to hell ! When the law gives the authorities power to hunt them out," the official went on, "we could arrest them, but as the law now stands, if a woman wishes to give the 'pimp' her ill-gotten money it is no business of the man in the street; it is no business of ours: it is a free country and a free flag and a free trade and free Babylon under our law." If the "pimp" and his woman have an open quarrel, jealousy on the part of the woman sometimes induces that climax, but even then she does not hand him over to the law. What she does is to give her late hero money to quit the country, and she tells him to be gone. He goes, making a pretence of being broken-hearted and drowned in tears, and shortly he returns smiling, with another fair-headed and blue-eyed, golden-slippered recruit to the sisterhood, a person who is perhaps fonder of him than is his first "missus." But only a few of the girls are petted, or are kept by the "pimps" for themselves. They are most of them simply slaves; they never handle the money that is due to them from their terrible work. They have no right to make any objection to any man who may be sent to them. I do not feel able to describe the agonies and horrors which these girls endure, it seems almost too much to ask of a woman; but it is right, nevertheless, that we *should know* these things in order to be prepared to help the victims and wage war against their captors.

A curious point with regard to the men who beguile women into slavery is that they are not by any means all of them fine-looking.

8

Some of them are very ugly, and yet they get perfectly-developed and quite good-looking women to follow and obey them. A case in point, Mr. Willis writes, was told by a brother officer who had done service in South Africa. In Johannesburg under the old Dutch rule, where the laws regarding houses of ill-fame were very stringent, a certain "house-keeper" had for her "pimp" a German—hideously ugly, square-faced, mole-eyed, with a receding forehead and thick, protruding lips.   His shaggy, red-haired head and non-picturesquely pock-marked face would frighten most women. A thick-set, slovenly individual past middle life, with a temper and disposition of a fiend ! Yet this man owned the woman who was supposed to be the most attractive prostitute in Johannesburg.   She followed this repulsive creature as if she were charmed.   The authorities at Johannesburg arrested them both, and they were committed at the preliminary trial, and offered bail of £1,000 each. Unfortunately the woman had only £1,500 in shares in Safe Deposit.   The hideous German demanded of the woman that she should sell out her stock and pay *his* £1,000, and give him the other £500 to get away with. She complied with his demand, and he left the country.   She stood her ground, and at her trial got twelve months in prison for her pains.   When she came out she had no home, scarcely any clothes, no friends, and, to add to her sorrow, she was ordered by the Johannesburg authorities to quit the country

as an undesirable. She went somehow, and
set to work to find her lover. He knew she
was serving twelve months', and knew also
the date of her release, but he was determined
that he would be no more troubled with her,
as he had now become enamoured of a pretty,
fair girl at Cape Town. He departed with
her for a rest-cure to Siam, where he lived
for some months in security on the ill-gotten
gains of this girl, whom he compelled to
charm a high native personage in Siam,
having found that this dusky princelet had
plenty of money for the girl with the
golden hair. The German monster was "in
clover." But the old Johannesburg woman,
now released from her sentence, tracked the
pair by land and sea, until she landed in
Bangkok in Siam. Infuriated and maddened
by jealousy and bad usage, she pleaded, with
tears and sighs, with her former master to
abandon the Cape Town girl, and come back
to her; but he refused. Driven to bay, the
Johannesburg woman began to fight with
the new favourite, and made things so hot
for the German that he retreated to Java,
taking all the belongings of the two women.
The Cape Town girl took to drink, and de-
scended by rapid steps to the Chinese quarter,
where she was murdered, and the Johannesburg woman became the mistress of an
Englishman and amused herself by smug-
gling opium.

The "pimps" make themselves extremely
agreeable at first to the girls whom they wish

to decoy. They amuse them and entertain
them, playing with them almost as if they
were children. They take them to places of
entertainment and to the seaside, and make
themselves pleasant until they gain a very
strong hold on the girls; then they take them
abroad, and if the girl is troublesome they
kick and beat her, and brutally ill-use her
till she is utterly terrified and willing to do
what is asked of her.

On the way out to the East the girls are
often made very useful to their masters by
being set to decoy some young Britisher who
is travelling. The girl is compelled to attract the young man and begin a flirtation.
The slave trader so contrives that the guilty
pair are caught in a compromising situation,
and as what he wants is money the young
man who has been trapped is unscrupulously
blackmailed. The girl is ordered to keep to
her cabin, while the "pimp" extracts the
young fool's money from him. Another trick
which is quite a favourite one with these men
is to make the girls rob men of papers or of
cards, and to use these stolen documents for
blackmailing purposes. A well-known princelet in the East with a very bad reputation
has been compelled to pay fabulous sums
for the return of documents stolen by some
of the white women whom he bought. The
women unfortunately get nothing out of it.
It is the men who owned them originally
who reap the harvest. This and similar cases
are quite well known by those who are aware

of what is going on in this particular part of the world.

Mr. Willis was told of one official in Siam who paid two thousand dollars for some papers which were taken from him in a house of ill-fame; and it is common knowledge that in London a very enormous amount of blackmail is extracted from men who consort with common women. Another man in Singapore who was tempted once—and only once—by a "pimp" to enter one of the houses in Malay Street was drugged, and had his papers stolen. A few days passed, and then the "pimp" visited him at his office. He had to choose between a heavy levy of blackmail, or the serious consequences of his affairs becoming known; either alternative was so terrible to him that he quietly went home and blew his brains out. Yet another phase of this trade in the East is that many of the native dignitaries, who have many wives and possess great wealth, are simply animals in most of their habits and ideas. With them it is not a sin to gratify any passion, and sensuality they freely gratify. So the traders in the East find it a desirable part of a very lucrative trade to pander to these men. They are offered by these rich natives thousands of pounds and jewels if they can procure for them a pretty young white girl. They will have nothing at all to do with the *demimonde* in the East—the girls they want must be brought especially for them, and they must be respectable. The only way to get the girls to the houses of these men is by drugging them and taking them while unconscious by night; and it must be said that the fate of these girls is generally very much better than that which befalls the unfortunates who are taken to Malay Street or to the Chinese quarter in Hong-Kong. But if there is a child the girl's fate is very sad, as she and her offspring are very much despised, and they are often both murdered and put out of the way. Mr. Willis sketched a picture of a beautiful Italian girl who had been brought to Burma from Europe, on order. She was quite beautiful, an Italian who had been sold to a native man. When she had a child she was put into native dress and thrown out into the compound among the servants. The sketch—drawn from life —is reproduced on the outer wrapper of this book. It is a strange picture of a beautiful white girl with a half-caste child in her arms living in an alien community— an outcast and wretched, having almost forgotten her native tongue.

A very well-known "pimp" trapped her and "married" her with the aid of a bogus priest and brought her to the East to the express order of the rich man to whom she was taken; and there she is now, discarded and degraded. The way in which slave traders marry girls is simply astounding, and shows quite a genius for planning and plotting. Once the "pimp" attracts and interests a foreign girl who is good, he quickly sees that the only way to get her is to pretend to marry her. This he manages secretly at the house of some distant " registrar " who is generally one of his own gang. If the girl protests and wants a priest's blessing that also is obtained for her, for the " pimps " are experts at disguises and have no difficulty in playing the part of a minister of religion. Another method followed is to take the girls to France or Germany and there arrange for a pretence marriage, the ceremony being performed by one of the " pimp's " co-villains. Once this " marriage " is over the " breaking-in " process begins. The girl has broken with her family and can seldom return. She drifts farther and farther away from help and closer to the end that awaits her in Malay Street or the opium dens in Hong-Kong. She is ruined and ill-treated, and the moment she reaches the East she is sold either into an opium den or into Malay Street and her accursed tempter starts out on a further hunt for girls.

CHAPTER VII

MADAME V.'S STORY : THE DEVIL'S AMBASSADOR

THE means by which Mr. Willis got into communication with the author of this story is as follows : He had become very friendly with an official in the Straits Settlements, and being aware of his intimate knowledge of the affairs of the place, he explained to him that he desired to do something to check the white slave traffic. The gentleman was in sympathy with this desire, and in pressing him to talk of some of the facts in connection with this matter which had come under his own observation, Mr. Willis put before him his duty as a father who loves his own children, and as a citizen who fights under the flag, and begged him to speak openly. Mr. Willis's friend was much impressed, and acknowledged that hundreds—perhaps thousands—of innocent girls were yearly decoyed to the East, there to succumb inevitably to disease and horrid deaths. He ended his sad recital, saying, "I have told you frankly what I know, and most of these cases are recorded in the police court proceedings of the country in which they occurred. I will risk something," he went on, "to give you more information; but if one or more of these girls could be induced to speak and tell the whole truth about her life from the moment she was decoyed from her own home until she became a wretched outcast, the lowest of low things in the East, the publication of such history would, I believe, reverberate throughout all Europe and perhaps awaken the consciences of legislators the world over. It might indeed awake the slumbering intelligence of the Western people who think when they withhold knowledge of these fearful crimes from the public that they are keeping society pure, little understanding that it is upon this very ignorance that vice lives and flourishes. But," said he, "the unfortunate part is that the women will not speak. They destroy themselves, they smoke opium and drink spirits and deaden their feelings and kill memory, and to get them to talk is almost an impossibility. But," he said to Mr. Willis, "I will meet you to-night in the billiard-room of the Hotel Adelphi, when I may be able to tell you of a plan I have formed in my mind."

Mr. Willis writes: I spent quite a restless afternoon waiting for the evening to come, and at the hour named I betook myself to the noisy billiard-room, where my friend soon appeared.

" I think I can fix you up," he said seriously.
" I will only do so, however, on your solemn
assurance that you are acting simply in the
public interest, that you are going to do
something definite with this information, and
that my name is to be kept out of the thing,
as it would not do, having regard to my
official position, for me to be connected in any
way with this matter."

I promised on my honour that I would
respect his wishes.

" Well," said he, " there is a noted woman
here who keeps a house of ill-fame. She is
an Austrian by birth and is not at all a bad
sort, and although she is chained to her work
by the devil's hooks of steel, with patent
fastenings, there is much in her that is good.
Her life, as I imperfectly know it, seems to
have been a very strange and very tragic one,
and what attracts me to the house is this—that
she has saved many a girl here, and she is a
perfect terror to the giddy young men fools
who at times infest these houses. She makes
them behave themselves as far as it is possible,
and often speaks with uncompromising plain-
ness to them. It is said that she has a son
somewhere in France. Now, if you could only
get her to tell the story of her life for the love
of that son, and to save innocent and ignorant
girls, it would be the most wonderful weapon
in the fight you want to make against the
white slave traffic. The woman's heart is
capable of being touched, and to-morrow I
shall find her lawyer, who is a real good sort

and has a good influence over her. He may be able to help you."

On meeting the lawyer I found that he was quite a good fellow. The moment he knew who I was and the business I was on, he consented to take me to Madame V.'s to see if she would tell me the truth about the horrid traffic that brought her originally to the East, and which is bringing hundreds of other girls to these places of infamy. We hailed a rickisha, and my friend instructed the Chinese runner to " Pigie, pigie—Malay Street."

The rickisha man grinned a broad grin, and was soon trotting along *en route* for Malay Street, which is known as the "Babylonian Hell of the East." It is the show street of the East for women of ill-fame from every nationality under the sun. It is said that there are 510 Babylonian houses in this street and that each house contains from eight to thirty women of ill repute. Fabulous prices have been paid for the good-will and stock-in-trade of some of the " best houses " in the street, one woman— a notorious character—having, it is said, paid as high a figure as 22,000 dollars for the goodwill of a "good" house. Each house has a large stone veranda, with overhead balconies, where from three o'clock in the afternoon until ten or eleven o'clock in the evening the poor, painted creatures, bedecked in their tinsel, sit sipping coffee, smoking cigarettes, and accosting passers-by with the invitation, "Come in here, please." These prostitutes are one of the sights of the East, and strange though it may seem, no tourist who visits Singapore dreams of leaving without at least driving through Malay Street to gaze at these "show women," of every nationality and protected by the British flag. In fact, I understand that when the Crown Prince of Germany was in the East arrangements were made for him to drive through Malay Street and see the Babylonian quarter at its best. Once a girl is known to live in Malay Street she is tainted and tarnished beyond repair. Each house has its "missus," among whom there is an *esprit de corps*, the observance of which restrains one "missus" from taking a girl from another house, and no "missus" will allow any of their "young ladies" to respond to pitiful cries or sighs or sobs of any strange girl brought to Malay Street and going through the process of "having the nonsense knocked out of her."

Malay Street shelters thousands of Japanese women, ninety per cent. of whom, it is said, are diseased; thousands of Chinese women; and hundreds of women of Germany, France, Austria, Russia, and other countries. No English woman is allowed to live in Malay Street unless she evades the law by marrying a foreigner. When passing through the street one sees the outward show of these fearful dens, but no pen dare describe the doings of the damned within. The women are not under Government control, nor are they in any way supervised by the authorities. Many of them are licensed by the Government to sell spirits, and in nine cases out of ten the spirits are manufactured on the premises. If a death takes place within the Babylonian walls a certificate is given by a registered Chinese or Hindoo doctor. Murders, robberies, and seductions take place weekly in Malay Street, but the police aver that there is the greatest difficulty in getting evidence respecting such atrocities.

Madame V.'s house was in Malay Street, and she keeps what is called "the best house" in Singapore. Madame V. herself is a stout, fair, and much-befringed lady who showed little outward sign of the weary life she led. She had been perhaps for the last twenty years ploughing the fields of death and pestilence; but she was still alert, her face was pleasant, and her grey eyes keen but not unkind. Her hair was dyed a bright auburn—"ginger," as it is generally called—her face was painted and powdered, her eye-brows were pencilled—altogether, she was very much "got up." She was extremely well dressed and looked very neat and clean. She had no jewels except a wedding ring. She spoke with a pretty accent, smiled very pleasantly, and gave herself quite important airs as she invited us to sit down and make ourselves at home.

Her house was sumptuously furnished. A Chinese waiter presently brought in champagne on a silver salver; the glasses were beautifully cut, and everything about the house was very rich. The man who brought me to this house of sin was madame's legal adviser and confidant. He gave madame some wine, after which she became quite vivacious, witty, and merry. I ordered more wine, and madame laughed, and drank, and chatted in a semi-confidential way. Then the lawyer talked a little to her about me, begged her good offices for my work, and departed, leaving me with her. Alone with this image of twenty years' sin, I let her have all the wine she wished for, believing in this way she would be induced to talk to me of her life. It was extremely difficult to get her to face the question at all. I asked her point-blank, "Why will you women keep bullies and 'pimps'?" "Oh, it is natural," she replied; "women who lead a life of pleasure want some controlling influence over their nerves. It is the nature of a woman to be influenced by a man. Respectable men will have none of us; so what are we to do? We also want protection. You must not suppose that all the men we have to deal with are pleasant and easy, and so a 'bully,' as you call him, on the premises is mighty handy. Besides, one wants to talk of one's life to some one who knows the best and worst of one—some one of one's own: and the 'pimp' gives his woman all she wants of him, ministers to her vanity, consoles her when she has a bad time, protects her, and amuses her also."

"Yes, and takes her money," I suggested.

She laughed outright.

"Yes, yes, we women are infernal fools—we always believe in our man. We pay him, we worship him, mistrust him, and curse him in the same breath; we praise his goodness before our abuse of his vileness has died away. He beats us, robs us, pets and coaxes us, and we are happy."

"Is it," I asked, "because of the physical necessity that women allow these 'pimps' to live on them?"

"Oh no," she said; "it is exactly the reverse. There are some women who will hardly ever allow a 'pimp' to approach them in the way you suggest. To women who are sold into this life there is no question of physical attraction. The 'pimps' take, of course, almost all the money that a girl earns, unless she lives long enough to grow wise and to fight him on his own terms; even then the man always has the best of it. One 'pimp,' a Russian, brought a very fine girl here last year. He had abducted her, I understood, from Vienna. She was quite a beauty to look at, and I was quite pleased, and congratulated myself on having procured the catch of the season for my patrons who come to my 'quiet house.' The girl, however, did not know to what kind of place she was being taken, and did not find out until she awoke the next morning from her stupor—for the man had been obliged to drug her. When she woke and found a strange man in her room, she screamed, and would have waked the whole neighbourhood. I sent for the Russian at once to go to her. A fierce altercation took place between them, and I heard the girl say she would rather live on bread and water than submit. Then the Russian told her that he had " done his time " on bread and water in St. Paul's fortress, St. Petersburg, and knew all about it; but it was now necessary to speak plainly, and he told her why she had been brought to the place, and that she was to do what was expected of her. She began to scream horribly. Then I heard a crash of crockery, and a call for police and of murder—and the next moment all was still. When I went in I found that he had strangled the girl, maddened by her calling for the police. Young ladies who come here," she added, "must not call for the police; it is highly dangerous.

" A Chinese doctor gave a burial certificate. The 'pimp' took her belongings and fled to Siam, taking with him a nice, childlike school-girl, whom he decoyed from the roadway as she skipped home from school. You can see," she went on, "how difficult it is for us to do anything in this matter. The chief thing is to keep quiet and out of trouble, and not to thrust ourselves on the gaze of the authorities. We must always try to lie in the shade quietly, if we wish to succeed. So, however much we may wish to punish these brutes, we would practically be cutting our own throats if we made much of a fuss. All we can do is to keep the bad sort out of our places. I do try very hard to keep a nice, quiet, respectable house, where gentlemen may consider themselves safe. A quite safe house pays best in the long run."

I begged madame to tell me the story of her life. She hesitated, and then very sadly said, "Well, if telling all that has happened to me would prevent any poor young sweet girl following in my footsteps, I will certainly tell you, for, after all, it is ignorance and innocence that cause so much havoc among young girls. Had I not been an ignorant wench, I would not now be here —that's very certain."

I ordered more wine, and asked her if, in the early days of her career, she had been an artist's model. "No," she said; "nor did I go off with a medical student; nor was I a parson's daughter, led astray by a bold, bad curate. None of these foolish stories belong to me," and she laughed, quite naturally. "My history," she said, "is an ordinary one. My father was an artisan in one of the rural districts far away from Vienna. My mother was a good and pious soul, who managed the affairs of our little cottage and eked out the meagre income by doing plain needlework and crotchet-work for the gentry of the neighbourhood. I was the only child; the hope and joy and the dearest thing life had given my parents. For the rest, they had incessant toil and the manifold burdens of poverty. I

9

went to the village school with other girls, helped my mother with her household duties, fed my rabbits, sang in the church choir, and sometimes recited poetry at our school gatherings. I was considered a very bright pupil.

"Thus my girlhood passed, and I grew to be a strong, healthy, and happy maiden. My good father worked early and late, toiling to pay the premiums of a small annuity policy which was to give me £200 on my attaining the age of twenty-one. We three used to talk over all the wonderful things that this precious £200 was to buy for us. Now, it was to be a cottage for my parents, where we could have a little farm and live in peace on our own spot of earth; now, we would buy a horse; and, again, we would decide upon a shop, which would have a millinery department, and my name printed over the door; then my mother was to have a black silk dress, trimmed with jet, and a new armchair. Ah, me!" exclaimed Madame V., "when I look back to those happy years and those peaceful evenings spent over the fire in the long winter months, when we made our suppers of home-made bread and sweet-scented honey from the comb, I am almost choked when I think how far away it all is. Then, after supper, when my hair was plaited for the night, my mother and I said our rosary, and my good father joined in the responses.

"I have heard it said that we are all masters of our own fate, but this is not true; we seem to be the playthings of those who can deceive us. My girl friends and I were accustomed to play in the fields and roam about in the summer evenings sometimes, often going to the village church for the benediction; and we were so light-hearted, so pure, so young, we would stop our joyous games and walk demurely into the church for Vespers. Of course, like all girls in the world we gossiped with each other, and each told her particular friend her hopes and romances. We all expected that some day a prince in disguise would by chance come by and maybe he would choose one, and then there would be wealth and fairy castles and jewels and all the beautiful things which seem to belong by right to beautiful maidens with the warm blush of maidenhood glowing in their cheeks.

" One evening the night came in more sweetly than I had seemed to feel it before— there were more roses out, and the whole air was so filled with their scent. A number of us girls were wending our way homewards along a path which led to the door of my father's cottage, when we all got a great fright."

Here madame became silent; tears were standing in her eyes, which gave them a curious glare; her thoughts had carried her back to the golden days of her girlhood. She tossed off a glass of champagne, and then she continued :

"We had just crossed the last stile when a tall gentleman in black suddenly appeared, 'Which is Fräulein V.?' he asked.

Some of the girls ran away, and others kept close to each other. At last one pert little puss stepped forward and said, 'This is Fräulein V. Are you the fairy prince going to carry her off?' We all laughed at the silly girl, but the stranger said, 'To-morrow will be your birthday. You will be twenty years old. I present you with this bouquet with every good wish for your future and happiness.'

"I was paralysed. My hands refused to take the gift, my brain was in a whirl; I trembled and stood still. The girls pushed me forward: one took the flowers, others thanked the stranger, others laughed and chaffed. The stranger bade us be silent and not talk of him, as that would spoil any chance of good fortune reaching us. With downcast eyes I walked on. Once out of sight of the stranger we found our tongues. 'That was indeed a knight-errant,' one girl declared; 'an ambassador from somewhere, and they know you; you have been chosen out of all.'" Madame laughed through her tears. "One girl—I have forgotten her name now, although I remember her face: a fat, good-natured, child-like face—made me promise that if I became a very great lady I would not allow my servants to worship me, as it was not pious.

"When I returned home I could not eat my supper. The man who had come into my life disturbed my thoughts, and it was only when daylight peeped through the window

of my little room that I went to sleep, holding my secret preciously within my heart.
Ah, monsieur, the cross had come to my life.
The accursed power of the devil's hand had
been drawn across my path; hell had, indeed,
opened its jaws for me. But all this I,
ignorant, did not know. In one night I was
changed from a child to a woman; I had
fallen in love with somebody, though even
who the somebody was I did not know. But
I lived in a strange world for weeks. My
knight of the flowers saw me often; almost
every night he brought me home from church.
My girl friends deserted me, and neighbours
began to talk. They shook their heads and
sighed, but my heart was very light and
proud. I was important and pert. The devil's
poison, vanity, was in my heart.

"My friend called himself Count Jansen;
he told me tales of nobility that fairly turned
my brain. Yet he steadfastly refused to come
into our humble cottage; and as he had said
at first that love is destroyed by publicity and
talk, as a fine flower is spoilt when the hard
wind blows over it, so from the very beginning
he put an air of mystery over our friendship,
which, while it attracted me, led me on to
my doom. The man only came to our gate.

"At times he would go away for weeks, but
he always returned more ardent, and with
gifts—bonbons, chocolates, and other little
presents that please the heart of the young.
I offended my father and my mother, who
began to be alarmed. They had heard the

gossip about my meeting with this stranger,
and warned me against him. But I was self-
willed and self-important, and I began to
believe they were ignorant and dull and had
no knowledge of the world. But alas! I had
not reckoned on what was to come upon me.
The result of my friendship was that I
was ruined almost before I understood what
was happening. When my parents discovered
the coming burden they broke down, and my
father became very ill. Then the devil who
tempted me, and whom I trusted and loved,
came to the cottage, and by some means
cajoled my mother, and tried to make my
father believe in him. In his weakness and
misery at my condition this was easier to do.
My lover told me that as I had arrived at
twenty-one years of age it would be a
wise thing for me to collect the two hundred
pounds due from the insurance company, and
seal my trust in him by allowing him to invest it for me; and then he would marry me
and look after my father and mother and do
well for us. I gave him the signed papers,
with the power to collect the money, and
then my child was born. My father died at
its coming into the world, and he cursed
me as he died for bringing shame and misery
on his house. But somehow my baby seemed
so beautiful that he came as a consolation for
all I had gone through, and I believed all was
to be different now: I was soon to be married.
and take my place in the world. My father
now being dead, my lover came to the cottage,

and my mother took a great liking to him. He arranged for us to remove to his part of the country and turn our backs for ever on the contempt of our neighbours. Thus, everything seemed perfect.

" One day, however, as I was seated in our little garden with the baby, my would-be husband appeared with two military-looking men. They passed without a word into the cottage and closed the door, and there without explanation they rummaged all our boxes. When they emerged my lover kissed me and told me that State affairs called him forth and that he had no control over what was happening; and then he disappeared down the flowery lane. The two official-looking men, who looked to me like Frontier Police, had taken many of our papers away. Even then the truth did not dawn upon me. Had I known I might have been saved, but I was still in dreamland, believing everything that was told me, and my mother was as simple as I was. My lover had said that nothing but death could part us, and yet days and weeks passed and he did not come, and he had taken all our money. I rarely went out, and could not endure the sneers of the people who passed us by. My clothes were shabby, and we had a hard job to live. My mother aged rapidly, and between us grew up a dreadful cloud; but the baby was the darling of both our hearts and the only thing we had to console us. After two years the man who had betrayed me returned, and I called to him, ' Paul, Paul,' and fainted in his arms. He said to me that we must leave the place for ever, get our things together and take only necessities. 'Any jewellery you have you had better let me keep for you. We must catch the 5.30 to Vienna to-morrow.'

" ' But, Paul—— ' I said.

" ' Come or stay,' he said; 'it is a vital matter. You go at once to Vienna with me. We shall be married, and you will return queen of the village, with fine clothes, rings, and your marriage certificate. For political reasons I cannot stay. The Government is against my party, and I have to be careful. If you love me, come.'

" What was I to do—to suffer another two years' bondage in the accursed village where all mocked me? I loved him, trusted him, and would follow. While I was preparing to start, he said, quite coolly:

" ' You will leave baby with your mother for a week or two.'

" ' Leave my child ? ' I said. 'Never ! I would die first.'

" My mother now appeared on the scene. She felt quite competent to look after the baby; so I deserted my baby and followed my master like a dog.

" Whither we were going I had no knowledge whatever. We took train for Vienna. In the train I felt like a child, everything was so strange, so new. My lover took no notice of the people, the station, or the crowds. He seemed sullen, reserved, and very quiet. He pulled his cap over his eyes and slept. He gave me the tickets to show the guard, saying he did not wish to be disturbed. At night we arrived in Vienna. Three or four men met us on our arrival. They were all muffled up, and I could not see what they were like. I was hurried in a closed cab to a house which looked dreadfully dark and gloomy from the outside, but it was very gay within, and very bright. Several men and women were seated in one of the rooms as we passed through. They were noisy, and were drinking wine and smoking cigarettes. They scrutinised me, and joked about my dress. One gentleman, who was, I think, a Russian, said to my lover:

"'Where did you pick up this queen of the forest?'

"The joke seemed to affect the whole company, for they all roared. One bold girl, very scantily clothed, came to me and offered me wine, which I refused. She threw it on the floor, and said:

"'Soon you will be very glad of it; you are merely a tender chicken now—wait until you are an old hen and you can only cackle, and no one wants you: you will be glad enough of a glass of wine then. Damn you! Who are you to turn up your nose at good wine?' she shrieked.

"The men were apart, talking in a low, earnest tone, and my Paul was evidently very excited. His face was deadly pale and his eyes flashed. What could the meaning of it

be? This strange place made me shudder.
I was wretched, but not suspicious.

"At last the suspense was broken by a
dreadful old woman, who came in and took
me by the arm and warmly welcomed me to
her house. She said she would order coffee
and get my room ready, and the girls who
were drinking called her 'missus.' Ultimately I was taken to my room, where coffee
and cake were served.

"'Now, my child,' said the 'missus,' 'you
must have a hot bath and an hour's rest, then
put on this underlinen and this silk wrapper,
and prepare to look your very best, as we have
arranged to make you the "Queen of the
Night" to meet your husband's friends.'

"She brought some jewels for me, and told
me when I was fully dressed I was to lie on
the grand couch that was in the room. I was
bewildered, and horribly tired and sleepy, but
Paul did not appear at first. After a time
he came in, flushed with wine and very
sullen.

"'Oh, Paul, where have we got to, and why
have I to put on these things that do not
belong to me?'

"'Why,' he said, 'you fool, one would
think any child would know why; and you
will have the goodness to stop all this nonsense, for you must get to work to earn
your living. This is the only place where
you can earn it.'

"I went to him trembling and implored him
to tell me the truth.

" ' What is the meaning of this house, these women, these ill-looking men, these clothes? Oh, Paul, think of our child, and think of your wife.'

" He pushed me from him as though I were a leper; and what he said to me froze me to the heart.

" What was I to do ? I wished to escape, but how could I escape with nothing but a silken wrapper left to me. My clothes had all been taken. I had no money and no friends. I was a stranger in a strange city. My protector, the father of my child, was unkind and brutal. Paul left me with a curse, and at last I was awakened from my false trust. I drank a glass of wine that the 'missus' brought me, and lying upon the bed cried myself to sleep. I dreamt of baby and of my mother, and then of shipwrecks and a thousand dreadful things. When I awoke it was all dark, and the rain was pelting against the windows. There was a storm raging outside. I shivered and sat up in bed, and then I saw that Paul was in a chair near a lamp. I shall never forget the look on his face.

" But he came to me, saying :

" ' My love, you are killing me; yes, it is my love for you that is killing me. I am trapped in my own net; I set out to trap you, but I am undone myself. All is lost unless you can help me. I am only the wretched creature of circumstances and the plaything of the devil; and if I cling to you they will kill me. Already they are complaining.'

"I put my arms about him.

"'Cannot we escape from here?'

"'My soul is too much disturbed, and if I remain your lover any longer, as in the old joyous days, I am lost for ever, and so are you. You alone can save me and help me.'

"There was no one to help or advise me on that dreadful night," said madame, shivering.

"'Promise me one thing,' went on Paul, 'and only one thing; and that is that you will do all you can to help me. You do not know the strength of the awful chains that bind me to this life.'

"'Oh, Paul,' I cried, 'I will do everything for you,' for I felt that he loved me then, and my woman's heart forgave him, and I only knew I loved him before everything on earth.

"And then, with quivering lips and moist hands, and a cold, ashy face, his heart beating close to mine, he told me what he expected me to do for love of him. Each word seemed to burn me up.

"The only way of safety for him and for me from some terrible danger which, he said, threatened us, and which I could not understand, was to make myself pleasant to an old Count who was to be kept pleased. Paul told me it was an opportunity for a beautiful woman to save her lover. He said I was very beautiful—and, after all, what other virtues had I to boast of, I who had been the mock of the village? Paul told me this old Count was all-powerful, but a drunken fool, and said to enjoy pretty women. If I enslaved this old reprobate, and got him in my power, I would do a great service to my lover, and, in fact, save his life, for the Count had some political secret which he could use against him; and so, with these explanations, which somehow confused and overwhelmed me, he departed.

"The 'missus' of the house came in, and expended all the cunning of her art in making me a beautiful creature. And then the Count was introduced. He was accompanied by a young man, tall and broad, but of almost boyish appearance, and beautifully dressed. The Count was old, very ugly, also very well dressed, and he wore some sort of an Order on a blue ribbon. The two men asked permission to order wine and to smoke.

"'Ah, you see,' exclaimed the Count, 'you see we make it our business to enjoy ourselves here and be happy.'

"Then the old gentleman said to his young companion, 'Claude, you may go now,' and the old wretch took my hand and kissed my fingers.

"Claude rose to depart. Holding out his hand to me he squeezed mine three times, and seemed to look at me as if he had some message for me. I could not understand at the time what he meant, but later I understood.

"Left alone with the old Count, I longed to escape, but there was no place where I could turn, and the man seemed to be getting stupid and dull. I had to submit to his degrading caresses, but before half-an-hour had passed he fell fast asleep.

"His breathing was so heavy I was afraid he would die. But I was saved further insufferable humiliation at the hands of the maudlin, sensual old beast, and I was grateful for the respite. This ended my first experience of the 'licentious old reprobate.' Would that my career had ended where it began. Alas! I was not free. I moved about the room and examined everything in it, wondering whether Paul would come to me soon.

CHAPTER VIII

"My destroyer had been stricken down by the quantity of wine he had consumed, and it was only too late I learned it had been drugged. I opened the window casement and gazed out over the city of wealth and luxury, of sin, poverty, and shame.

"Many thoughts raced through my brain, tumbling over each other. First in my mind was my baby, and my old home, where I had known the extremes of happiness and misery! Then my mother's face came to me; she, poor old soul, was waiting with a breaking heart until God in His mercy would call her from the world of sorrow.

"Whilst wrapped in these memories a hand touched me on the shoulder. I was startled. It was Claude! He had appeared like a ghost, clad in a long white wrapper, with slippered feet.

"'Hush, madame!' he exclaimed, 'hush! he is asleep'—pointing to the Count. 'I saved you from his cruel embraces by drugging

143

the wine he drank. Yes, madame, I drugged him.'

" He drew a chair to my side.

" ' I am here only for your good. My uncle, the Count, thinks nothing of destroying a good woman. He is outrageous in his desires for the young, the fresh, and the beautiful. But once he uses them they are cast off like faded roses. You must not be here when he awakes. I have come to conduct you to another place where you may rest safely. Come, madame.'

" He took my hand and helped me with his strong arm to rise, and without another word we left the room where the drunken Count still snored in his heavy stupor. We went through a long, darkened corridor, then ascended a small back stair which opened out on to a landing-place which was evidently on the top of the three-storied house.

" Claude half carried me, half dragged me, in his hurry, until we came to a large oak door that stood ajar.

" He pushed the door wide open and took me into a large, spacious room, in the centre of which stood an old oak bed of the Louis XIV. fashion, with large massive posts and mattresses, and hangings of heavy silken damasks.

" ' Here you will be safe,' he said.

" Then he locked the door and came back to me.

" ' Read, madame,' he said, handing me a note.

" It was from Paul. It ran : ' My love,

trust this gentleman. Do all he tells you to do for love of me. I shall be away two weeks. Love.—Paul.'

"I stood in the centre of the large room, bewildered.

"Why had Paul deserted me? Why was I in the room with this young nobleman, this Hercules? who had evidently divested himself of his day-clothes and wore now his sleeping suit, which was judiciously covered by a long wrapper.

"'Are you the Count's nephew?' I asked.

"'Yes,' he quickly replied. 'I am his nephew—and I am your protector. I will see you made comfortable, and depart.'

"This was the only gleam of comfort I could see—his departure.

"'You tremble. Do not fear me, dear madame. No harm will come to you here. I shall defend you with my life. Here, take this glass of wine: it will put you to sleep.'

"I mechanically drank the wine. It quickly fired my blood and made me giddy in the head.

"'Let me help you to take your ornaments out of your hair,' he said, and without waiting for my assent he proceeded to fondle my hair. Then he took me in his arms. Oh! those strong arms. I can now feel their vice-like grasp.

"'Oh, please leave me alone,' I pleaded.

"'Yes, yes, I will leave you alone when you are comfortable.'

10

" He took the ribbons and ornaments out of my hair, which fell in its great wealth about my shoulders.

" ' Now take this one little glass of wine and tumble into bed. Remember your husband told you to do all I ask of you,' he said.

" My senses were confused. I could not muster up courage to be rude to the man—for man he was, in the physical sense of the word—and I was but a woman—betrayed, confused, my brain in a whirl. My husband's command to me was to obey his friend, and such a friend as this any woman would readily trust. He was certainly moulded in the giant's mould.

" I drank the wine. After a moment I reeled, almost falling to the floor. My protector caught me in his arms.

" Oh, what a tide of misery, joy, ecstasy, and sorrow mingled rushed through me at that moment. My power of resistance to his will, his love, his *mad* love, left me. He imprinted hot, burning kisses on my lips, and whispered his love for me. Youth claimed its due, and Claude plied me with romances.

" He would make me a Countess : he would be gallant and good to me. In the whirl of excitement I almost fainted. He took me in his arms and laid me like a baby on the bed. My head rested on the perfumed silk pillow. The joy of sensations passed through my blood. He kissed me ' a thousand times good-night.' I was almost motionless. One kiss more, and then a final ' good-night.'

He dropped my hand, drew the curtains, extinguished the lights, and was going.

"I heard him turn the handle of the door; the lock fell into its socket. I saw his shadow still in the room. It hovered over me in the night, like an evil thing that loves before it destroys.

"I was drugged, maddened with the fiendish 'dopes' these men use on innocent girls. I thought he was my protector. Alas, alas! ignorance and the accursed drugs made me think so; but my——"

Madame stopped: tears filled her eyes, her lips quivered. She remained silent and sad.

At last she said:

"He proved to be my destroyer. For this fiend in human form, I forgot my baby, my mother's tears and prayers.

"I lived in the paradise of his strong love—young love that laughs at all obstacles. But happiness was for me only while the effects of the drug and my intoxication lasted.

"The curtain must fall on the wild doings of that fearful night that sealed my fate, and wedded me for ever to the life I am leading. 'Lead us not into temptation,' the prayer says. Some of us are led into a temptation we have no power to resist: 'tis a cruel fate that so places us."

Madame stopped. The long, long thoughts came back to her of that youth which had fled for ever; now only the grave opened its jaws to receive her as the result of twenty-five years' sin and shame.

"It is the old, old story," she went on. "Next day the Count's nephew took me from the house.

"Rooms were taken for us in a snug little suburb, where everything was plain and homely, and we could love each other undisturbed.

"I loved Claude, he was all kindness—never happy when not by my side.

"Thus weeks and weeks went by. I could have lived for ever in the paradise of young love; but the devil amuses us with little things, only to slay us with them in the end.

"Paul was gone—where I knew not; but time and new things were speedily effacing him from my memory. One evening Claude took me to the Opera. It was a gala night. The Emperor and party were present. I was very happy.

"As we were leaving the theatre, an official-looking man, in full uniform of some kind, accosted Claude.

"'You are still in Vienna?' he said. 'Remember my warning. Who is this woman?'

"'My wife,' said Claude, without hesitation.

"The officer smiled, saluted me, and marched off. Claude was much disturbed. He said the officer was one of his Count's guards, and was always chaffing him about his love affairs. Of course, I believed him—young innocent fools believe anything. Why are girls such fools? Most of our class of girls only learn sense when they have nothing to protect.

"Next day Claude was very dejected, and full of uneasiness. When he came home to dinner he was very downcast.

"'We must leave here to-morrow,' he said to me: 'your husband is abroad, and wants you to join him. Get ready. Our boat leaves at 2 p.m.'

"This was news, indeed. I commenced to pack up in the morning. In the midst of my work a young woman was announced. She wanted to see me. She was admitted. She was a mere child—a pale-faced, blue-eyed, flaxen-haired child. She looked like a delicate flower reared in a hothouse.

"'Oh, madame, madame,' she cried, running up to me—'I have come to warn you. For God's sake mind what you are doing. You are in the hands of a set of bad men. I have come to warn you of the fate that awaits you. My name is Nelly.'

"'Nelly?' I echoed. '.Nelly, eh?'

"'I have been in the house of the damned, where you were brought also, at first. It is the worst house in all Austria. What is your real name, madame?—pray tell me.'

"I gave her my name. She wrote it down, and quickly placed the paper in her bosom; then, taking another sheet, she wrote her own name and address on the back of it.

"'That's my full name and private address. We may in future help one another, but now take my warning. It's true, true as

God is in heaven. Your husband Paul is a notorious——'

"Here she broke off: the voice of Claude was heard at the street door. She peered through the blinds.

"'My God! I am caught, I am ruined. One word, madame: they are taking you to Singapore. It is a fearful place. I will write to you, care of the Post Office. Ask for letters *in your own name*, remember. Get my letters—they may save you—and write back. Hush! The monster of all monsters comes.'

"Claude immediately bounded into the room, and at the sight of the young girl his face changed, and his look grew dark and threatening—the very *devil* glared out of his eyes. . . . Oh, I shall never forget that look on Claude's passion-distorted face!

"'You here, you imp of hell! What mischief are you making? Why have you left your mistress's house?' Claude demanded; and, catching her roughly by the arm, he tightened his grasp until the poor child screamed with pain.

"'Claude, Claude, what are you doing? You're mad! Let the child go! She only came to wish me good-bye. For shame, Claude! I am shocked at your brutality. Poor little flower!'

"Poor child! I pitied her, and she almost sobbed her little heart out. She drew near to me for shelter and protection.

"'Curse her! If you knew her as I know

her, you would say she should be burned at the stake—alive: she is a *police spy*. She has already sent two men to jail.'

" At the words the child raised her careworn little white face, and shook her head indignantly: her eyes flashed defiance for a moment—only for a moment.

" She was soon cowed again. His look struck me to the heart. She was silent.

" ' A police spy ? What's a police spy ? ' I asked.

" ' Here, you must get out of this and return to your " missus." '

" ' No, no, for God's sake, madame, don't let him send me back to that house. Pity me, madame : you do not know the fate of all who enter that hell. It *is* hell—hell on earth. Oh, madame, save me. Is there no God in heaven to protect me ? Madame, madame, for God's sake ! '

" She clung to me frantically; and now my ' brave protector,' Claude, threw off all restraint, and rushed madly at the child, brutally dragging her from the room by the hair of her head—yes, by the hair of her head.

" Still the poor child screamed. A little later her voice was muffled, her struggle seemed to end ; all was still. I stood petrified. What terrors was life unfolding to me ?

" I waited, waited one hour . . . two hours. The suspense was intolerable. At last Claude came to me. His looks were wild.

" ' Oh,' he exclaimed, ' what a time I

have had! The girl is mad. She belongs to one of the best families in Vienna, and is placed under madame's care for restraint and protection. If she got abroad, and a scandal were created, all would be lost. She, in her insanity, thinks and says all kinds of things. My dear, I'll tell you a secret. She is my uncle's illegitimate child. Her mother died mad, and the girl inherited her lunacy from her mother.'

"'What have you done with the child, Claude?'

"'She is safe with madame,' he replied, 'I took her there myself—so let us be gone, out of this accursed city.'

"I was shocked and troubled over this episode. I became suspicious: *the first suspicion I ever had.* My mind was puzzling over many things, chiefly concerning the ways of the world and the sort of men in particular by whom I now seemed to be surrounded.

"I mechanically packed my boxes.

"Claude then commenced to play with me and chaffed me, kissed me, and did his best to dispel my gloom.

"Like all my sex who are allured away from home, from duty, from their prayers, by the accursed spell these 'pimps' put on us, my love for him soon returned: when his embraces, his fervent vows were renewed, I soon, too soon forgot the white-faced little girl. Poor pale-faced creature! It is part of the 'pimps'' duty to teach their victims to be lascivious, and forget all things that are good.

"Thus we started. Once on board and out at sea Claude told me we were bound for Singapore, the key of the East—to me it has been the golden key of hell!

"He told me of millions of money, of mines and plantations, where I should be 'Queen of the East'—poor painted 'Queen of Shame,'" said madame, laughing.

"He told me fairy tales of the dusky sultans who occupied gorgeous palaces in vast domains of the 'glorious East.' He was at much pains to enlarge on the passionate desires of the native rulers and sultans, who had all the arrogance of ruling Eastern races in their veins—how the black sultans gave away palaces and jewels and plantations to white women who 'caught' them; how the husband of one white woman whom a sultan took on a boating expedition made a fortune out of the adventure!

"It was quite easy to 'catch' the presumptuous black spider, who always desired a white woman when he saw one.

"Why we wanted to mix up with this kind of man-devil I could not divine. Was not Claude the nephew of a Count, reputed to be very rich?

"Why, then, come in contact with the low-minded offspring of an adulterous race? What were palaces, motor-cars, diamonds, etc., which had to be bought with the poisonous love of sensual black sultans?

"But," said madame, "I was going through the process of 'getting the nonsense knocked out of me' and the 'notches taken off.'

"One day—a beautiful day when we were sailing on the placid seas of the Eastern Archipelago, Claude spoke to me—remember he had now grown rather rough and spoke to me with much licence and unreserve. He seldom fondled me now, and took his pleasures without any efforts to please me. I felt myself greatly dependent upon his good humour. He often refused to allow me to go on deck at night. I was not allowed to speak to the officers, his excuse being that they were a poverty-stricken lot, who wanted everything for nothing.

"The captain, an old grizzly Scotchman, with a red, shaggy beard in the process of turning grey, was my only companion, besides Claude himself. I had to mend my own clothes and look after his things, pack and unpack his belongings, and finally wait on his lordship as though I were a coolie servant, to study his will and his pleasure. He was, indeed, lord over me.

"It was just the process of 'breaking me in.'

"'You see that young fellow, that English johnny?' Claude asked—'the fellow with the watch-bracelet and green socks on—well, he's a fool! I want you to catch him.'

"'Catch him?' I said.

"'Oh, don't be so stupid. Shake yourself

up. What do you think we are travelling about for ? Not for the good of our health, madame, and I am not here to preach the gospel. I want you to *catch* him, and by G——, if you don't I'll throw you overboard.'

" He hissed the threat into my ears.

" ' Remember what I say. Have done with this infernal humbug and prudishness ! Do you understand, madame ? You are now out for money. So get to work on the fools with money and no brains to hold it.'

" Here he pinched my arm until I fairly screamed. With that he banged the cabin door and went out. At last the Eastern veil was lifted, my mission pointed out. I did understand, alas, too late !

" I had a good cry then. The new life was appearing before me, my future dawning on me. Alas ! What could I expect ? I had deserted my beloved baby, forgotten my old mother, abandoned even my God, to follow this young Hercules like a pet sheep wherever he led me. Why ? Simply because my will could not resist the physical power he had over me.

" Claude came back when it was nearly dinner time. He apologised for his rudeness, and coaxed me to ' set my cap ' at that young fool, for mere fun.

" ' He has a splendid diamond ring on his finger,' Claude explained. ' Fool with him until he allows you to try it on—try his temper—try his depth of understanding—

fool with him. I want to know his business, for reasons I will tell you later.'

"For peace' sake, I agreed. After dinner I sauntered on to the upper deck with a passenger.

"The young Englishman accosted me with great politeness, and I smiled at him.

"Soon the Englishman and I got to be very friendly. He was a nice youth, very polite. He was a gentleman. He laughed and chatted and complimented me on my general appearance, and at last asked if I were married.

"I replied, 'Yes, worse luck!'

"He took my hand, and asked me where my ring was. I asked him if his diamond ring were the symbol of *his* marriage tie, and he laughed outright, took it off, and allowed me to play with it. He was very nervous and hesitated a lot. However, after a while his arm stole round my waist—we were on the upper deck quite alone : at least, my new-found friend thought so—I feared that Claude was not far off.

"'Now, I'll make a bargain with you, my Austrian "grandee." I will give you that ring for a dozen kisses,' said my gallant Britisher.

"I hesitated. The ring was on my finger; he was playing with it. He pressed nearer to me, then drew his arm tightly round my waist, drew me to him, and kissed me three or four times.

"There was nothing slow about this innocent

English youth, once he started. All Britishers are slow to begin. I drew back. I did not want to compromise this young man.

" ' Oh, you must not think it wrong, nothing is wrong until you are found out,' he laughed, tussling with me for another kiss—when we were startled by Claude's angry voice.

" ' What, you dog ! What ! Seduce another man's wife ? '

" With that he sprang like a wild panther between us. With one whirl he threw the young Englishman, with a fearful bang, against the side of the vessel, then roughly caught me by the arm and, half dragging, half shoving me, hurried me off in tears to my cabin.

" When we arrived at the top stairs leading to the end deck, he roughly snatched the diamond ring off my finger and gave me a push that nearly sent me headlong down the companion way. I was in tears, and trembling from head to foot.

" Claude returned to the discomfited Britisher ; high words passed between them ; the mate, captain, and one or two passengers came on the scene, and the altercation became stormy. Once in my cabin I quickly divested myself of clothing, tumbled into bed, and cried myself to sleep. I liked that young Englishman. He was at heart a gentleman. I felt guilty, as though I had committed a crime. Next day Claude ordered me to keep to my cabin until I got his permission to leave it, which I willingly did, after the fuss about the young Britisher.

"I never saw the Englishman until five years after. He came into this house: all was then explained. He never got his ring back, and he was compelled—to avoid scandal —to give my beautiful (?) Claude £100 as 'hush money.' Pure blackmail. Oh, what fools the young and innocent are! What food they are to the blackmailer!"

Madame laughed heartily and polished off a further glass of wine, refilled her glass, and continued :

"Once in Singapore, Claude took me to an hotel, and told me to dress my best, as 'His Dusky Highness' the Sultan of some Eastern province was in town, and would dine with us.

"'I am a servant of the Sultan, and don't you forget it,' he said.

"When I was ready for dinner, Claude said :

"'Remember, my love, it is your business to catch this black pig. Why in the name of the devil should he have money and I none? So *catch* him. It's money down: in case of fire, he must pay before the band plays. Do you understand?'

"I did *not* understand, so nodded my head and said nothing. The Sultan came, and the dinner passed off like a funeral. The Sultan was very nice, polite, and considerate; he ate little, but seemed to feast his dark, cat-like eyes on me. I wore a low-necked pink silk

evening gown, trimmed with old lace and
tiny golden buttercup buds. My shoulders
and bust were well formed. I really think I
looked well. Claude said so : he had dressed
me up for show purposes.

"After dinner we went for a motor drive.
The Sultan was all attention, telling me tales
of his tiger hunts, his ancestors, of old sea
fights, of the crown jewels, and all the things
that would interest a silly, brainless woman
in the hands of a cunning 'pimp,' who was
bartering for her like so much merchandise.
I was young and silly, and felt somewhat
gay. I liked the Sultan—he was manly,
good-looking, and polite—and I would have
gladly gone off to his home in that far-distant
land where lions breed like rabbits and tigers
infest the jungles.

"Claude seemed happy. He was now all
attention. He said a dozen times to me, 'If
you only play your cards well, we will land
this presumptuous black spider. Fancy the
" cheek " of the black mongrel, wanting a pure
white woman to embrace him!'

"The Sultan left us, and we had heard
nothing of him for weeks. I fully expected he
had forgotten I was on the face of the earth.
Claude grew restless. I think his funds were
flowing away from him. One night he invited
a well-known Singapore dignitary to dine with
us. He and the invited friend drank much
wine : they were both very flushed. We
adjourned to the hotel balcony just outside
our bedroom, to enjoy the fresh breeze from

the sea—the only pure, invigorating tonic in Singapore.

"Much wine and liqueurs were brought up to our party. I refused point-blank to take any; I was getting to know my little book. When they were fairly drunk Claude rose to leave us. I protested.

"'Oh, d—— your whining!' he growled. 'You can stay,' he said to the official friend.

"'Right O,' returned he, very much the worse for liquor. I rose to say good-night. Claude scowled at me.

"'What d'ye mean by this d——d affectation?' he demanded. 'You know full well what I want you to do. You understand? This man stays to-night. Is *that* plain enough for you, madame?'

"I stood erect, and stared at him in defiance. I was getting on in the 'breaking-in' process.

"'Yes, it's plain enough. But I will not do as you or he wishes. What do you take me for? Are you mad?' I queried.

"'Take you for?' he laughed. 'Why, an adventuress—all the way from Austria. Ha, ha! This is really funny. It's good enough to write home about.'

"The truth was out. He had thrown off the mask. I burned with indignation.

"'Dog!' I said, going, 'if either of you lay a hand on me I will stick this knife into your black heart. Leave me, you miserable hound!' I screamed. 'Police, police!' . . .

He drew back, like an infuriated tiger at bay, then made a mad rush at my throat, and crash . . . crash . . . went over me on the floor. The high official took to his heels, good, careful man, and left me in a death-struggle with the man to whom I had looked for protection.

"He punched, tore at me, bit my shoulders, and dragged me by my hair into the room, where he kicked me until I could not offer resistance. Finally he threw the contents of the water jug over me, and left me wet and bleeding, more dead than alive, bruised all over. My eyes closed up with his blows, my cheek cut with the ring he had on his finger —thus bashed, bleeding, battered, I lay on the floor of a strange hotel in a strange land . . . a helpless, broken mass. Ah!" said madame, with a sigh, "God was indeed punishing me for my sins. Misery had indeed overtaken me, broken, cut up, penniless, deserted. I was alone . . . alone in my misery!

"My heart was breaking. Nothing but the burning indignation at the insult cast upon me sustained me during those awful hours of tribulation. The indignation I felt saved me, kept me alive!

"Some one sent for a doctor, who ordered me to occupy another room; a motherly old Eurasian came to nurse me.

"I took all the money and jewels I could lay hands on"—madame here laughed out, and tossed off another glass of champagne,

11

saying, "I was getting on. What do *you* think? The funds were not much, certainly, *but something*: and once in my own room, I began to mend.

"Within a week I was almost all right. One day I received a letter with the Vienna postmark on it. It was from the white-faced girl, Nelly. She commenced:

"'Oh, madame, forgive me. Your first husband has been convicted of murder; he killed a young girl he decoyed away. He was a "pimp." His mate is wanted by the police: he is the same fellow that took you away. He is called "Juno, the Woman Tamer"; he is wanted for decoying young girls into bad houses, and worse. Get away from him quickly: he is worse than your first husband was, and if the police catch him he will be hanged—and a good thing if he *is* hanged.'

"Poor girl! She went on to tell me all her troubles, and begged me, for Our Dear Lady's sake, to get in a situation as servant in Singapore. I had just finished reading my letter, and placed it in my bosom, when the Sultan was announced.

"All smiles, all inquiries, all goodness, he came to my room. He had heard something of my troubles and wanted to help me. He was shocked at my appearance, and offered me his purse and protection. I thanked him from my very heart. I wanted a friend. As we were discussing the situation on the veranda, Claude appeared. The Sultan rose to go.

" ' No,' I said. ' Do not go. My business is soon settled with this man. What do you want? I am done with you for ever.'

" ' Oh,' he cried, ' you think to chuck me over for this black scorpion, do you? Do you forget I am the Woman Tamer? I have bashed into line worse women than you. I will take you to Malay Street. If you are not contented to allow white men your favours, well—I will put a Chinaman or two on your highly-strung nerves. So get ready and come! If you want this fellow here,' pointing to the Sultan, ' and he pays up, well! he can have you out on hire! You're mine, kick as you will!' A mocking sneer followed this speech. Claude was half drunk and wholly mad. When aroused he was as strong and savage as a jungle tiger.

" The Sultan's eyes flashed, the fire and anger of his race awoke. I motioned him to be quiet. I rose without a murmur and went to my room.

" Claude laughed in triumph, saying:

" ' That's the way to train up these hot devils, your Highness.'

" The Sultan answered nothing.

" In my room I wrote a hurried note to the hotel proprietor, and sent it by my nurse down the back stairs. The work started. The telephone rang below.

" Claude continued in his bragging fashion for some time. The Sultan grew weary and seemed to wish to take him by the throat and squeeze the life out of him, then throw him over the balcony, as report says he had often squeezed a tiger to death in the jungle— out Borneo way.

"At last heavy footsteps were heard on the stairs. It was a desperate game I was playing, but I had to play my best cards. Three figures well known in Singapore appeared. I rose.

"'Are you officers of the police?' I asked, trembling all over. Still I was fighting on.

"'Yes,' came the firm reply.

"'Arrest that man. Secure him instantly: lose not a moment—do you hear me? He's a murderer, wanted for murder in Vienna!'

"They moved to where Claude was sitting.

"'Stand back, you dogs!' he hissed through his clenched teeth.

"'Seize him! arrest him! he is a murderer! Officer, do your duty!' I screamed, frightened out of my very life. 'Will you let him kill some one before you move?'

"They pounced on him, and the fight was deadly. He struggled as no man but a murderer could struggle: the odds were three to one, and yet they could not master him!

"Oh, what a world of love I would have given to a good man endowed by nature as he was! Every part of him was magnificent, but his heart. That was vile. At last they pinioned him down, fairly wrenching his strong muscular arms behind his back. Then he lay face downwards, panting, bleeding, cursing me and my work. Three frightened

Malay policemen kept watch over him. The officer asked me what the charge was, and I coolly replied:

" ' He is a " pimp," and is wanted in Vienna in connection with the decoying and murder of a young girl; one of his accomplices has already been convicted. Alas! my first husband and father of my child! Take this letter with you, a girl's letter to me. Search the Austrian *Police Gazette*, and despatch him to the place where he will be shown as much mercy as he has shown to me.'

" Claude heard all that passed, and hurled out fierce imprecations on my head: but the information I gave the police chilled his bones. He knew the truth of the allegations: it was murder he was wanted for.

" Claude was bundled off: investigation followed, and he was tried in his own country and convicted of murder. Thus ended, on the gallows, the life of as fine a sample of physical manhood as ever charmed a woman. He had a handsome face and figure, and a golden tongue, but the heart of a devil!

"After Claude had been taken away, I turned my attention to the Sultan. I ordered tea, and told him plainly of the plot that was set afoot to entrap him, and assured him I would have told him in any case. He seemed highly pleased and grateful: he asked permission to settle my bills, opened an account at the largest shop, gave me his motor-car with attendants, and finally left three bank-notes for a thousand dollars each on the table. He was respectful, even shy. I spent a month motoring, buying dresses, and receiving presents sent by the Sultan from his land far away. Many Singapore people called on me for afternoon tea, and men and women of all sorts paid me attention. It was well known that the Sultan was in love with me; so the men and women with axes to grind expected me to turn the handle and let them have a grind in turn.

" With all the favours and consideration the Sultan had shown me, he still—true to his Malay breeding—had me closely watched, night and day. I knew I was watched, I knew all his paid eyes and paid spies were on my track. I never went abroad without my nurse. She was an old hand at shepherding girls for the Sultan; she knew his history by rote. I had sent for my pale-faced Nelly: she would soon be with me, poor child, poor white-face !

" One day, the Sultan, who had come from his country over the seas, made a suggestion to me in a roundabout way. He asked me to decide, saying :

" ' If you stick to me, I will stick to you. I cannot marry you : I am married now. You be my friend and I will love you after the fashion of my race.'

" I at last consented. After all my troubles, I would trust him implicitly. He promised me a good home, a fair settlement: all promises were honourably performed.

" We were faithful and true to each other.

Thus commenced the illicit drama of black and white. I was taken to a beautiful bungalow, splendidly furnished, with lots of servants, all black and all spies, and was installed as its mistress, a real 'Sultana.'

"At last Nelly came to me, poor child. She was a great comfort. She had gone through enough troubles in her short life—having been kidnapped as a child and taken to that den of infamy where I first met her, where girls were provided for rich adventurers who infest Vienna. Nelly became ill, very ill, poor child. The illness seemed to grow on her. She was pale—almost as white as the lily of the valley. She always looked beautiful. She was of that white, transparent, wax-doll-like beauty. Her mind was pure, her thoughts were heavenly. She prayed incessantly, and was pious and good. Her scrap-books, postcard collection, old ribbons, and the photo of her mother and brothers were her heart's joy. Licentious love she never knew; she was simply a pure victim. I at once loved her as a daughter; she loved me as her mother. Now her honour and her health were my care; thus we lived on in a sort of twilight of calm on the verge of sin. The best doctors came to attend the child-girl. They shook their heads; her complaint was not easily cured; the world knows no cure for it but death.

"At last the Sultan's interest grew cold. He had taken up with a certain horsey man's daughter, with whom he had started a secret liaison. We quarrelled. I grew tired of him and decided to separate. To this the practical Sultan agreed, and that we should continue friends. He furnished and set out for me this house in Malay Street; he saw me fairly launched—a full-blown 'missus' in this house —and through his agency I received many fresh girls from abroad, and very soon established a quiet house, where gentlemen could come without fear.

"No danger signals were required in my house. I did not like bringing Nelly to an immoral house, but I kept her good in my own private rooms. Nelly could be good anywhere.

"Only last year the Sultan cast his deadly eye on this child. He was after her to ruin her, of course. I told him that my death alone would open the way for him to ruin the little creature.

"Whenever the black prince came to town he took Nelly and me about, gave us presents, paid our bills, and generally made my home his home. We were very select. 'Pimps' and runners, carriers and fetchers, were not allowed to enter my house. No one was paid for bringing drunken men in; all liquors sold were of the best; no man was drugged, robbed, or scandalised in my superior house. His dusky Highness, however, often got drunk and made a scene: drink made him mad.

"When intoxicated he was a beast, and used actually to bite the girls, and pinch pieces out of their flesh ; but he always paid well for these gentle frolics !

" Yes," said madame, " he always paid well ! He was a real good payer. I'll say that for his Highness beyond the seas.

" The police are very good to me because I keep a healthy house. The horrors of most bad houses are the diseases that follow. I have known youths—mere children—ruined for life in bad houses such as we are discussing. The awful plague that follows a visit to some of these houses should be known to the young and innocent. The public should know it. Some one should speak out plainly to save the young from disease—perhaps death.

" I never allowed young, inexperienced youths to use my house for their destruction. I always take care that they are soon bundled out. I always advise them for their good. This is the real truth. It is the sacred duty of the Government to regulate such houses, and not allow disease and death and destruction to spread on all sides.

" I could name at least one hundred splendid men called to their graves through diseases contracted in such places. The people who govern us are not ignorant. They know what is going on, but still they stretch out no hand to save the young from the terrible consequences of sexual diseases.

" Now, if you are going to write, take care to warn the mothers and fathers of the youngsters out here, and tell girls what they may expect if they allow men to trap them into secret

marriages and hie them to the East.   It is
ignorance, the accursed ignorance which
sends victims to these death-traps, these
rotting pitfalls of disease, that makes the
dreadful toll—death.   But for ignorance I
would not be here now.   Yes, ignorance
alone caused me to place my soul with the
devil !"

Madame stopped.

"And Nelly ?" I asked.

Madame's eyes filled with tears.

"Nelly, my sweet, pale-faced child ! . . .
died of the terrible disease that yearly claims
tens of thousands of the human race, the
disease that modesty and hypocrisy will not
name.   Many know its ravages, but, alas !
those who know most may not be heard, and
those who have authority will not speak.
Hypocrisy and false shame forbid it !   People
who can write, and owners of powerful newspapers and journals, could do much to save
thousands of young innocent girls from these
pitfalls.   But, alas ! everybody seems to be
too busy or too afraid to touch a dirty social
evil that must be touched if it is to be
regulated.

"Nelly contracted a complaint when she
was first seduced by her infernal 'pimp'
decoyer.   Soon after her capture she knew
she was diseased.   The doctors told her so
plainly, and she smiled and said: 'Oh, then
it won't be long before I die.   Our kind
Father in heaven, through the sweet Jesus,
said that the greatest sinners may find salva-

tion if they repent. Oh, I have prayed so long, I know I will be saved.'

"Even to the hour of her death she smiled sweetly, though the ravages of the fearful complaint, which was doing its work, were horrible.

"Luckily for Nelly, she knew little, after all, about the life; the disease took hold of her almost at once after she was kidnapped. She came to this country ill—her sickness slowly developed until the worst symptoms were visible.

"She was happy, poor child, right up to the moment death claimed her. She loved and was loved. Young ——, of the Bank of ——, met her here months and months ago. He liked her from the first. He and she used to sit and play like two children in my private parlour at the back. As I say, she would never allow him even to kiss her; yet she loved him. He wanted badly to marry her, but she would not agree; the spectre of her illness was in her mind, a fearful disease was eating her heart out. She would not allow the man she loved to run the risk of the curse that was already in her blood and bones.

"I truthfully told her lover of her life, her real virtue and goodness, though human devils had trapped and hurt her. All the story he heard of her persecutions only brought him closer to her. After she died he wrote several pieces in her scrap-book.

"It is here," said madame, handing down

the book from a large shelf in an old cup-
board where she had hidden the ribbons,
hair-pins, postcards, and a hundred playthings
and belongings of the dead child. Poor
madame could hardly handle the little ornaments and purse and other of Nelly's childish
treasures. They moved me deeply, too. Many
scrawls of poetry were written in the scrap-
book by the boy who had loved her. Poor
Nelly! He must have cared for her, that
chap!

Here is one:

> Little hands that I have kissed,
> Finger by finger to the tips,
> And delicately about each wrist
> Have set a bracelet with my lips.

Yet another verse from the pen of little
Nelly's boy:

> I met her in a house of *Blank*:
> Her face was pale and white,
> She looked like a flower not yet in bloom:
> She had missed the road to right.
> She pined and sighed for her mother's voice,
> She shuddered in silent dread
> At the waning Day and the coming Night—
> When her wages were paid . . . in bed!
>
> She lived a month, or two, or three,
> Perhaps a full whole year;
> She died, like a flow'ret plucked too soon,
> And was buried without a tear.
> Now she fills an unknown grave
> Scorched by the Eastern sun.
> Poor child! she's gone . . . where her sisters **went**
> Since the world had first begun.

Doggerel, of course, but human; and the lines touched me as fine poetry has failed to do—for so many tragedies lay behind the foolish rhyme.

When I had finished looking through the scrap-book, I involuntarily sighed for poor Nelly. The God of Justice will be merciful to her, poor trapped innocent—trapped and ruined by a "pimp" from the inferno—yes, with the ashes of his abode still on his fine clothes.

I rose to go. With outstretched hand I said:

"Goodbye, madame. Only one word: where is your son, the bright, brave boy you loved so dearly and left so desolate with your old mother?"

Madame faltered.

"My boy is in Paris, being educated. My mother, my poor old-fashioned mother, she is, poor soul! in heaven, let us pray God, with my father, whose daughter broke his good heart. He, good man, came of a proud race of soldiers. His grandfather fought with honour for his country against the great Napoleon at Austerlitz. His daughter's dishonour broke his heart."

"But why, madame," I pleaded, "do you not abandon such a life? You have unfolded your terrible experience to the world for the direct purpose of saving innocent and ignorant girls. Why not——"

"Stop! Stop!" exclaimed the wretched woman. "You do not know what you ask!

I am chained to a stake with the devil's links. No hope is left for me in this world. No reparation can I make."

The distressed woman paused, and I relieved the painful silence by remarking :

" Go to your son."

" My son is safest away from me," said madame. "If he knew that his blood was tainted with his mother's sin, he would kill me—yes, kill me ! "

A flood of tears stopped further talk. Madame was completely unnerved. She took my outstretched hand and said :

" Goodbye—goodbye, my friend. Keep away from those houses of disease and death in the East. Think kindly of me if you can. God bless you, and forgive me. I am a wretched woman, but still a woman. For God's sake, awake the people of England ! The 'pimps' are agents of the devil: stop their hell games—crush them out."

Madame disappeared through the rich hangings of the doorway at the end of the room. I sauntered out to the busy streets of crowded Singapore, deeply impressed with the story she had told me.

I then determined to make public this traffic in European girls—English, German, Italian, and French ; girls who are taken out and sold to any kind of heathen, to any sort of dreadful animal who can pay for them ; who are sold into coolie opium dens ; who are given over to the Chinese and the lowest classes.

This trade must stop. It is a well-known fact that if a woman is too troublesome to deal with in an ordinary way in a bad house of Malay Street, she is made over to various low brutes who can break her and kill her if necessary. It is not possible to print, nor even to let one's self write of all that is done to these unhappy girls.

Once some of the nauseating facts are known, once public opinion is properly roused, the traffic in women and the trade of the " pimps " and the procurers will, let us hope, receive its quietus at the hands of Parliament.

CHAPTER IX

MARTYRS

THE stories of the two unhappy children which are here written were told to Mr. Willis by a Government official in the Straits Settlements.

One of the men who trade in girls happens to be a young, handsome, and well-made German. He appears to be, among the set which he honours with his presence, quite a ladies' man. But the history of his crimes has revealed him to be cruel, cold-blooded, and relentless. He seems to be one of the most successful of the fraternity of "pimps," and manages to obtain women who fetch great sums of money for him. He "gets himself up" regardless of cost, and for years he has been bringing girls over, most of whom he takes to Malay Street. Often he gets special orders from native princelings to bring out girls for them; and it has been his boast that he always has "spot cash" before he fills the order. On one of his trips to Europe he managed, by the devil knows what specious lies, to entice a young German girl. It is said he trapped her somewhere in England. He actually married her, and on the voyage to the East there was nothing in his conduct which aroused her suspicions. But on arrival in Singapore he took her direct to Malay Street. He landed this young creature in a bad house, leaving her in charge of the "madame," and it was not long before she was made aware of what her fate was to be. She flatly declined to live a bad life, and fought with all her strength against it. Every persuasion was tried and every argument used, but the girl was good, and nothing would induce her to consent to their overtures. Then they sold her for one week to an Arab with plenty of money. He took delivery of her at Malay Street, but he could do nothing with her—she fought like a tigress—and he returned her and demanded his money back. Next they locked her up and starved her and beat her and brutally ill-used her. She was found dead in a drain in Malay Street, and had met her death fighting. A Chinese doctor gave a certificate for her burial.

But there was yet another martyr—only one of many—for the fates of all are not published. And this girl was also brought by the same man into Singapore. She was very fair. The brute who brought her used to say he liked these blonde women, as they were as a rule more easily managed and endured the "breaking-in" process better than the dark or red-haired girls. This young girl was also a German, and she, like the other sheep for the slaughter, was taken to Malay Street. She refused point-blank to follow the horrible life that was set before her. The usual trouble took place; the old hag who kept the house screeched at her and told her it was a most respectable house, and the "pimp" who had married her, as he had "married" dozens of others before, pretended to be broken-hearted. When that game failed he ill-treated her horribly. But when the girl's jailers found that nothing would cow her they resorted to the fearful expedient that is not uncommon in these dens. In a book that was published some time ago, the life story of a girl who had been taken to the Argentine for the purpose of prostitution was given, and there was a description of how she was bound hand and foot and given over to a terrible negro. The name of the book was, I think, "Lima Loo," and it was an exposure of the terrible fate that befalls white slaves in the Argentine. In all these houses the same fearful expedients are used. If the girls are utterly unmanageable, the most horrible of all things is tried with them. This unfortunate girl was sold for three days and three nights to two hideous Chinamen. She saw no one else, and they occupied her room with her. Her terrible cries were heard all over Malay Street, but there was no one to help or assist her, and she was soon quieted. The third day a doctor had to be called, as the girl was thought to be dying. She had then become quite calm, as she believed, poor creature, that God would really take her out of the hell she was enduring by opening for her the gates of death. It mattered not now what happened to her. But Nature cruelly asserted herself. The girl's strong constitution saved her, and in spite of her longing for death she actually began to get better.

The "pimp" came to visit her occasionally, and was quite satisfied and delighted at the change in the girl—she was so quiet. At the same time she had a strange look about her that made him observe some caution in dealing with her. She made no complaint, and when in desperation he struck her, trying to rouse her anger, she did not even try to ward off his blows. She simply prayed in silence. No Christian martyr has ever suffered more than this girl suffered in Malay Street from the hands of those whom we, if we chose, could utterly destroy and render powerless. After weeks of atrocities, the unfortunate girl being so submissive and so still under her agonies, the terrible old woman who kept the house and the "pimp" decided that it would be quite safe now to introduce her to the licentious gatherings which took place in this house. She was attractive, and they hoped to reap a rich harvest from her. It was Thursday night, which happened to be what was called "real red night," and the officers of a foreign ship-of-war were in the harbour of Singapore. The officers of this vessel betook themselves to the town to see some of the sights of the East.

When a great company of men had gathered in the house where this young German girl was confined, she was sent into the room to entertain them. She was painted and powdered and glittering beads were wound about her. She wore golden slippers, but her clothes were all taken from her, and she was led in practically nude. The drunken men hailed her with delight, and she was forced on to a table and told she was to dance for the entertainment of the people present. "Remember," said the "pimp" as he left her on the table, "I am watching you, and you have got to do your best." Then she spoke: "Yes, and God is watching, too." She seemed to see a sudden vision, and called, "I am coming, I am coming! Lord God of my fathers, help me!" Before any one could prevent her she sprang with an almost superhuman effort and crashed against the window-frame, which gave way under the unfortunate girl, and she fell with a sickening thud to the pavement below. She was broken and bleeding, but not quite dead. When picked up by a passer-by she smiled and whispered, "I know that my Redeemer liveth." She smiled again and whispered something of what had happened to her, and then, shuddering, she closed her eyes and died.

The unfortunate girl's death was taken up by the police, and an inquiry held in open court at Singapore. The foreign officers were exonerated of all blame; "madame," the keeper of the house, was acquitted; the "pimp" departed to Java, where he lay quiet and secure for some time. But it is said that by-and-by he came back to Singapore and still flourishes in these cruel parts. Were any of Nero's Christian martyrs treated worse than that poor German girl was treated in Malay Street, Singapore?

That great prelate Bishop Oldham, of the American Missionary Society, preached a sermon on the death of the poor German girl, but the trade still goes on—the flag still flies—and the churchyards fill up with an appalling regularity that must please even the devil himself.

In a small town not far from Singapore, a horrid Chinaman with abundance of money has already paid a well-known "pimp" three separate sums—large sums—for a beautiful European girl whom he has ordered. She has not up to the present moment been delivered, but there is little doubt when the "pimp" whom he has trusted with this money thinks he is coming to the end of his tether, and that he can squeeze out a larger sum by producing the woman, he will do so. The market is endless for these girls. They are not required so much, however, for Europeans settled in the East for business or for any other purpose, because it is well known that European men generally content themselves with the women of the country.

CHAPTER X

AMERICA's quota of women to the dreadful banquets of disease and death in the East, writes Mr. Willis, is infinitely heavier than that of Great Britain. The unrestricted riot amongst American women and girls taken by devious means to the East is, in certain centres, appalling. The American is quite unlike the Britisher, who is slow to think and slow to act. The American is always active —never idle. He is heedless of trifles, avoids trouble where he can, with honour, and neglects much domesticity to keep on his eternal hustle after the " almighty dollar." Yet, when once convinced of the seriousness of a proposition he must handle, he handles it smartly and effectively.

The Americans, of course, have their unfortunate street women. They have their Forty-second Avenue and Broadway prostitutes, their room women, their time-payment women, their swell houses with women—where silver doesn't count—their fearful slum women to whom a dollar is " big money," and their women as show prostitutes in Chinatown, New York, where for two dollars the revolting sight may be seen of a Chinaman snugly smoking opium by the side of an American woman. These sights, and thousands of others—many of which are to be seen in London, and all of them, with scientific variations, in Paris—are social plagues within the American gates. Time and wise legislation may or may not eradicate such evils or control them, but these plagues are to-day within America's gates, and the purpose of this chapter is to show, or attempt to show, civilisation the awfulness of the trade *outside* the gates—far away in the East, where America has great business propositions on hand, and where America has established herself as a first-class Western Power within the bosom, so to speak, of the great Asiatic Powers. America very properly aspires to become a leader among the great Western Powers in the East. She is now standing as a " good stepmother " to China—a vast territorial area covering nearly one-twelfth of the known surface of the earth and inhabited by a population of anything from four hundred and fifty million to five hundred million souls. America has certainly got half her foot in China, and by many diplomatic acts of statesmanship has impressed the Chinese. Her last great act of " policy " towards China was to reduce the fearful indemnity claimed against China by the allied Powers for the late Boxer rising.

America commands a great trade in Shanghai, Hong-Kong, Singapore, Burma, India, Siam, Japan, and China proper. Her individual merchants in the East are respected and trusted by the Asiatics. Indeed, no commercial effort is spared by "Uncle Sam" or his "great trading sons" to impress the Asiatic's mind with the fact that the American is the right man in the right place in the East. Why, then, are all these splendid efforts so miserably discounted by the great Republic allowing a flood of brazen American prostitutes and low-down "pimps" to descend upon the East and, by their presence and their terrible traffic, to taint the Asiatic mind? Let Americans pause in their hustle and their "dollar hunt"—pause for a small breathing space, and take stock of the number of their daughters who are yearly done to death in the East. At each harlot's death in the fearful Asiatic Babylonian dens a big percentage of American influence over the Asiatic mind is lost.

As lovers of that land where freedom lives and flourishes, may we ask the authorities at Washington to stop, once and for all, American prostitutes and "pimps" plying their "profession" in the East? Surely it is the duty of the Legislature to do a great right, even at the expense of doing a little wrong! If women of ill-fame are kept out of the East and lose their unsavoury trade, compensate them with coin nobody will miss, and save the honour of the nation and the reputation of the womanhood of the nation in the eyes of the Asiatics

upon whom, at the moment, America is spend-
ing millions upon millions of dollars to maintain
a favourable impression. Let Washington well
consider the seriousness of this aspect of the
subject, for no man or woman, or set of men or
women, should claim licence to injure the name
of the national womanhood of the mothers
and daughters of America. To ask for such
licence is a step beyond freedom or freedom's
claims; yet the American prostitute in the
East claims this licence. The individual
liberty of the subject at home or abroad,
wherever the American flag flies, is amongst
the most treasured assets of the American
people; but licence to prostitutes to lay siege
to the East, and sell their bodies and the
bodies of American girls for coin to Asiatics,
is something ahead of liberty. It is licence
on the high road to licentious riot, which can
only bring about a state of affairs that outrages
liberty and makes the defenders of liberty
blush.

The British authorities in the East are wiser
—for once, at least—in the policy they adopt
in regard to British prostitutes plying their
trade in the East, in those quarters, of course,
where the British have control. A British
woman in the East following the oldest "trade"
the world knows is, when discovered, uncere-
moniously banished—that is, deported, without
trial and without bother or fuss : simply for
the public good. Any British prostitute plying
her "trade" in Calcutta, Bombay, Madras,
Delhi, Rangoon, Burma, Penang, Singapore,

Ceylon, Hong-Kong, Shanghai, or Borneo, is, when discovered, at once shipped to London or America. By this strong and speedy action the public good and the protection of the national name are secured. It is a splendid policy for a nation to adopt. Any Western nation that coolly stands by and views with complacency their women prostitute their bodies to Asiatics—who, of course, include Indians, Malays, Chinese, Cingalese, Siamese, Filipinos, etc.—quickly loses the last fragment of respect the Asiatic may have for it. An Asiatic will sometimes pay ten times the usual price to associate with an American woman, and such association will serve him as a thing to sneer and gibe over at the expense of the Western whites for a full year.

The Asiatic mind is volatile. It is easily swayed or inflamed by incidents that to the Western mind would be something idle and not worth bothering about. Once taint the Asiatic's mind by allowing him to have dalliance with our women, and we speedily lose control of him, lose his respect, and, incidentally, lose his trade. The Asiatic soon learns to despise the thing he can freely and cheaply use.

It was my painful experience when travelling through the East to see much evidence of the contempt that the advanced Asiatic has for a nation like America, which allows its women to openly live in bad houses and in concubinage with natives in the East.

A case is reported from Siam. It was one of those painful sights that American men in the East have perforce to witness. An American prostitute travelling with four young American girls, who, it was alleged, had been decoyed from California to the East, cleared the population of its dollars in the manner a circus is expected to. This woman did a " roaring trade " and " coined " money, at the expense of the health of the decoyed girls and the American national honour. At one town in the East where she arrived like an earthquake, the American Consul took counsel with his British brother in a like position, as to what means could be adopted to stop this "travelling hooker" and be at once relieved from the sneers and gibes of the Asiatics. The British Consul strongly advised deporting the "missus," but the American Consul trembled for the consequence of public opinion at home if he interfered with a daughter of the nation, even though she were a bad woman. So nothing was done. The "missus" sailed on, leaving a flourishing trade for the quack doctors in her track.

At Hong-Kong, Shanghai, Siam, Borneo, and Calcutta, a well-organised system of supplying the demand for American women exists. The markets in those centres are controlled by gangs or agents or "trusts" at New York and California, and every detail of the unsavoury business is organised. Some of these "trusts" or "rings" are said to be influential and wealthy. One thing is sure— they boldly carry on a fearful trade in American girls, and most, if not all, of their number do not know what the inside of a gaol is like. The orders for girls for the Eastern " trade " are generally booked, by cable, with the agents in the New York or Californian centres. Hundreds, if not thousands, of American girls are yearly hustled off to the East—seldom to be heard of again.

The East is considered the best place to " plant " any troublesome girl who has friends who may ask questions. The agents of the " rings " or " trusts " get rid of her for so much cash. They pass her on to a noted " missus " at Hong-Kong, Shanghai, or Siam—and that is the end of her. If she does not " fall to the life " and " get going quickly," she simply disappears—perhaps over the " fatal bridge at Shanghai."

One pitiable case came under my direct notice in the East. It was that of a young girl whose parents were good people in the fruit-growing business in California. The girl—a child of the nation which claims in the face of Christendom to have a well-registered mortgage on all that pertains to liberty—was entrapped by a procuress, seduced by a man in high authority in California, and secretly kept in hiding for months. Of course, her parents became alarmed for her safety, but by some pretext this young girl was induced to leave California and go with a motherly-looking person to New York, preparatory to her proposed marriage with her seducer. The unfortunate child-girl was only one night in New York—the next day she was *en route* for Shanghai. When she landed at Shanghai she was dumped into the " house with the golden stairs," but as her sobs and sighs, her tears and her importuning for her mother, her brother, and her little sisters became nauseating to the strong-minded " missus " of the " house with the golden stairs "—who was out for money, not tears— the child-girl disappeared so completely that not a trace of her or her having lived in the fearful Babylonian house now exists. It is freely whispered that this unfortunate daughter of America crossed the " fatal bridge at Shanghai "; if so, poor child, she was, or is, in the " ante-room " to hell itself. It is simply marvellous what some of these American " missuses " can do with young girls who pass through their hands in the East. A pretty girl will be laughing and joking in a house of infamy on, say, Monday; by Wednesday she has vanished, disappeared completely, Heaven knows where. These disappearances are " table-talk " in every hotel in Shanghai, but nobody seems to bother. The lines—

> Rattle her bones over the stones,
> Only a prostitute whom nobody owns—

are an epitaph callously applied to the American daughters in the East when the hour for their disappearance or death arrives.

As already stated, the Hon. John Goodnow tried to stop the traffic of American women in the East, but he failed.

JEZEBEL AND THE CONSUL

I was told the following incident by an attaché to one of the Consular offices in the East when he and I were at one of the hotels at Tiffen. He told me what *he* was pleased to term "a good joke on the Governor," the "Governor" being the American Consul in charge. The good, easy-going Consul had settled in his own mind that the traffic in American women in the East had better be stopped, and for the purpose of making a start at the "stopping business" the Consul sent for a bulky, brazen "missus" who traded heavily in young girls by direct cable to New York and California,

This generously proportioned woman obeyed the Consul's demand, and bounced into the American Consulate, shaking the building as she progressed. The American Consul informed the weighty "missus" that she would have to give up the "free trade" traffic in American women, and that she must "cut out and go."

The Consul was firm. So was the "missus."

"Madame, you are leading a life of shame. You must 'quit' it," urged the Consul.

"Quite a lot of people are leading lives that they should be ashamed of, but they ain't 'quitting,' and don't seem to be making any preparation to 'quit,'" suggested the "missus."

"The American nation blushes for you, madame," said the Consul.

"Well, I've done my share of blushing for the American nation when I see what folks can do with the dollar, with which, at the moment, folks at home are trying to buy up creation. They've got tired of buying up Congress, municipalities, preachers, and the like. But say, hadn't we better 'ring off' these 'jam-tart' tactics, and get right down to bedrock in this little campaign you are hustling on to me?"

"As you please, madame," agreed the Consul.

"Well, we'll start off at 'scratch.' I am an American woman—and don't you forget to mind it—and I intend to stop 'right here' as long as I have a mind to. If you put your Consular laws on to me, I tell you, without chewing a word, I've blown the sunspots off better men than you, and I've poked holes with my 'gingham' in your Consular laws times out of reckoning before to-day. Outside and away from that, what call have you to interfere with me or mine? You preach an unwritten law and quote some unregistered authority when you tell me I must quit. I use but what is my own, and if I've a mind to boil tea or stew coffee in a utensil that society says mint sauce or ice cream should be served in, where is the law to make me obey society? Society is pretty rotten at all times, but when society is old and cold and washed out—well, it's beyond the limit. In your hurry to harry

me, Sir Consul, don't forget that the 'sky
pilots,' the 'pulpit-punchers,' and 'Bible-
bangers' don't own creation; they don't even
own America by quite a lot. If you stop my
progress out here in this hell-on-earth, where
all the plagues of Egypt are bottled together,
and may be sampled without the asking—if
you stop me, I say, I'll shake eternity to its
foundation to get even with you. I am out
for business and dollars, Sir Consul. You,
sir, are out for morality and hypocrisy. When
you were a young man you were a noted
'lark.' Now you are old and grumpy you
are a 'nark.'"

" But the honour of the nation," the Consul
pleaded, "demands that the prostitution of
our women in the East should stop."

"The honour of the nation," the " missus "
rejoined, " demands that you get busy and
stop the 'rings' and the frauds on the people
by the 'bosses' and 'dollar freaks' that
'run' America, and leave us stray women to
toil out our account on earth, and then fight
single-handed with the devil when we 'hand
our cheques in.'"

The Consul was silent.

"Well," said the "missus," with a loud
laugh that reverberated throughout the building, " what will you do, Sir Consul—'follow
suit,' 'reneague,' or 'go to the pack'? It's
all one to me. You're 'done to rags,' anyhow,
if you lay hold on my position."

The Consul " went to the pack."

He had no power to interfere with this bold

American "missus" or to order her off the Eastern premises. She was a smart woman, a woman who would have made money—good money—in any line of business outside the harlot traffic. Yet she feared the Consul; so she played her "ace," and invited the Consul to "follow suit" or "throw his hand in."

The next day she married an "Italiano" cool-drink-vendor, on condition that he should keep cool and stick to his drink-vendor business while she would continue to manufacture "drug cocktails" in her house of infamy. She wanted his name to protect her from the Consul. He wanted her money to send to his deserted wife in Italy to stop her sending after him. So the satisfaction in the nuptials was reciprocal.

A day or two after this episode the American Consul received a card announcing:

MADAME ALBERTO RAGAILLO
LAMBEGRO

presents her compliments to the Consul, and will be at home to receive her visitors at such and such an hour.

This fearful woman played the "strong suit," "led trumps all the while," and finally she and her "mates" drove the worthy Consul out of the East and out of the American Consulate in utter disgust. The poor man tried to do some good, but Washington deserted him.

13

AMERICA IN ASIA

It is beyond question the national ambition of America to become an Asiatic Power—or rather, a Power in Asia—with her possessions already in hand, and the extra footing she expects to obtain in China. It behoves America to be at least circumspect in Asia, and she cannot start better than by prohibiting her daughters from immorally inter-mixing with Asiatics. For good or for evil, America has settled herself in the Far East, with her Philippine Islands under the guns, so to speak, of Japan, and as remote from her home base as it is possible to get. Being a Western Power in the Far East, the obligations and responsibilities of America to Christendom are, to say the least, very great. Beyond this, she has her actual enemy, Japan, armed to the teeth outside her Eastern gates, and she has a myriad Japanese ex-soldiers and ex-sailors inside her gates. Therefore it behoves America to be doubly circumspect and watchful of her Eastern possessions. But she is not watchful. Wise heads in the East declare that if she does not quickly take stock of her methods in the Philippines, and keep her men in order, there will be a repetition of what took place at Port Arthur and Dalny, where the Russians were hunted out of that corner of the East by the Japanese after they had spent millions upon millions in making harbours,

waterways, wharves, public buildings, forti-
fications, etc., but neglected to preserve a
tone with their people which is decent and
dignified.

The Japanese openly boast to-day that
America is but building up the Philippines
preparatory to Japan's occupation. The
Japanese declare that they can take the
Philippines from the Americans any morning
" before breakfast."

When America took the Philippines from
Spain, President McKinley, addressing a
religious gathering at the White House,
Washington, on November 21, 1899, said :

" Before you go I should just like to say
a word about the Philippine business.
When I realised that the Philippines
had dropped into our lap, I confess
that I did not know what to do with
them. I sought counsel from all sides
—Democrats as well as Republicans—
but got little help. I thought first we
would take only Manila, then Luzon,
then other islands, perhaps, also. I
walked the floor of the White House
night after night, and I am not ashamed
to tell you, gentlemen, that I went down
on my knees and prayed Almighty God
for light and guidance more than one
night.

" And one night late it came to me this
way—I don't know how it was, but it
came: (1) that we could not give them

back to Spain—that would be cowardly
and dishonourable; (2) that we could
not turn them over to France or Germany—that would be bad business and
discreditable; (3) that we could not
leave them to themselves—they were
unfit for self-government and they would
soon have anarchy and misrule over
there, worse than Spain's was; and (4)
that there was nothing left for us but
to take them all, and to educate the
Filipinos, and uplift and civilise and
christianise them, and, by God's grace,
to do the very best we could by them as
our fellow-men for whom Christ died
also. And then I went to bed, and went
to sleep, and slept soundly, and the next
morning I sent for the chief engineer of
the War Department (our map-maker)
and told him to put the Philippines on
the map of the United States (pointing
to a large map on the wall of his office);
and there they are, and there they will
stay while I am President."

How has the promise of that great dead
President been carried out? To-day, licentiousness and concubinage run riot throughout
the Philippines. American harlots of every
grade abound and flourish in the principal
towns. Opium dens, cocaine dens, and dens
for nameless other evils are to be pointed
out and viewed for the asking. The American
man associates with the native woman

and thinks it his prerogative to do so. The Filipino women adopt airs, and sneer at their own countrymen. The soldier and the sailor live in open concubinage with the black woman. The licentious life led by the populace, including the American soldiers and sailors, with the Filipino women, is an open and unhushed scandal in the face of Christianity which is doing and will continue to do America and Western civilisation a fearful amount of injury. Yet while one deprecates the concubinage between the soldiers and the Island women, bringing about, as it does, the bastardising of thousands upon thousands of copper-coloured half-castes —poor, helpless youngsters brought into this world to be despised and kicked by the whites and loathed and spat at by the dark-coloured races—while all this is terrible, it must be frankly admitted that America has many examples of other nations before her in this respect. It seems to be the custom of the East—at least when the Eastern woman meets the Western man. Divines preaching the pure religion of love, of charity, of righteousness, and of forgiveness of sins, too often, by their own evil ways, set an example to the ignorant Filipino which makes one blush for Christianity.

That great man, Bishop Brent—who is, perhaps, the best living authority on all matters relating to the Philippines—writing on the subject of the morality amongst the people and their Christian teachers, says :

"No one but a blind partisan seriously denies any longer the grave moral laxity that has grown up and still lives under the shadow of the church and parsonage in the Philippines. Inch by inch I have been forced back by the pressure of facts from the position I originally held that there was a minimum rather than a maximum of immorality. The cumulative testimony that has come to me has been chiefly incidental and unsought, containing in it the witness of Roman Catholics of good standing. When the new hierarchy sets to work I can imagine from my small experience that they will have an unsavoury and anxious task.

"It is considered to be no special discredit to either party concerned—certainly not to the man—if a temporary contract is entered upon between a man and a Filipino woman, to be terminated when expedient. A man may, according to this *mal costumbre*, have even more than one woman without transgressing propriety, though a woman must abide faithful, as long as the contract is in effect, to the one man. It is unfair to jump at the conclusion that such a lamentable practice has grown up because the country has been under Roman Catholic rule. The question, however, may be justly asked whether Latin Christianity has honestly grappled with it. The answer is found in a fact. Many—I use the conservative word— many Filipino priests have a personal lot and share in the *costumbre* under discussion, either in its less or its more revolting form. Their grown-up children bear witness to the long continuance of the custom. I know one old priest who lives openly with his Filipino wife—for that is what she really is—and family in the town where he has served, if my memory is accurate, for more than half a century. I have no reason to suppose that his ministrations are not acceptable to his flock—and yet the common folk believe that a lawfully wedded priest would, *ipso facto*, be incapacitated for the priestly office!

"No doubt the Church has, in the past, spasmodically struggled with this be-setting sin of the Filipino. But, in spite of everything, by degrees its filthy stream trickled into the sanctuary, and apathetic quiescence in a seemingly hopeless situa-tion ensued. A council for the reorgani-sation of the Church so far as possible along American lines has been summoned by the archbishop, and an effort is being made to secure the aid of the American priests, thus far without much success. I believe that the American archbishop and bishops in the Philippines, nearly all of whom I have met, are the type of men who would be as shocked as you or

I at what they see. It is, beyond per-
adventure, their desire to mend matters.
I am sure they will try, but their hands
are tied by the ordinance of a council of
A.D. 1059, which in the long run and
broadly speaking has been a failure.
What the Philippine hierarchy should
be free to do, according to the principles
of justice and honour, is to relax the
rule of a celibate clergy locally, to pro-
nounce the Church's blessing on every
priest who has been and is faithful to
one woman, and to excommunicate *con
amore* those who have various *queridas*.
The question is not one of doctrine, but
of common morals, which strikes at the
root of society, and in which every
citizen is concerned.

" Again, it is all too common to find
the parish priest an accomplished
gamester. The stagnation of topical life,
the absence of other amusements than
the *baile* and a mild game of ball played
by the men, make the prevailing excitement a powerful temptation to the least
viciously inclined."

Under America, the moral standard of the
Islands has not improved from the fearful
state they stood in under the rule of Spain.
Manila is the chief centre of America's
Babylonian Eastern world. There are,
certainly, under the American rule, more
churches and more schools there are also

more houses of infamy and more concubinage and illegitimacy than ever before. But again I say that these are questions that affect almost every nation in the East. Time alone, with prudence, may yet bring about remedies of the evils in the East where the population is mixed and the environment of the national life so licentious.

The object of this chapter is to point out to America the evil that exists through her daughters of shame in Asiatic countries, including the Philippines. The remedies are within America's grasp if she will devote a little time to dealing with the cleansing of this moral slough of infamy. America can deal with her women of ill-fame in the East by arranging with the other Consuls to assist in deporting white prostitutes from the East and by laying the "cat-o'-nine-tails" on the bare backs of "pimps" when caught. This would certainly be a strong beginning, and as the matter is serious beyond question, the work should begin at once.

CHAPTER XI

PLEAS

FOR many years both of us now writing of this book have been constantly among the working classes, who form, perhaps, the most sensitive audience with which one can deal. Therefore, if we could put before the mass of people in this country, and before the working-class men especially, the horrible cruelties that have been practised upon unfortunate girls, we believe that they would take the matter in hand and deal with it. *And they have votes.* One can see how quickly politicians run to the people when they want anything from them, and, once they arouse public opinion, nothing can interfere with the course the people wish to pursue. We do not mean to say that this is the only power to be invoked on behalf of the unfortunate women we plead for here—the slaves of this horrid traffic. The educated and cultured, and those who have money, position, and power, could of course do a very great deal if they wanted to. The question always is, Will they want to? And the Press?—we are hoping much from the British Press. The British Press could present this subject to the people, and tell them what the white slave traffic in the East really means. It is, indeed, the British Press that must make public the facts relating to this slave trade, in order that this subject may be adequately presented to the people, the difficulty about such things always being to get the question placed before the nation with sufficient publicity. Before beginning the fight we have tried to enlist help, so that the matter could be taken in hand and the battle against the white slave traffic, especially in the East, be begun.

It was only a few days ago that a young lady told me that she was followed as she came out of a large London store by a nasty, sleek-looking, well-dressed, well-oiled-looking foreigner, who tried to attract her attention and induce her to go with him. Asked why she did not give him in charge of the first policeman, the young lady said the disagreeableness following this course of action was so great *to the woman* that she did not like to do it. Now, this is one of the hard things we must put before respectable women as being their duty to the State and to their sisters ; they *must*, when they are accosted by these men, give them in charge of the police. Of course, it will be made disagreeable enough for them, but it is a public duty to do this, and when a few cases are proved, genuine public opinion would vere round to the fact that women were putting themselves in this disagreeable position, not because they wished to do so, but as an act of patriotism and duty, simply for the protection of others. It is, of course, very safe as a general thing for girls and women to travel about—thousands of them do it every day—and it is only very rarely that one gets spoken to ; but, still, these things do happen.

At a woman's club some time ago the wife of a very well-known barrister told me that she was followed all along the Strand, as she was walking from Charing Cross to Treloar's shop to buy some carpets. She was pursued by a nasty-looking man, who kept on speaking to her, and called her " My dear." This lady was then on the Education Board, and beyond all question reliable in every way, and yet even she felt she could not face the difficulty of giving this wretch into the charge of a policeman. Women hate doing this sort of thing, and we shall never get them to do it until we have put before them the necessity there is for them to sacrifice their own feelings in the matter for the sake of countless numbers of girls who are victimised. A friend, who is in the City—he is one of the partners in a very large business—says that one of his clerks informed him that a nasty, vulgar, flashy man they have in their employ makes it a practice every evening, after office hours, to dress himself up very smartly and go to the West End, or to the East End, or anywhere else

he is likely to come across poor seamstresses
and shop girls. He gets quite a good salary,
and makes a fair commission on his work.
He provides himself with attractive presents.
and practically every evening of his life
he goes out with a new girl to dinner; he
flatters her, gives her food and wine and some
present, and—ruins her!

It is almost unbelievable that these
wretches can exist and go on as they do,
and it is only when women hold together and
try to serve each other, forgetful of their own
personal inconvenience and comfort, that we
can hope to throw a shield of protection around
these girls, who from very sad economic conditions are so easily made victims of men of this
sort. Many come to Mackirdy House for help.

Before my marriage I travelled a good deal,
and for nearly six months toured in America.
I also went all over the Continent, and I did
not encounter many disagreeable experiences,
I am bound to admit. Still there were some,
but I was well off, and had scores of friends,
and went to safe places. When I went to
make social investigations abroad I had two
men on my staff with me. A very curious
thing, however, happened to me one day *after
my marriage*, when I was travelling *with my
husband*. He put me into the train at Victoria—and it happened to be a first-class
carriage too—and left me to get an evening
paper. He was delayed a few minutes, and
as I sat waiting for him, a flashy-looking,
vulgarly dressed sort of foreigner—I think

now he must have been a "pimp"—got into
the carriage. Of course I took no notice of
him, but he sat down exactly opposite to me,
and put his foot across the door, which he
shut, and then he addressed me as "my dear."
I still took no notice of him, but he went on
talking, and offered me a ladies' paper. I
thought it better to say nothing. Then he
began to indulge in what I suppose he
thought was wit, and to chaff me on my
silence. He told me I looked "far too sweet
and good-natured to be disagreeable" to him.
Just then, to my great joy, I saw my husband
coming down the platform, and the train was
about to start. My husband flung open the
door and jumped into the carriage. I suppose he noticed that something had upset me,
for he asked what the matter was, but I
said, "Oh, nothing." Not satisfied with this
answer, he insisted on knowing why I looked
worried, and I told him that the man opposite
had made a mistake, and thought I was
travelling alone. Just then the guard blew
his whistle and the train began to move out
of the station. My husband said nothing at
all, but simply turned round and took the
man by the collar of his coat and somewhere
round the waist line, kicked open the door
of the carriage, and with a dreadful bang
bumped the creature down upon the platform. He never said a word, but quietly
sat down near me. I could hardly help
laughing at the helplessness of the wretch
as the train passed out of the station leaving

him sitting on the platform. I said to my
husband :

"What a dreadful thing to do! He might
have been killed."

"Well," he said, "what if he had? It could
not possibly matter if a 'thing' like that had
been killed."

And that was all I could get him to say
about the incident.

But suppose now that flashy and well-
to-do individual had found, instead of a
married woman with a protector, some poor
shop girl or village girl who knew nothing
about life, how easily he would have got into
conversation with her! He could have given
her something to drink, and have taken her over
to France almost before she was aware that
anything was happening. It is not difficult
to do these things when men have to deal
with uneducated, ignorant girls—and they
always make an effort to choose their victims
with great care. I have often heard it said
that no woman or girl is ever spoken to who
goes along her business in a quiet way; but
this is an absolutely false statement. Hundreds
of women are accosted who are perfectly quiet
and inoffensive, and who would not for a
single moment think of giving any encouragement to a man. Of course, when girls
know what they are about they take no
notice, and the men generally find that they
have made a mistake, and leave off worrying
them.

If you care to walk down by the large

West End shops, or, better still, if you will go about closing time to any of the large work-rooms even in the East End, you will see hanging about the doors in the street men whose calling is written plainly all over their faces and forms. These men are simply "pimps," who are on the look-out for girls whom they can entrap. They are not always seeking the women for themselves, but they are seeking them for sale in bad houses.

It is a matter of vital importance that we should look after these girls *before* they get into the grip of the white slave trader. The conditions under which so many of them live are so intolerably dreary and sad. If they have to work in a shop where the living-in system prevails there are probably a large number herded into one dreary room. The houses they live in are cold and barely furnished. The food in these establishments is generally bad ; the hours of work are long, and the wages for young workers very small. On Sundays many of the houses turn them out to fend for themselves. They are not supposed to come in or give any trouble ; so even if it is raining they have no place of their own to go to. A great deal has been done towards improving the condition of women workers of this country, but very much still remains to be done, and until some sort of minimum wage is established, and until living-in houses are all under *constant* inspection of *qualified women* who will report upon their conditions, and until Government will compel employers to both pay their women well and to house them well, we cannot possibly hope that prostitution in its entirety will cease. As long as women are cheap, so long will prostitution flourish. Of course, "the profession" offers many inducements to women. About five years ago a friend of mine told me of a girl who came to her mistress, a lady of title, whom she had served for some years, and said to her, "My lady, I wish to give notice to leave." "Oh," said the lady, "are you going to be married?" "No," said the girl, "I am not going to be married." "Well," said the lady, "I do not wish to interfere with your business; but are you going to a fresh situation, or is there any reason why you should leave my services? You have always seemed very happy here." "Well," blurted out the girl, "I am not going to work any more. I am going to become a fallen woman." "Good heavens! what on earth is that?" asked the mistress. "Well, my lady," said the servant, "it is this way. My sister, she is a fallen woman, and she lives like a lady. She has silk stockings and silk petticoats, and she earns from eight to fifteen pounds a week. That is why I want to be a fallen woman too." No persuasion could affect her. Of course, her mistress would have thought it extremely shocking and not the thing at all to tell the girl the price she would ultimately have to pay for her way of life! The girl could only see the present, and as she was young, good-looking, and fresh there was perhaps a likelihood of her earning sometimes eight to fifteen pounds a week. But it must not be supposed that this amount is easily earned : it is assuredly made occasionally by prostitutes in a good position, but the earnings fluctuate a great deal.

We must quote here a paragraph from *Prevention*, the organ of the National Council of Public Morals, which has on its committee some of the most distinguished men and women of the day, many eminent clergy, including archbishops and bishops, peers, and well-known social workers. In an article on " The Common Lodging-House " the paper says:

" Another urgent necessity is the provision of lodging-houses for women. At present the common lodging-houses for both sexes are such that it is difficult for a woman inmate to preserve her purity. Moreover, the by-laws, framed so far back as 1877, regulating their internal arrangements and governing their management, need both revision and reform.

" With regard to fallen women, there is remarkable unanimity amongst those who know in stating that the great majority of them begin their downward course before they are eighteen years of age. Therefore it is urgently necessary that the age of consent should be raised from sixteen to eighteen. There are two other amendments to the existing law—the Criminal Law Amendment Act of 1885 —which I wish to urge for reasons that have come within my own experience of the courts. (I ought to say, by the way, that this paragraph is a quotation from a speech by D. Lleufer Thomas, stipendiary magistrate.) First, in the case of debauching a girl between thirteen and sixteen years of age the accused is entitled to an acquittal if it shall be made to appear to the court or jury that he had reasonable cause to believe that the girl was 'of or above the age of sixteen.' Now as this offence is not triable summarily in a police court, but the accused has to be committed to the Assizes, there may well be an interval of three or four months between the police court hearing and that at the Assizes. Meanwhile the girl has developed rapidly, so that when the judge and jury see her for the first time it is not difficult for them to be persuaded that the accused may have had reasonable cause to believe her to be 'of or above sixteen.' More prisoners get off through the benefit of this proviso than in any other way, and *the proviso should be struck out.* Secondly, no prosecution in respect of this offence can be instituted more than six months after the commission of the offence. The time ought certainly to be extended to nine if not twelve months, for in many cases it is only when a girl becomes a mother that the police first get to know of the offence; and as the law now stands it is then too late to do anything."

This magistrate also makes

" *A Plea for Policewomen*

" Has the policewoman no place in our national life? Is it not desirable that the Home Office should permit and even encourage the appointment—at least as an experiment—of a limited number of high-minded, specially - trained police-women for special duty in some of our larger towns? Such an innovation would inevitably tend towards the introduction of more humane methods into police operations, and it would probably enable much more to be done for the protection of children and young girls, and also in giving warning and advising women leading lives that are likely to ruin them. Whenever women prisoners are kept in custody in police cells or stations, whether on their arrest or on short remands, not exceeding three days, it is unsatisfactory that there should be only male officers to attend to them. . . ."

Mr. Thomas's whole address is very well worth reading, but there is not space to do more than quote from it; and in respect to lodging-houses and hostels for women we give from the same paper, *Prevention*, a report from Mrs. Mackirdy's speech made at the Cory Hall, in Cardiff, on this subject:

"Hostels for Women

"Every girl and woman on the streets is a menace to some home and some life. It is quite impossible to have a neglected and cheap womanhood and with it a fine and progressive manhood. What a nation's women are, that the men must also be. No man can be better than his mother or his mistress. It is for this reason that we are so set upon ending all opposition to these hostels for respectable women. We long to go forward all the time, and step by step, to uphold and to care for the woman before she has fallen. We feel that a woman degraded is such an awful stumbling-block to little children and to young people who may see her.

"*Women Need a Home*

"I dare say 'rescue homes' are all right in their way, but real homes are of far more value to the nation. To give a woman who is on the verge of ruin a taste of home is to wake in her heart a desire for home life—the most whole-some desire, next to the love of God, that a woman's heart can know. This desire will inspire quite hopeless women to efforts of self-respect and ambition. I saw one day a young street woman with a number of *little children* round her. She had been drinking, and was saying such things as Satan might well hesitate to utter ; and there were the children ! I wonder whether ever in her life that unfortunate wretch had any chance given her to be good.

" *Industrial Conditions for Women*

" The industrial conditions for women are very bad. Yet there is work for the *fit*. Now we want to make fit people out of the unfit. The stress of modern life, the bad industrial conditions and sweated women's labour, the restlessness of the time, and the curse of sin which offers so much and conceals the price to be paid— all these things make it imperative for every thoughtful man and woman to join together in working for the protection of women and the safeguarding of our girls. Let us in every city be ready with inviting, welcoming homes to take in the unfallen girl and the respectable poor woman. This is a good and practical way of lessening immorality and putting a spoke in the wheels of the white slave traffic. Barracks and institutions will never compete with or lessen immorality.

A woman wants home and companionship.

"*For the Sake of the Men*

"It was a broken-hearted mother—a widow—whose only son had paid with his life for consorting with a 'fallen girl,' who came to me with sobs and prayers. 'Tell them,' she said, 'to prevent the women from going on the streets—tell them to take care of the girls for the sake of their own sons.' I have never forgotten the plea. It is for the sake of our men who are so precious to us that we must take care of our women.

"We hope there will be in all the cities, and everywhere, hostels which are homes in charge of really experienced workers, open to respectable women and girls; and that many organisations will be able to find work for those needing it."

All of those who are interested in the protection of girls are anxious that they in case of necessity should be able to go where they can be taken in at once into homes which are not called "preventive" or "rescue homes," but simply hostels or shelters, where the inmates will be well treated as ordinary human beings, and where they will find friends and be helped to get work. In this way many a girl who has been tempted by some wicked "pimp," perhaps to wander about with him, could be saved before it is too late.   It is often the case that these men who wish to secure girls for the white slave traffic do not dishonour them themselves at once, or at any rate they do not take them until they have quieted their suspicions and have acquired a hold on them.   So between-times, while the girl is hesitating, she might be saved.

Only the other day a generous lady who had read Mrs. Mackirdy's speech in *Prevention* sent an opal and diamond ring which she wished Mrs. Mackirdy to sell for the benefit of this home for girls and women. She felt so strongly that women, at any rate, ought to help to the uttermost the cause that has for an end the protection and help of girls and women.   The difficulties girls have to face in these days when they are obliged to work for a living are very great. Some of the less-enlightened firms, and those who have determined to get every pennyworth of use out of their employees, treat them in some cases in a very disgraceful way, and any shop-girl may be dismissed instantly on a complaint of a shop-walker, although a week's notice is her due.   They often pay a woman her week's wages and turn her out; and if one could only inquire into all the cases it would come as a shocking revelation to find that in many cases the girl's chief sin consisted in not making herself agreeable enough to the shop-walker.   Of course in good establishments the girls have a much better time, and they are much better looked after.

As girls have been taken by white slave
traders from England to the Continent and
to America, and as from the Continent they
drift sometimes to Egypt, where the conditions will bear no speaking of at all, or to
China and various places in the tropics, we
ought to enter into some sort of agreement
with other nations to hunt out the procurers
and "pimps," who are called in Europe
souteneurs.

There are between seventy and a hundred
places in Buenos Ayres alone to which English
girls are sent. It was stated some time ago
by a police officer that the police were always
seeing suspicious people going to and from
England to Buenos Ayres, but that it was the
most difficult thing in the world to apprehend
them. As English girls obtain the best sums
of money both in the Argentine and in the
East, it is not difficult to see why the trader
who deals in them is always hunting. Italy
and Austria provide many of the Christian
girls who are taken to Singapore and the
East. And in a very large majority of cases
they are absolutely innocent and quite un-
aware as to what they are being taken
abroad for. We ought to provide, in every
town of this country and at every sea-port, a
certain number of police especially to watch
the comings and goings of men and women
suspected of being engaged in the slave
traffic. Many of them are already more
than suspected, and if they knew the very
instant a procurer or *souteneur* had set foot

in this country he would be watched until he departed, it would be the easiest thing in the world to find out whether the woman he was taking with him was one in whose company he had any right to be. These wretched men feel more sure of their money and more sure of their victims when they send them off to distant places, and this is why the white slave traffic extends over such immeasurable distances. The great idea is to get the girls away from any one who might protect them. They are never allowed to write to any one, and thousands of difficulties surround them if they wish to escape.

A governess—now happily married and living not far from London—relates an adventure she had some years ago in London. She answered an advertisement for a governess to a motherless child who was in the house of her father and in charge of an aunt. It all sounded perfectly natural and reasonable. After a little correspondence the girl was asked to send her photograph; this she did, and then she was engaged and was to go to her post, which was a house in a rather unfashionable and decaying square in London. On her arrival she was received by a woman who announced herself as the aunt of the child; but the girl did not like her appearance, as her hair was dyed and her face was painted; moreover, she smelt of liquor. Presently the supposed father came in, and he was still more objectionable-looking. They offered the girl wine, and in looking round the room she instantly saw that there would be no way of escaping. Gathering all her wits together she maintained as unsuspicious an attitude as she could, and answered all questions very pleasantly and naturally. They asked her if she had a father or brothers, and before she realised she was making a mistake she said she had not, and it quickly occurred to her that she should not have allowed these people to imagine she had no one to protect her. However, she was shown up to her room, and found it was a large bedroom with a big double bed, and that it communicated with another room. Here she was told to take off her things and have a rest. Before the woman left, the governess asked if there was a letter-box near, as she wished to post a letter, but she was told that all letters would be posted for her and that she need not trouble to go out. The girl waited until she heard the woman who had accompanied her upstairs descend, and then very quietly she came out of the room and peered over the bannisters. She could see down into the hall below, and as no one seemed to be moving about, with a fervent prayer that she might be protected and enabled to escape she very softly crept downstairs. Several times her heart almost stood still as she thought she heard some sound. She managed to get to the front door, and had almost opened it when she heard the door behind her open and the man and woman tumbled out and made a grab at her. The girl said that she was so absolutely terrified that she felt paralysed, and she thought that she would never be able to get the door open; but fortunately she did—she managed to squeeze herself through and pull the door to and fly down the steps. Before she got to the last step she noticed that the square seemed quite deserted, and a man ran up the area steps to give chase; she simply flew along the pavement, and luckily before she had gone many yards towards the post-box a policeman turned into the square and she called out to him. Her pursuer immediately fled. The girl told the policeman everything, and was horrified to find that the house had already been suspected and was under police surveillance. She had only just escaped in time. If stories like these were put into sensational novels one would believe of course that they were quite impossible and were invented simply for the sake of creating a sensation and writing a good story. The fact is that infinitely more sensational and terrible things happen in real everyday life than are ever written about.

Sir Percy Bunting, editor of the *Contemporary Review*, made a speech at the International Commission on the White Slave Traffic which was held in London some years ago. We quote a portion of his speech, which appears in a book on the white slave traffic which has done much, we hope, to make public things that are going on in this country. As the writer of that book says:

"Quite naturally the unsavoury nature of the subject has prevented its general discussion, and the great majority of parents are therefore ignorant of the danger which threatens their daughters should they allow them to accept situations at home or abroad without first instituting the most searching inquiries."

He goes on to say:

"Hence, prevention being better than cure, only one way remains of combating the scourge, and that is through the medium of the Press. Great Britain is literally honeycombed with this pest; and its appalling dimensions are largely due to the ignorance of the great mass of the people as to its methods and its ramifications, which spread throughout all classes of society."

Sir Percy Bunting said:

"No one can be surprised that, while vice is practised and money can be made out of it, it should give rise to a trade carried on by a third person, *entrepreneurs* and their agents, or that the trade should, with the facilities of modern civilisation, have command of large capital and resources.

"Certain it is that there is a regular trade in young girls who are bought and sold, imported and exported to and from the ports and cities of Europe; that the trade is influenced by the ordinary laws of supply and demand; and that the capitalists have their purveyors and agents in other countries than their own, who recruit likely subjects for the business.

"It will naturally occur to remark that such traffic involves slavery, whereas the status of slavery is abolished in civilised Europe, and any person can claim her freedom. The answers are, first, that a girl once compromised tends to fall into an obscure pariah class, which has not the usual protection against oppression afforded by the habits of society; that the unprotected condition is doubly dangerous when she is once in a foreign country in which she has no friends, and of which she does not understand the language; that many of the girls are minors, and in such circumstances acquiescence may be easily enforced."

Will the most cold and incredulous of the law-makers at Westminster doubt the words of such a thinker and such a critic as Sir Percy Bunting?

CHAPTER XII

REMEDIES

THERE is not the slightest doubt in the minds of any of those people who have been considering this problem of the white slave traffic that the remedies for it are within our reach. There is not a single philanthropic society of any responsibility which would not hail with delight any laws that could be passed which would kill this traffic, and we feel confident in saying that all organisations which have for their aim the social betterment of the people would join without question in any crusade that might be made for the suppression of the white slave traffic.

It would be quite easy to introduce into Parliament one Bill which could be divided into several clauses dealing with all the phases of the white slave traffic in the East and also here.

The first act of this law must be that, as a murderer can be arrested on suspicion, so also must the police be given power to arrest a *souteneur*, a bully, or a " pimp," all of whom are creatures akin, *on suspicion*. There is no respectable person of the community who can object to this being done, for the simple reason that accidents are well-nigh impossible. Business men going to and from the East, the Argentine, and the Continent are not in the habit of travelling with different young girls on these trips; and those of them with their wives, daughters, nieces, or any female relatives can generally be known at once. We have seen at the docks of many countries travellers of all descriptions; and so far as our observation goes we cannot think for a single moment that the police would have any difficulty at all in arresting *on suspicion* the people who are really suspicious. No man ought to be allowed to leave this country for any continental port, whether it be Copenhagen, Sweden, Austria, or *any other* port, with a girl or woman, until he has given the address of the place where he has been staying, and the address of the place to which he is going; also the age and descriptions of the women. Unless they are obviously prostitutes, with whom, of course, no one need interfere, the particulars should be required by law. And the police in every port to which these people are going should be warned. They should be followed from port to port, and the destination of the girl ought to be ascertained. This is by no means so difficult as it might appear. Merchants going to and from the Argentine are quite well-known people, as are also merchants going to and from the Continent. They go to reputable places, and stay in known hotels and boarding-houses, so that cases of suspicious conduct would resolve themselves into a class which would be easily dealt with. But the first thing we must endure in order to secure the protection of our young girls is to face the vague risk or inconvenience on their behalf when travelling. Supposing even out of ten thousand cases one person was wrongly suspected, within two hours, at the very most, he or she could produce credentials, an apology would be made, and nothing more need be said about it. What creature on earth who cares about the safety of the young and the helpless would ever object to a remote possibility of inconvenience to themselves, if by including that vague possibility in our scheme a great protection is to be thrown around those who are so helpless and so cruelly wronged ?

We must have a law which deals with the *first offenders*. It is this mistaken system of requiring that a man should be caught and convicted several times before the law can deal with him severely enough, that is the cause of a great deal of the mischief. Once let it be proved that a man has procured a girl for immoral purposes, whether he has succeeded in accomplishing his purpose or not, so only it be proved that he *is* a procurer let the punishment be for him one dozen

15

lashes and a year's hard labour. This sentence should be imposed the *very first time the conviction is made.* It should be the *legal punishment* for this offence in every case.

Then another matter, though needing a little money from the public, ought not to prove at all difficult. In every port which can be used by procurers and their agents, there ought to be *two mission workers*—a man and woman. If they are a married couple belonging to some good organisation, well and good ; but if they are not married the man must have his own quarters and the woman hers. There must be a room into which a girl can be taken on landing if she wishes to escape. In Singapore, in Java, say, in fifty different ports let us place two thoroughly reliable and good men and women workers— that is one hundred people who are to be on the look-out and to attend every single boat that comes into port, night or day. I feel quite convinced that the story of this hideous traffic has only to be told to the public, and our people have only got to be made to understand what it means to these girls to be taken prisoners and sold to a slavery whose most horrible features we cannot in decency speak of fully, for every decent person in this country to give, according to his or her means, something towards the battle with these atrocious criminals, the white slave traders. It will easily be understood, of course, that the people sent out to do this work must be experienced, and they must be good Christian people. It is not likely to be easy or pleasant work, and in fact in the East and on the Continent it is a labour which will have its dangers. But if lives have been sacrificed freely to convert the Chinese to Christianity, to carry the Gospel to Arabs, to cover India with a network of missions, surely we can afford to support one hundred soldiers of Christ to do such service for their betrayed and injured sisters.

Another very important point. Any steamship company which has taken out to any foreign port a girl who is found to be enlisted for immoral purposes must be responsible for returning that girl to the country from which she was taken, free of all charge. The American Government has made it a law that all steamship companies bringing into the country emigrants who are rejected at the port shall be compelled to take these people back to their homes, and they have to do it. What is there to prevent our Parliament passing a similar Act in regard to these girls and women who are taken out to foreign ports? This law would strengthen our hands immensely, because it would make the steamship companies themselves extremely careful about their passengers, and it would make it increasingly difficult for these procurers and white slave traders to take their victims abroad. It might be made a matter of international courtesy that other countries should join in this crusade, and that the Governments of each country should contribute some small sum to these houses which are to be kept for the benefit of women taken from all countries in Europe.

Women who are convicted of procuring girls for immoral purposes should be sentenced to three years' penal servitude for the first offence, and if a second conviction be brought against them they should get a seven years' sentence. There are horrible old hags going about London now—I have met two or three of them myself—who ought by all the laws of justice to be hanged. How many an unfortunate child they have caused to be done to death no one will ever know; nor will they ever get their deserts in this world. They go from street to street, from lodging-house to lodging-house, they hang about outside churches at night and in all places where they are likely to meet clean, respectable women and girls, and get into conversation, worming themselves into their confidence, and they offer to show these distressed and hard-driven sisters of ours the infamous way of escape from poverty and hunger and friendlessness. For this service they are paid by the men for whom they procure these girls, or by the keepers of houses of ill-fame, or by the bullies. The only person who gets nothing out of the contract is the victim herself. Therefore, it is simply sentimental wickedness on our part to deal easily with these women. For foreign procuresses there should be a severe sentence of imprisonment *with hard labour,* to be followed by deportation; and

should they be found in the country again,
then let the sentence be doubled. They are
not here for our country's good, nor for the
good of any one, so why should we endanger
the girls of the nation ?

Every theatrical agent and concert agent
should be registered by the County Council,
and should be held responsible for the engagements which he obtains for women.
Many of these men are nothing more than
agents for the procurers and for immoral
houses abroad. It should be required by law
of an agent that he keep a list of all engagements procured by him for women, and that
he must have the addresses, a photograph,
and full particulars of those taking them,
their home addresses, their parents' signatures,
and the addresses where they are to be sent.
Further than this, it must be made compulsory for him to notify to the police when
he is sending a party of English girls out of
this country, or even when he is sending *one*
English girl out of this country. The girl
need not necessarily be interfered with ; she
need know nothing about the matter at all.
But if the police know where she is going and
the people with whom she is going to stay,
and they are in communication with the
police of the foreign country, it can instantly
be seen how very careful the agents will be
about sending girls to bad cafés and dancing
saloons and houses of ill-fame abroad. The
people of this country should demand that,
whether they like it or not, the theatrical

agent of every sort and description, and concert agents, shall be bound by these rules. And let us see that they do not get out of it. Many of them have done too much mischief already. The responsible agents will really be helped by these means, but the bad men will find their criminal path made less easy. Decent people have no cause to fear the law. To us all our laws and our justice are splendid things; we are not afraid of them. We look upon them as great possessions, something for our protection and the advancement of civilisation and religion. It is only the evildoer who fights shy of being brought within proper bounds. It is only the shady trafficker who cannot carry on his business in the light and face inquiry and just regulations. Therefore the objection raised by these people ought not to weigh with us at all.

The directors of steamship companies should be approached and asked *by the Government* to communicate with the captains of all vessels under their control, requesting them for their country's honour to be on the look-out for any young girl travelling alone or in company with a man or woman who is in the slightest degree suspicious. The captain of a vessel has opportunities of observing very closely his passengers, and he and his officers might very well form an opinion in the case of suspicious men and women taking girls and young women abroad. Although they might not be permitted to interfere with their passengers, which would, of course, cause a great deal of trouble and be quite impossible, the captain might be asked in cases of suspicion to make a point of lending to a girl or woman a little book on the white slave traffic abroad, which must be written for this purpose. It need not be luridly written, but it must truthfully set out, faithfully enough to make it worth considering, the fate of a girl who is taken abroad for immoral purposes. In this pamphlet might be given the names and addresses of the workers whom our Government, our people, and other Governments and other people have placed in the ports for the protection of the undefended, of the innocent and ignorant. If the girls know where they may apply for help, and know where they will be taken in without question, many of them will gladly leave their procurers. It must also be pointed out to them in this pamphlet that once they get to a street like Malay Street or the dens of infamy that abound in the great cities of the Continent and China, or even India, they need not hope for any rescue. If these measures were carried out the white slave traffic in the East and abroad would be dead within five years—dead as a door-nail. It is a traffic that is carried on simply for money. Those who pursue that trade have no other object in view at all. Therefore if you make it impossible for these traders to make money, and make their way of life so difficult and so dangerous that in order to follow it they run twenty risks every time they enter and leave a country, they will soon abandon their detestable trade.

I have never known a case of a man who lived upon the immoral earnings of a woman who did not ill-treat her, brutally very often. It seems strange that the women should go back to these men; but they are bound by a thousand ties, and they are very helpless. Also they live under a system of terrorisation hardly equalled in the worst annals of Russia. I have known some girls and women who have been compelled to earn their living in the streets, and many of them, poor creatures, have told me of the horrible usage to which they have been subjected. Some of them got away, but outsiders would hardly credit the difficulty there is in rescuing one of these women from the men who trade on them. The last thing in the world these creatures want to do is to give up their victims and the source of their livelihood. They follow them, and write to them, and in many cases threaten the workers who have taken them away.

Mrs. Booth's workers will tell you, so will the workers of the Church Army, how the houses where they take their girls are spied upon, and sometimes a veritable besiegement goes on. The women are simply terrified, and it is with the greatest difficulty that they can be coaxed into quietness and into the feeling of safety at all.

The law should be amended to raise the

age of consent from sixteen to eighteen, without the proviso about the girls *looking* sixteen.

The loophole given to procurers by the foolish and cruelly unjust proviso that if a girl *appears* to be sixteen or over her destroyer is free of responsibility, has sent many a girl to her doom. The Criminal Law Amendment Act of 1885, which says, " It shall be considered a sufficient defence if the accused can make it appear to the Court or Jury that he had reasonable cause to believe that the girl was, or above, the age of sixteen," makes it very easy for men to escape.

Criminals and procurers are rather fond of the disguise which a clergyman's garb gives them; but their behaviour, faces, and manners, if watched for a little while, generally give them away. Every railway station is the haunt of the procurer or of a female creature of this species. The railway officials are somewhat on their guard, but they can hardly be expected to watch individuals in all the rush of their business. One can see any day of the week, if one cared to try the experiment, in almost any of the large stations, especially those stations which are used for continental services, foreign men very much dressed, but possessing nearly always a rather nasty appearance, who hang about the station, and if you watch for a little while you will see them accost a girl now and then. If one happens to be a woman who looks young, one has to take great care

not to be accosted one's self. It is a very disagreeable thing for women to wait about a
railway station. There is always a liability of
being spoken to by strange men, and these
wretched foreigners of bad character are very
difficult to throw off.

Girls who are travelling alone ought always
to be warned that, if they have to wait for
any one, or for their trains, they should
always wait in the ladies' waiting-room. It
is the only place where they will be out of
reach of those who prowl about stations.

We want to kill off the human wolves who
destroy girls and women, and it is for this
purpose that this book has been written—as
anything which has been written on this
subject must have had for its object the
stamping out of this evil. But it is the
constant dripping that wears away the stone,
so we hope to press the matter on the public
conscience, and bring it before the public gaze
repeatedly, until the nation says, " Enough !
this evil must cease." Then the work will be
done. In this way only can we hope to have
the law amended and *new* and *necessary* laws
passed regarding this traffic; and also new
and necessary precautions taken at our cost
and our charge—yours and mine. I am quite
willing to pay my share. If I were not, I
would not ask you to help—to destroy the
plague-germ and to make free the Christian
slave.

Mr. Willis further suggests some drastic
measures which he, in common with many

of the police authorities, thinks would help materially to remove the worst phases of this trade. For myself, I would not put my name to any recommendation that would involve putting unfortunate women into the hands of *men* doctors. The thing to me is monstrous, shocking, and cruel. But why not employ *women* doctors? *They* are the persons who should deal with their own sex. *Men* doctors are often simply impossible and brutal in their dealings with these poor women. We must have women doctors, *appointed by the various Governments.*

REMEDIES SUGGESTED BY MR. WILLIS

1. A law should be passed by Parliament empowering the police to arrest procurers or " pimps " (whether men or women) who are known to the police as such, on suspicion of being white slave traffickers.

2. Men and women leaving this country for the East or other foreign ports to travel abroad with girls for suspected immoral purposes to be compelled (when required to do so) to give their names and addresses, occupations, and destination; to produce evidence of the age of, and their authority over, such girls; and generally to satisfy the police controlling the white slave traffic as to their *bona fides.*

3. The law to be amended respecting *first offenders* for procuring women for immoral purposes; such offenders to receive, on conviction, one year's hard labour. For the

second offence the punishment to be two years' hard labour; and, for the third offence, three years' and twenty-five lashes.

4. Any man convicted of living on money earned by any woman as the wages of immorality to be sentenced to one year's hard labour for the first offence; to two years' hard labour for the second; and to three years' penal servitude and twenty-five lashes for the third. The fact that a man is living with a woman who plies for hire in prostitution should be prima facie evidence that he is living on monies she so earns.

5. In all ports on the Continent and in the East two mission workers to be placed by some philanthropic institutions, *aided by Government*, for the rescue and protection of girls who desire to leave procurers or houses of ill-fame, and every assistance should be rendered to girls wishing to be so protected.

6. All shipping companies taking to foreign ports girls and women enlisted for immoral purposes to be responsible for returning, *free of charge*, such persons to the country from which they were taken.

7. All theatrical, concert, or other agents instrumental in taking or sending girls and women abroad to be registered at an office of the police or other authority having jurisdiction over the port of embarkation. Such agents to be held responsible for the *bona fides* of any engagements which they may obtain for women; and to register the names and addresses of girls and women engaged for

positions abroad and the addresses at which such employees may be found in a foreign country. In the event of any misfortune happening to the employee, the agent or the employers to bear all the expenses of returning her to her own country and provide for her until such time as her relatives or friends are able to take charge of her.

8. Any man found taking a girl to a street of sinister reputation in any port controlled by Great Britain to be arrested *without a warrant* and dealt with as a " pimp " or procurer.

9. The age of consent to be raised from sixteen to eighteen years; and no man or woman to be free from responsibility for procuring a girl or using her for immoral purposes, even with her own consent, unless her age exceeds eighteen years.

10. No man or woman to be permitted to sue or obtain judgment against any girl or woman who has been under their protection for immoral purposes—*i.e.* any debts contracted while under such `protection to be void.

11. No white European woman, of *whatever nationality,* to be allowed to ply the trade of ill-fame in Asiatic countries under British control; or, in the alternative, (*a*) such women shall not be British and shall remain in one recognised quarter of the city or town; (*b*) the premises occupied by such women to be licensed by the authorities and kept clean by the licensee; and (*c*) the women to be

registered and kept clean by the licensee, under Government medical supervision.

12. No intoxicating drinks to be made, sold, or used on premises occupied for immoral purposes, either by clients visiting such places or by the owners or occupiers of such houses.

13. No girl under the age of eighteen years (proof of age must be established), or youth under the age of twenty-one years, to be allowed to frequent houses of ill-fame in Eastern countries.

14. No men known as " pimps," "bludgers," or " women breakers-in " to be allowed to reside in the quarter containing houses of ill-fame in Eastern countries.

15. In the event of robbing, drugging, imparting infectious disease, selling spirits, or allowing girls or youths under the prescribed age to frequent the immoral houses in an Asiatic country controlled by Great Britain, the licensee to be fined for the first offence, and for the second to be imprisoned or deported.

16. Every woman or girl, not being British, above the prescribed age, landing for the purposes of an immoral life in Eastern countries controlled by Great Britain, to report herself to the authorities and be registered as a public woman.

17. Any unregistered girl found on premises used for immoral purposes to be deported, and the owner or occupier of the house to be fined or deported.

18. Owners or occupiers of houses keeping young girls against their will, or acting in collusion with " pimps," to be imprisoned or deported, and the " pimps " decoying such unwilling girls to be imprisoned and flogged.

19. All Asiatics or persons of coloured races to be prohibited from entering or frequenting quarters where white women reside as prostitutes.

20. Any " pimp " or procurer convicted of decoying, falsely marrying, or inducing girls to travel to the East for immoral purposes, to be flogged and sentenced to penal servitude.

21. All European policemen to be empowered to detain men suspected of being " pimps " landing in Eastern ports with women.

22. Women of ill-fame of any nationality whatever to be prohibited from plying outside their own compounds.

23. Diseased women of ill-fame from foreign countries, including Japanese harlots, not to be allowed to land in any Asiatic country controlled by Great Britain.

Mr. Willis also suggests that the British Government should generously endow lock-hospitals in India, Burma, Singapore, and Hong-Kong—the ward for women to be staffed *solely by women doctors.* That at all China Treaty Ports the British Consul should endeavour to induce all nations interested to maintain lock-hospitals; and that in the Argentine the British Government require that an English woman doctor be employed for the benefit of the British women taken there, and that a lock-hospital be provided for them. Further, that the police authorities in the British Isles should have power to cable the movements of suspected "pimps" to the country where they are booked to disembark, that evidence should be taken in the said country as to the nefarious trade of the "pimp," and that if a prima facie case be made out the "pimp" should be sent back to the place of embarkation, to be dealt with as the law directs.

We further suggest that the commissioner of police in charge of the white slave traffic, the prevention of men living on the immoral earnings of women, and the bringing to justice of procurers and procuresses, should be assisted by a Special Service Brigade, no member of which should rank lower than a detective-sergeant. Also, that only members of the Special Service Brigade, and other officers ranking not lower than a detective-sergeant, be empowered to arrest *on suspicion* men or women coming within the category of white slave traffic offences.

A grave warning we have to add. As a nation we have a habit of "cooling down" and growing indifferent after a subject has been touched upon. We suppose other countries have it too—it is human nature to get very much worked up and troubled about certain matters—an enormous fuss is made about them—and then the fuss is allowed to die down, public interest allows itself to be occupied with other things. The slave trader is no fool. While there is any agitation brewing and disturbance going on, he comparatively speaking "lies low." As soon as the disturbance is over he begins his operations with a greater access of vigour. We do not want to save our girls for two, five, or ten years, we want to save them as long as our country lasts and as long as our religion holds good. Therefore the last thing in the world we wish to do is to get up a sensation; to do that would simply be to frustrate our own object. What we want is not a *sensation* but *a national awakening* to our responsibilities, a dignified, determined, strong, and persistent resolution to kill this white slave traffic.

There are a few millions of us who might be expected to sympathise with and help in this matter; there are only a few thousands of the wretches who live on infamy. But those few thousands are enough to poison our national life, to inflict grievous and shameful injuries upon the daughters of our land and upon other Christian lands, to degrade us in the eyes of the heathen, to pull down our honour about our ears, and to drag our religion in the dirt. They are able to do all these things, and they do them. Therefore we think we are quite justified in saying that they shall no longer exist. They have forfeited all right to the consideration of decent people. They want justice, so in God's name *let them have*

16

justice—so far they have had too much consideration and indulgence. Let us give them justice now.

A girl I once engaged for secretarial work related a dreadful experience. She had been engaged as secretary to a registry office of a very "swagger" description in the West End. It was run by a smart woman who was as wicked as she was clever, and who lent herself with alacrity to the procuring of girls for immoral purposes by men. In one case a man had engaged from this woman's office six girls one after another. He was a rich man, and had a nice house a little way from town. It was in a lonely place and he had a housekeeper, a woman also in his pay. He paid five pounds down for having girls sent to him. The girl afterwards told me that when the sixth engagement was made, five girls had already returned furiously indignant at the insults to which they had been subjected during their first night in the house. She remonstrated with the woman for sending another girl to this place. The woman was very much enraged and told her to mind her own business, and within a week the girl found herself dismissed.

All these cases accentuate the dangers which confront young girls, and all those societies which exist to help them need our loyal support. We would commend to the notice of the public who are interested in this question the splendid work done by the

Y.W.C.A. Far too little is said or known about this work. The homes they have established for girls of all classes, not only in this country but in foreign countries, have proved a godsend—and such places of refuge and deliverance are a godsend indeed to many a hard-pushed girl or woman. The homes are not free : the girls all have to pay, nor do they take any girls without references and good characters. This is quite right and very necessary. It is quite impossible to mix up different classes of women and girls who need our protection and help ; and the Y.W.C.A. provides for the class which is very close to us and which demands our respect and consideration, and that is the better-educated and better-born girls who are obliged to work for their livings, and earn very small salaries. Those who are condemned to occupy lonely lodgings, where they are cheated and neglected, where they get bad food and have no single thing on earth to give them any comfort or pleasure, where they are subjected to a thousand temptations in spite of the fact that they are refined and well-bred girls—such girls as these can be provided with comfortable accommodation, cheerful sitting-rooms, and cheap food, all of which are the greatest possible blessings to them.

Of the work of the Y.W.C.A. homes I know a good deal personally, and I also know a great many girls and women who have been in them and whose independent reports I have had from time to time, and I may say I have never once heard any complaint of these homes—everybody praises them. It occurs to me that the people most likely to be able to place rescue missionaries in the foreign and Eastern ports would be the Young Men's and Women's Christian Associations and the Church Army and Salvation Army. Each of these organisations is so wide and large that they embrace the very best people to select and arrange for the workers at the various ports."

The fearful use which so many theatrical agents make of their licence has been described in a book which has been written by a gentleman I know, but we believe it is still seeking a publisher because he has spoken too plainly of the condition of things. As if one could speak too plainly if the object is to warn and help those who are victimised. It is high time that these theatrical agents who are supplying young women for immoral purposes to individual men and to bad houses abroad, should be brought within the grasp of the law and be severely controlled.

If the remedies we have suggested seem severe, we can only say that they are those which are recommended by every one who has had anything at all to do with the victims of the white slave traffic. There is not a single worker in this field who recommends leniency; indeed we have before our eyes the result of leniency. There is no other way to kill this infamous thing. But in the future let us hope women will have a real voice in these matters. So long as we can do nothing but plead, just so long the sorrows and pains of womanhood will meet with scant respect from law-makers and politicians. It is only by the great publicity which we hope for this book, and the enormous weight of public opinion which we are hoping and praying may be behind it, that we believe we shall be able to help the victims of the white slave traffic in the *East especially*. To write these things, to read them, and to know that such cruelties are being perpetrated every day makes one heart-sick and terribly sad.

It is easy enough to rid our minds of our neighbours' burdens; but, after all, conscience is a pretty good guide as to which way our duty lies in matters like this. It is not a question of inclination, nor even is it a matter of opinion. How can there be any opinion but one on a question like this? If you know that a girl is being ill treated; that some one young and innocent is betrayed, enslaved, and tormented; that some one who prays to the God that you worship, who has loved the things that you have loved — the happy country, the splendid cities, music, art, the many things which are precious to us all; who cares for what is beautiful, pure, and lovely: that such an one is dragged into some pit of infamy and degradation—how shall any of us have two opinions as to whether or not it is our duty to go straight to her assistance?

Although it is necessary to do individual

work, and it is necessary to help stray cases, as the National Vigilance Society and the Travellers' Aid Society and other societies do, *this is not enough*. We do not want to wait until our girls are tarnished and wounded; we want to set about them a high fence so that they may be secure in the garden of life, and where these beasts of prey may not come.

CHAPTER XIII

BURMA MARRIAGES: WESTERN MEN WITH EASTERN MORALS

MR. WILLIS having lived in Burma and been a close observer of the manners and customs of the country, we will here point out the difficulties and dangers of the situation to the American, English, and Canadian parents whose sons go to Burma to work for various companies or to the oil-fields, and just touch upon the question of the temporary alliances that something like ninety per cent. of these young fellows make in Burma.

A short while ago *Truth* published a series of articles under the heading "Western Men and Eastern Morals," which caused a commotion in this country. These articles dealt, quite thoughtfully and without the slightest exaggeration, with the situation, especially in Burma. But they elicited extremely indignant denials from some officials, and from the companies who send these young men out. Unfortunately the truth of the stories was far too absolute to be doubted. One has no desire to be an extreme moralist and to condemn the whole system.   It is not our part to sit at home and condemn people who fall into difficulties and temptations in other countries. But this might be forgiven us if we plead with the parents of lads likely to go to these countries where we have commercial and other interests, that they tell them what they are going to face and put before them ideals of justice and self-control.   In the distant oil-fields of Burma there are over five hundred Americans and Canadians boring for oil. These young fellows are many of them fine specimens of manhood.   There are, again, hundreds of young Britishers who are out in those parts working for various companies. Their labours often extend into very wild and desolate places.   It is so common for young men to keep girls that nothing is thought of it, and the whole country is flooded with poor, unfortunate, half-bred, illegitimate children who have no fathers and no one to be responsible for them.   It is horrible to think of; and the horror deepens when it is brought to light that many of the *little girls* of these unions are sold into immoral slavery for a few rupees.   They have no one to guide them, no one to defend them, no one to care what becomes of them.   They are so much human flesh, to be bought and sold for the only purpose for which in these countries female human flesh is of any use.   And for all the children, whether they come to this end or not, what fate is there in store?   They have not got all the instincts of the people of the country, they have none of their advantages, but they have every imaginable and unimaginable disadvantage to burden them from the moment of their entrance into this world.

The cheapness of young, clean girls on sale in these parts staggers the young men who go out there. At times very comely girls, fresh from the farms, are bought for 20, 30, or 40 rupees by young men who work at the oil-boring wells. A rupee is worth one shilling and fourpence. These young men see on every side examples of the lives led by their older comrades—even by their superiors—and it would, indeed, be a difficult thing for them to resist the temptations that are thrown at them. The girls who are sold vary in age from thirteen to sixteen. The older ones are not often bought, because the women age more quickly in the East and lose their beauty. As a general thing we hear that these girls are treated very well by the American and British men who keep them; but the arrangement can only be temporary, and the agony of parting is fearful for the poor Burmese girl who is left with several children with whom her own people do not wish to have anything to do. There are cases on record, in which, rather than face the position of a discarded woman, the Burmese girl has killed the European with whom she has lived. It is a thing easy to do. In Rangoon there is a school which is filled solely with these children, and the nuns of various Roman Catholic convents also take them in; but there is nothing for them, save misery. Nor can it be well for the men who go out from Christian homes to commit sins which bring such suffering on countless numbers of others. If it is a hard thing for a man to lead a lonely life, and if physical temptations *are* very strong and difficult to resist, why has *he* a right to ease and comfort at the cost of the lives and souls of hundreds of innocent ones? If there were never any children of these alliances, matters would not be so hideously cruel; but there nearly always are children, and this makes the injustice and cruelty a thousand times worse.

Even in Africa some complaints have been made about the way in which the men from Christian lands interfere with the women of the country. But the law in Africa is extremely severe against this offence, and it has been said that the attacks which have been made upon white women in the country are, after all, not at all surprising considering that the women of the country have not been sacred in the eyes of European men these many years. However, public opinion is now alive to the necessity of compelling Western men to respect the native women. But in Burma and the East—in China and in all these distant countries—can it be wondered at that we have to face the ghastly and horrible humiliation of having Christian European women taken out there for shameful purposes and for use by the men of the country? They have no cause at all to love us when we con-

sider that for scores of years our men have
done exactly as they liked with the women of
the country. This dreadful practice has become a recognised thing, but, nevertheless,
injustices of this sort cannot be perpetrated
year after year without ill-consequences to
the nations of the people who commit them.

A good deal of the trouble lies in the
fact that young men are led to believe
that it is quite impossible for them to lead
entirely chaste lives. They are even encouraged in this idea by some doctors. No
harm comes to men who exercise self-control,
but they have to fight against the strongest
passion which is known to the world and
to humanity. The instinct for mating has
been made so extremely strong that nature
scores a great victory in all cases where
human beings are not trained to fight her in
this particular. One feels helpless when faced
with problems of such alarming proportions,
and one realises that there is nothing on
earth that can redeem the situation except the
strength and moral rectitude of the men themselves. Of course laws might be passed, and
probably some recourse to legislation might
be taken if women were more generally interested in the affairs of the nation. But the
enforcement of these laws would be difficult.
When one remembers the great number of
very powerful companies interested in the
trade in the East, and all the influence they
could bring to bear on matters which affect
their own convenience and their own advan-

tage, we do not see that we can hope for anything except to educate, and to waken in the men who are to go out there some sense of justice and righteousness. We can only point out to them the horrid cruelty of which they are guilty. They may say, of course, that the women are much better treated than they would be by the men of their own country; and in the majority of cases this is quite true. But on the other hand the final desertion is so complete, and the fate of the children is so horrible that *nothing* can alleviate the suffering caused to them. If men will persist in having these temporary marriages, they might at any rate refrain from bringing unfortunate little children into the world to be kicked about and ill-used and despised by all with whom they come in contact. It seems such a dastardly trick for a little self-gratification and a little pleasure, or even for very much physical comfort, to require thousands of little children to pay a life penalty. If our men could be brought to think on this side of the question, a great many of them would be more careful of what they do. Also the more strict behaviour of our men in these foreign countries would give us a better chance of wiping out the white slave traffic which exists in so many of them.

CHAPTER XIV

TOUCHING UPON THE MARRIAGE LAWS OF VARIOUS COUNTRIES

It is a fact well known by the police and those who work among deluded girls that bullies and " pimps " often " marry " their victims in order to get them safely beyond the hope of rescue. English and foreign girls are married to these wretches under various names and disguises.

The Foreign Office in London has issued a book in English on the laws relating to marriage in certain foreign countries. This book is a typical production—heavy and ponderous—practically it cannot be said to be available for the public use. Moreover it would be very difficult for inexperienced people and those unacquainted with legal proceedings to understand exactly what the various clauses relating to marriages in foreign countries really mean. What we require is a very simple statement of what a girl may expect if she marries a foreigner either in this country or in any foreign country except under the exact regulations provided for these unions. Girls should be made to understand that marriages in foreign countries are often complicated, and the regulations appertaining to them are stringent. They ought also to be made to understand that marriages contracted with foreigners in England are in very many cases illegal in other countries. After the girl has been taken away from England she has very little redress if any flaw can be found with her marriage—indeed she has little enough redress if she should stay in England.

Last year a woman told a sad tale. She had been married, as she supposed, to a German. She lived with him for some time and had two children. When the man went away to his own country it was discovered, when she tried to get help from him, that she was not legally married at all and had absolutely no redress. She has never been supported by the man again, and nothing could be done to make him support her.

It is an act of absolute foolishness to suppose that ordinary people, or the general run of girls, would think for a single moment of inquiring for such a book as is published by the Foreign Office. To begin with, the girl is generally desperately in love with a man, who has attracted her in many ways; a man who has brought some romance into her life and given her presents, and who is, as far as she can see, a very superior person. He has acquired a hold over the girl, and has indulged her with fairy tales of all his possessions. It is hardly to be expected that such a girl is going to turn from her lover to wade through the pages of a Blue Book to find out for herself whether her marriage at Westminster, say with a " Russian Count," would be lawful. Many of these " pimps " give themselves high-sounding titles or represent themselves as being merchants of great standing, and there is always some wonderful reason why the girl should not draw them into any publicity. The fact of the matter is that the poor girls are often so immensely anxious to get married that it is very difficult to get them to understand that they are running any risks. In fact, one young woman departing to a continental country with a man who was going to marry her, as she thought, resented very strongly advice that she should go to the Consul of his country and find out something about the rules regulating their marriage. She said he would be very angry at her want of trust. There are two points that should be impressed upon girls by all their teachers in schools. One is that no man whose intentions are good ever resents inquiries made about him by the woman whom he wishes to marry. In fact, a decent man is most anxious to protect the girl he loves, and in many cases insists on her making inquiries about him. He never for a single moment attributes her wanting to know his circumstances and his history to want of trust—such an idea would never enter a decent man's head. Let girls be told this one fact on all possible occasions.

The second is that they should be impressed with the fact that even if the intentions of the foreigners who make love to them are quite pure and honest, there are technical matters relating to the marriage laws which have to be very carefully attended to, or else the marriage is illegal.

If we really wish to protect our girls from making pretended marriages, afterwards to be taken to the Continent or to the East, and there flung headlong into the houses of ill-fame, we should establish an Information Bureau in every city, or the Mayor or Registrar or some official of every town should have an hour on certain days a week which he could devote to interviewing parents of the girls or women who intend to marry foreigners. It should also be made known in the public Press and told to girls in schools and Sunday schools, in their confirmation classes, and everywhere as opportunity occurs for speaking to them about their affairs, that it is an urgent necessity for them, if they wish to be protected, to go to the Information Bureau and learn what the marriage laws of different countries are.

There are now being held in Great Britain various Mormon missions. For a few weeks there was quite an hysterical outburst against these people who are taking English girls and women to Utah. The excitement has subsided, and within the last few months several hundreds of women and girls have gone out by various boats. What their fate is likely to be in Utah we cannot, of course, exactly say. The Mormons do not tell them when they are taking them abroad that in the United States polygamy is illegal, and no one in Utah now can, without breaking the laws of the land, have two wives. But that a good many of them *do* have two " wives "— or three or four or twenty—goes without saying. It is entirely a mistake to suppose that these marriages are legal; and this is a fact of which girls and women are quite ignorant. We know this, because two separate girls in different places have told us that in Utah the Government allows the men to have two wives each, so long as they treat them well and provide for them both and keep them in separate houses ! We could not help being amused at this defence of the Mormon habits; but tried to explain that the unfortunate Government, which is responsible for a good many evils in the United States, is not to be saddled with the burden of authorising poly-gamy. In these Bureaux, which might very well be established, the parents of girls who are courted by foreigners could get information of an authentic and confidential kind—the position and status of the lover from abroad could be ascertained.

As a few instances of the difficulties which beset people of different nations when they desire to marry, it may be interesting to know that in Austria a marriage between a Catholic

17

and a person who professes no religion is held invalid by the law of the country. In Belgium, in France, Brazil, and Hungary, every citizen who contracts a marriage abroad must under the law notify the authorities of his own country of such a marriage within three months of his return to his native land. Thus, any of these people can go into England and marry an English girl, take her to his own country, or leave her in this, and if he wishes to get rid of her, he has only to remain in his own country for three months without notifying the authorities that he is married abroad, and such a marriage becomes illegal. A girl's marriage in England with a foreigner is no protection to her honour, her life, or her body, should she go abroad with the foreigner, unless the marriage is directly legalised in the country her husband claims as his own. In such event the man could be punished for any ill-usage to which he might subject her. The various countries help each other, of course, to punish some offences against the law, but they do not help each other to defend and protect women who are in an illegal position. Many a "pimp" who marries a girl in England takes her to the Continent and to the East and sells her for the largest price he can get. Then he returns again and marries some one else. One, a notorious "pimp," within the last year landed in Singapore no less than four beautiful Jewish girls. He is said to have entrapped them in the poorest part of the East End of London.

These girls, being scarcely more than children, did as they were told and swore that they were going to Singapore to their mother —a likely story! The poor creatures were not there long before they were taken to Malay Street. Now, if the police had had power to arrest that man—supposing he did find those girls in England—on suspicion, they could have discovered by cable in a few hours whether or not the girls actually had a mother in Singapore, and what the " pimp's " business was. The finger-prints of every suspected " pimp " should be obtained by the police, and they should have power to obtain them whether he has been convicted or not.

Mr. Willis says that when he was in the East a case came to his knowledge in which a " pimp " took an English girl away and actually sent obituary notices to the papers; some of these were sent to her people. These notices were written, too, with the greatest show of sorrow, and told how the poor girl had died in a foreign port—the girl in reality having been sold for immoral purposes. If these facts were made known and preached from the very house-tops, no young girl who is self-respecting and good would willingly put herself into the hands of these " pimps "; there would always be a chance that she would make some inquiries as to his *bona fides,* or her people would do it for her.

How to keep a great mass of girls well informed for their own protection is really a matter of some difficulty. Our population of women is now so large, and working girls like to feel themselves so entirely independent, that to teach them about these things is very difficult. If only we could open the doors of rescue homes and the Lock Hospital, or present to them, wholesale, books of this sort in order to give them actual examples of what is going on, and the fate that befalls their friends and companions if they step out of the straight way, they would starve and slave in their own land rather than be sold to ill-usage and infamy. Therefore, the question of instructing these girls becomes a real problem, unless indeed social workers, and especially clergy, will take it upon themselves as a binding and Christian duty to instruct them so far, at any rate, as to rouse their sense of caution.

One of the ironies of educational methods along moral and social-improvement lines has always seemed to us the fact that the people who attend lectures and meetings and conferences are already amply aware of their duty in regard to these matters. The audiences which gather at temperance meetings, for instance, as a general rule are really very amusing. At these meetings there are always a number of good old ladies, a few very particular men of advanced ages, perhaps one or two Sunday school teachers—and the lecturer holds forth for the benefit of this select audience on the evils of intemperance! Exactly the same thing happens in conferences and meetings of other religious and moral societies. The people working in these circles get so immersed in what they are doing that they really know very little of what is actually taking place in the world; and they do not realise that those people who are most affected by the evils which they are anxious to overcome, and upon which they dilate, are the people who never hear them spoken of at all—they never enter a meeting-house. The girls with whom we have to deal, and who are in danger from " pimps " and procuresses, are the girls who are likely to be frequenting places of amusement after their work, or are to be found wandering about the streets. The girls who are safely sheltered in homes and institutions are those who are in least danger.

During the last three years, I have heard three lectures on the " Disruption of the Home," and these lectures have afforded me quiet delight. Perhaps it is very wrong of me to say this: but they were delivered by terribly dull and prosy men, one of whom was unmarried, one was married and had no children, the other had several children and a comfortable income. It was most amusing to hear these good men lecturing women—it was the women with whom they were finding fault, not the men, as according to their statements it was the *women* who "disrupted the home," because they objected to having nine to one dozen children each. The audiences to which these gentlemen delivered their moral lectures consisted of highly respectable people, most of whom had quite large families, in fact nine out of every ten homes represented were certainly not in any danger of being "disrupted" on account of any lack of children under their roof. And the " society woman "—whoever this mysterious individual might be—against whom bitter scorn was levelled, was conspicuous by her absence.

Sometimes, of course, the moral lesson has gone home quite unexpectedly to the people who ought to get it. I remember rather a good story of my husband's about a minister in the Established Church in Scotland. It is quite common in Scotland for people to have a glass of whisky or some sort of spirit or wine before they retire at night. This minister was not a teetotaler. He was known as a man of wide culture, and he spent most of his money on the poor people in his parish, and was simply adored by them. He lived a frugal and somewhat austere life. His neighbour was a minister of one of the various sects, and he was a firm teetotaler, who called himself of course a "temperance man." He had a small family of nine children! One evening while my husband was in with the clergyman of the Established Church, chatting over a quiet glass of whisky, in came the other minister, who forthwith proceeded to lecture them both soundly upon their intemperate habits. They were both highly amused, but the Established Church clergyman asked his fellow cleric whether he called himself a " temperance man," and he replied that he certainly did. " Well," said he, " my interpretation of temperance is perhaps different from yours. Now you see I have been working all day out in the parish, and you probably have not been out to-day. I am not a married man, but I come home and take one glass of whisky, which you call intemperate." " Which is intemperance," cried the other. " Well," said the clergyman very good-naturedly, " look here, my friend : you have a wife and *nine children*; I have denied myself that sort of thing, and I do not think *you* are the person to talk to me about *temperance*." This surely was a very excellent retort ? It only shows that the people who *need* instruction are the ones who seldom get it.

No one in his senses would for a single instant decry the use and great advantage of meetings and conferences of thoughtful, responsible, and good people, and from these gatherings *does* emanate a great deal of good. Nevertheless, when one has to deal with delicate and difficult matters, especially those matters which relate to morality as affecting girls and women of the poorer classes, we must find a way of reaching them other than by private meetings and conferences. The subject requires *enormous publicity*, and however much we may regret that such matters have to be spoken of, it will be a

matter of infinitely deeper regret when injury
to the nation, and hideous injustice to the
victims of the white slave traffic, result from
our silence on these questions. It is admitted
that hundreds go to their doom yearly in
ignorance, and we neglect our duty when we
shirk making known the doings of those
wolves of the human species who go about
our cities seeking whom they may devour.

INVESTIGATIONS AT WHITECHAPEL
BY MR. WILLIS

DAUGHTERS OF THE POOR

AFTER gaining full information in the East, Middle East, and Far East as to the management of this awful traffic in white women, writes Mr. Willis, I determined to gather facts at this end and learn first-hand, so to speak, the methods adopted in London by "pimps" for filling the vacancies in the ranks of the unfortunates abroad, which death, disease, and mysterious disappearances cause with fearful rapidity.

It is well known in the East—known to those who care to know, known to those who want to know—that many white women and white girls are recruited for "trade" purposes at Whitechapel and the surrounding districts—the home of the poor, the overworked, the under-fed, and the scantily clothed and often brutally used women and girls of several nationalities.

Armed with a letter of authority, I waited on the chief officer at the Whitechapel police headquarters in Leman Street. Once authorised to speak on this fearful subject by their superior officer, the sturdy officers in charge of Leman Street Station unfolded chapter after chapter of the deadly work of the "pimp" and his coadjutor, the procuress. Facts, figures, and photographs were shown to me that would convince the coldest and most callous Parliament that ever existed of its duty to spare one day for the subject in their legislative hustle, and pass a law to fully protect the mothers and daughters of the nation from the machinations of the fearful "pimp."

Unfortunately, much that one is told cannot, for divers reasons—most of them weighty reasons—be placed in this book.

In interrogating the authorities at Leman Street, I was particularly inquisitive as to the doings of a well-known Eastern "pimp." When travelling in the East I have more than once come across the accursed tracks and unwholesome evidence of this notorious "pimp," who to this moment trades in human flesh recruited at Whitechapel, where, I am told, he was born. He is of Polish-Jewish parents, who came to this country to escape the awful atrocities in their own. The "pimp," being British-born, claims all the rights and privileges of British freedom, equity, and justice.

The particular "pimp" to whom I am now alluding "graduated," it is said, from the Whitechapel dregs of poverty, and passed through various prisons to his present position as "leader" in the business of "pimp-ing."

As a youth he always firmly declined hard work and being afraid to steal, beyond petty larcenies, he accepted the first "safe job" offered to him as a "sounder," or "nit," that is, general "look-out" man, for a notorious Whitechapel "fence." A "fence" is an individual who buys stolen property—one who controls the dangerous practice of getting on to the market the goods and chattels the burglar commandeers with the aid of the dark lantern and the "jemmy."

The burglar and the pickpocket are ever ready to inform the police that it is the easiest thing in the world to steal, but the trouble arises when the thief wishes to turn the stolen property into ready cash. So, to effect the sale of stolen property scientifically, the "fence" has come into being. Most "fences" who know their business give special attention to placing stolen property abroad—the East for choice, where good prices are obtainable and no questions asked.

It was as a "sounder" for a notorious "fence" that the "pimp" I am writing about (he claims many aliases, one being Lavington H.) first went into the East. He was a quick-witted and energetic offshoot of a sharp race; well spoken, well dressed, always in funds. Once in the East, his active brain quickly realised the fact that a big trade and "big money" were possible in landing white girls in the East for immoral purposes. Therefore, he returned to White-chapel and his familiar haunts and entered into league with several noted procuresses— one a notorious old Jezebel who has been regularly sowing the seeds of iniquity for more than thirty years. This old hag, with the assistance of male confederates, "spread the good news" of Lavington H.'s arrival from abroad, and the splendid future that was in store for girls who would go abroad and marry a real Sultan. Lavington H. "played safety" by staying at a first-class hotel in Piccadilly, meeting his agents from time to time, by appointment, on the Embankment, where arrangements as to the class of girls to be trapped, caught, induced, or, if need be, married for Eastern purposes, were discussed.

Sometimes only one girl would be obtainable; at other times two or three would be brought into the net at one catch, on one pretext or another, and then shipped off to the East in charge of this "pimp." When the white girls were disposed of or suitably placed abroad, the "pimp" would return for another contingent. On one occasion this "pimp" nearly came to grief. His partners in crime had secured for him a very pretty and virtuous girl. She did not find out the life she was expected to lead until the ship was between London and Colombo, and then it was the captain of the vessel who warned her. As she rebelled and threatened exposure, the "pimp" thought it prudent to quietly drop her at Colombo, and she returned to London.

The "pimp," as I have already stated, combined the selling of stolen property with the selling of white girls in the East. He can always "bring to light," as they term it, a fine diamond ring, a diamond pin, a high-class gold watch or two, watch-chains, earrings, bangles, etc.—all stolen in England or America, and altered in design and made ready for sale in the East.

To add to his other accomplishments, this "pimp" has lots of "push," and is nearly always to be seen at Eastern carnivals, race meetings, regattas, etc. Such gatherings help him to practise his nefarious tricks in selling stolen goods, but these exploits are only entrées or side dishes compared with the main business of his life—namely the selling of white girls to the highest bidder out East.

Last July or August—I forget the exact month—the big race meeting of 1911 was held at Bangkok, Siam. This despicable "pimp" appeared at the gathering, and, wearing fashionably cut clothes and diamond rings and pin, he elbowed his way among decent people. A friend of mine, a man whom I have known and trusted for twenty years, saw this pervert of humanity seated in a comfortable armchair on the large, hospitable veranda of the German club at Bangkok. The "pimp" had more to say than any of the decent men who were gathered in that quiet corner, trying to keep cool on a hot, sweltering day, and in his boastful fashion he let a ray of light into his fearful trade.

Those who know the East are fully aware that at race meetings or at great carnival gatherings, most of the clubs—especially the great Liberal German clubs—throw open their doors, in truly friendly fashion, to visitors, who are at liberty to saunter in and out, drink, play billiards, cards, or bet on races.

It was at one of these gatherings that this "pimp" elbowed himself amongst the horse-racing fraternity—all honest, straight men, who work for their living and despise the unclean monster who lives on unfortunate women's earnings.

The "pimp" was busy talking about his own ability, when one horse trainer—an Australian—being disgusted with the fellow's talk, stopped him by remarking, "If half one hears is true, the game you're at is a bit over the odds. I know what they would do with your sort in my country."

The "pimp" became indignant, and actually defended his trade. He said, with much vehemence, "It's all sentimental humbug about girls coming out here. In the first place, they want to come out; in the second place, they know what they are coming for—and they get what they expect. Here they get money, good clothes, good food, and a good time. If the life is short, it's merry. If they remain in England—well, they get what they're looking for, without money, or food, or clothes. If I bring a girl out here, I see she knows the business before we start.

"I am not on this earth to buy trouble, and if a girl is willing to undertake the trip, why should busybodies interfere? The first questions I always ask my 'sounders'" [agents who "sound" and procure the girls] "are, 'Does the girl know her business? Has she passed the probationary stages? Does she want change of air, change of climate, good food, and good clothes? If she does, bring her to me; I'll do the rest.'

"I never go near Whitechapel; it's not worth the risk," the "pimp" added. "If a girl is agreeable to go out of England of her own free will, who can stop her? Not the police—they have no power to stop her. Nor yet the so-called preventive societies who 'live on the game' and are not worth thinking about. So, if a woman observes the law —and it's a free country whilst you keep the law—where's the harm? It's the law that rules—not sentiment."

Such was the "pimp's" summing up of the horrible trade—heartless, inhuman, brazen, and defiant.

I went primarily to Whitechapel Police Station to question the authorities about this fellow. Whilst the officers would not commit themselves, it was clear, to my mind, that they knew their man, and may ere long give him a little more law and be instrumental in meting out to him salutary justice, with a plentiful supply of hard labour to balance the accounts they already have against him.

If there are any " doubting Thomases " as to the extent of this fearful trade, I would strongly recommend them to visit Leman Street Police Station, where—if they have proper authority to put questions—that clever officer, Chief-Inspector Wensley, will soon tell them of the awfulness of the situation and the crying urgency that exists for speedy remedies in the shape of Parliamentary enactments that would give the authorities a strong arm to speedily stop, and perhaps kill, the illicit trade of " traffic in white women."

Almost weekly, glaring cases of the traffic in young girls who are taken abroad come under the notice of the Leman Street police, but in nine cases out of ten the police are powerless. Now and again they do succeed in bringing home the terrible offence, but even when they do, the law deals mildly with the offender. It is, indeed, a fact that the " pimp " who breaks the heart, the health, and every hope on earth of a white girl and who lives on her awful earnings in London is, when caught—which is seldom—treated far more leniently than a women's franchise enthusiast who emphasises her Parliamentary inequality by breaking a window or two.

As recently as April 14th this year, one of the numerous gang who are living on the ill-earnings of unfortunate women was ar-raigned at Bow Street before Mr. Curtis

Bennett. The "sister of the pavement" who gave information to the police, complaining of the man's conduct in taking her immoral earnings from her, was a good-looking young English girl about twenty-five years of age. She stated that she had known the accused "bludger" for about fifteen months, and during that period, with the exception of some six weeks, he had lived on the money she had earned on the streets. As a rule he never got out of bed till about midday, and he had a fearful aversion to work. Sometimes, when she had no money to give him, he beat her most unmercifully. The result was that she was black and blue. Finally she left him. After that he wrote her letters threatening to "kick her inside out" if she did not send him money. It was quite true that this wretch had given her diamond rings, but he had purchased them with money she had made on the streets. The woman told the magistrate that she had given this "bludger" as much as £12 within a week, and that he had only given her a few coppers when she went out in the evening to look for more money. The unfortunate woman declared that she stood in hourly terror of the man's brutality.

The magistrate asked if the accused were a foreigner, and Detective-Sergeant Broadhurst replied, " No, sir, I wish he were."

The magistrate: " So do I."

The brute received sentence of three months for living on the results of the woman's

18

prostitution, and three months for beating her when she had no money to give him.

This is one of the cases where the "bludger" is caught and dealt with under the authority of the law; and, as the law now stands, this human monster is penalised in about half the sentence he would have received for breaking a plate-glass window if he had belonged to the suffragette league, or if he had not belonged to any league, but, simply as a matter of getting money easily, had stolen a policeman's watch, for which no British Court would have given him less than twelve months. But for living on the prostitution of an unfortunate woman—who is forced to sell her body to men and her mind to the devil—this "bludger" gets three months, and three months more for beating and kicking her when she has no money to give him.

A case is recorded at Leman Street against two oily-tongued wretches—young Jews, good-looking, well dressed, and apparently free with money—who decoyed two handsome girls, both Jewesses and, I am told, both well-behaved. These girls were trapped at White-chapel and shipped off to that fearful burial-ground for thousands of our girls—Buenos Ayres. The police showed me the photographs of these girls. They were well developed and comely. I also saw the picture of the "pimps." One would take them to be anything but "pimps."

The method they adopted to decoy these girls is the old, old story: fine clothes, silk stockings, a castle to live in, and servants to fan you. However, there was a noise about the disappearance of these girls. The Leman Street police got on their track, and as sufficient evidence was forthcoming, a warrant was granted. Chief-Inspector Wensley had the matter in hand, and the men were arrested in Buenos Ayres, extradited back, and convicted. One, named Cohen, received twelve months; the other, named Gold, fifteen months. Probably both names were assumed. The girls were restored to their parents. These men were only two of the many traffickers in girl-flesh, and how many girls they took off to Buenos Ayres, before they were caught, Heaven only knows.

Some cases that have come directly under police observation demonstrate the dreadful, deadly infatuation that often binds thoughtless, foolish girls to the "pimp." The police support the theory that girls are frequently hypnotised by the strong will-power or animal magnetism of some of these wretched "pimps."

An officer of the police, a man of the highest repute, pointed out a case to me where a "pimp" waited months and months to get proper control over his victim, who was a good girl. For a long time the fiend incarnate contented himself with merely "walking out" with the girl, taking her to cheap picture shows, buying her little presents and articles of clothing, meeting her as she came home from work, giving her tea and sweets, and doing everything that would take her mind off his villainy. But the fearful end came when his will-power mastered her mind. Once he had taught her to trust him, to love him, to watch and wait for his coming, he ruined her and then ruthlessly " dumped " her into the inferno at Buenos Ayres, where she poisoned herself.

A very pathetic case is recorded at White-chapel station—that of a nice-looking girl, who was a hard worker, well-behaved, and who tried hard to live a proper life. Many of the " pimps " endeavoured to catch her to send her abroad, but she was too shy and coy for them to master. At last, however, she fell to the wiles of an old she-devil who keeps a shop at Whitechapel. This woman, a noted procuress, introduced the girl to an old re-probate whose only business is procuring girls for the South American trade.

The old hound was called " Uncle " by some persons ; by others he was more affec-tionately termed " Papa." He caught this young girl in his meshes, with the assistance of the procuress, and, by means of fine pro-mises, she was taken to Buenos Ayres to fill the duties of a barmaid at startling wages ; but on landing she was simply " dumped " into a " bad house." The " missus " of that den of iniquity, with, of course, assistance, did the rest. The girl's clothes were taken from her and she was ill-treated and half starved.

The "missus," growing tired of the girl's "nonsense," as she termed it, reserved this unfortunate—who was fighting not only to protect her honour, but also her health—for the roughest of the rough, mongrel-breed of men, the half or quarter-caste breed, the cross between the desperate cut-throat Spaniard and the Red Indian woman—probably the worst cross of breeds in the whole world. When these tame savages came to town from their far-off cattle ranches in the country to see "life," the "missus" would introduce them—half drunken and boisterous, fearing neither God, devil, nor man—to this unfortunate girl, Miss B. In consequence of the fearful knocking about this girl received, she became almost a wreck in health, broken in heart and spirit, and was penniless, friendless, alone in a hell upon earth in a strange country.

By some means she had a note conveyed to the British Consul at Buenos Ayres. That worthy gentleman lost no time in visiting the house, and, with the authority of his position, rescued her, treated her with all Christian humanity, gave her clothes and medical attention, and caused her to be returned to England. She came back to her native land—not the bright, healthy girl she left it, but a derelict of womanhood, broken in mind and in body. I dare not mention her name— it would be cruel to do so—but her photograph and the record of her case is with a great pile of such cases at Leman Street. Poor girl! Murdered by a system that allows trafficking in human flesh in a great Christian country like England!

What of the thousands upon thousands who die unknown, uncared for, unassisted? They die off as the flowers of the field, and no real effort is made to save them or bring their destroyers to justice. They are, of course, alas! the daughters of the poor.

In the case of Miss B. I have quoted, nothing was done to the "missus" of the house, nor was the old "pimp" called "Uncle" leg-ironed to stop him from destroying more girls. Such is the law. Such is the hypocrisy of our dealing with this subject that everybody but the "pimp" and the "missus" wants to avoid the unclean thing of trafficking in white women.

Quite recently this old "Uncle"—whose more appropriate name would be "Old Nick" —was seen by two Leman Street detectives on an outgoing boat bound for the Argentine with two young girls, good-looking Jewesses, bound for that bourn from which few white girls ever return unless broken in health and their bodies in such a state as to force them to pray for death. The officers knew the fate of these girls, but they were powerless to interfere with the "liberty of the subject." So the ship sailed with its human freight, and the "pimp" laughed at the inglorious laws of glorious England!

Another very painful case was unfolded to me at Leman Street. It was the same old, old story, with, however, this variation—the culprits were caught red-handed and were promptly landed in gaol. An old beldame, it is alleged, enticed into her shop a pretty young Jewess, a daughter of southern Europe : she, poor child, was another daughter of the poor. When, indeed, may we ask, do procuresses or "pimps" interfere with the daughters of the rich or the powerful ? Very seldom. It is the daughters of the poor always who are sacrificed on the altar of sensuality ; it is the daughters of the poor who are decoyed, waylaid, trapped, ruined, and damned to satisfy the animal cravings of animal man. But to proceed. This young girl, not yet sixteen years old—girls of southern Europe develop quicker than the children of the West—was enticed by this old beldame, who systematically set to work to poison the girl's mind, by holding before her a dazzling mirror reflecting beautiful finery and adornments that might be obtained by the child consenting to receive a "lover," a lover who loved her for herself.

The next step of the beldam was to hand the girl over to the "pimp" to prepare her for the life she was to follow. He took the child to his rooms and kept her almost a strict prisoner for days. When he considered her sufficiently tamed he sought out one of his chums, to whom he imparted the information of the "treasure" he had secured for a good customer abroad. The "chum" was taken by the "pimp" to inspect the child, and after a few days all three seemed to be fast friends.   Eventually, however, the two men quarrelled as to who should have final possession of the child.   The police had suspected that each wanted her for shipment, and when news of the quarrel came to their ears the old woman and one of the men were arrested and committed for trial.   The second man took to his heels, and is now hiding in Amsterdam.   Happily, the girl was rescued, but her story is fearfully painful.   In this case much credit is due to the effective manner in which the Leman Street police pounced upon and gaoled the ruffians.

Another very bad case, which occurred quite recently, came under the notice of the Leman Street officials.   A certain half-bred, worthless German Jew, living in the neighbourhood of Whitechapel, had such a strong aversion to working for his own living that he hit upon a plan—unfortunately not by any means new or singular—of living without work.   He married a young, handsome girl, a Jewess, and then bundled her off to Buenos Ayres as a married woman to earn her living and remit to him money whereby he might live without work.   He did not mind if she sent him the wages of sin, the wages of pleasure, or the wages of thieving, so long as she was prompt with her remittances.   Weak-minded, she obeyed her husband's orders, and led a life of shame.   She hardly ever failed to remit a good part of her earnings to the man who had sworn to protect her, but her health gave way under the abominable life.   So she gathered all the money and worldly goods she could muster, and, broken in health through disease and debauch, landed back at Whitechapel.

The monster whom she called "husband ' was at first all kindness and consideration. He proposed that they should buy a shop with her money and end their days in peace. The woman agreed. They bought the shop, and she paid over her "devil's counters" as the purchase-money. But the shop stood in the husband's name—naturally this was his first concern. Once all was secure this man-devil brutally told his wife that she must go on the streets and earn something to keep the home together.

The unhappy woman—now broken in health and suffering torments of pain—refused to further damn her soul, more especially as a young, dark-eyed recruit to the "sisterhood of the pavement" was then serving her probationary course with the husband. In despair, the wretched wife appealed to the authorities. But, alas for our laws!—which have taken centuries to make through our Parliamentary system—nothing could be done to help the woman, because, it seems, the delightful point as to the validity of a wife's evidence given against her husband—though a contemptible "pimp" he may be—has not been finally settled. A celebrated test case under this head is now before the High Court, and will probably remain there until it is forgotten, or until the schedule of wronged women and wrecked lives is multiplied by three !

Another human monstrosity at Whitechapel answering to the name of "man" married his own cousin and sent her forth to battle in the Argentine and remit her earnings to him. The police suspect this fellow of afterwards marrying another girl and sending her out to Buenos Ayres to follow the same evil course mapped out by him for wife number one.

Chief-Inspector Wensley showed me the photograph of two pretty-looking girls who had been kidnapped in France and brought to this country for immoral purposes. Luckily for the youngsters, the Leman Street authorities "got wind" of the affair, rescued the girls, and sent them back to their sorrowing parents. The "pimp," of course, took to his heels. So the nauseating record goes on *ad nauseam*—still nothing done, by those responsible for the laws of the country, to protect girls, or indeed to protect children.

We hear of enthusiasts at Westminster bringing in Bills for every conceivable object except the protection of the daughters of the poor. We read of Bills being presented to prevent youths of fourteen, fifteen, and sixteen years of age selling newspapers in London streets to earn a crust —often a dry and hard crust. But whilst the Bill takes the crust out of the hands of those unfortunate youngsters, no proposal is made to replace it with wholesome bread and butter. Of course, the youngsters have no votes, some have no homes—so, naturally, they must accept what Parliament enacts for them and abandon the paper-selling business for that of thieving.

One of the main difficulties the police encounter in dealing with the machinations of the "pimp" when he is beginning his trade of trafficking in women, is the evil spring from which much misery flows. The difficulty under the existing law is to convict men of the "pimp" class who live and fatten on the earnings of women of ill-fame. All the intelligent heads of the great police organisation in England will tell you plainly that if you stop men from living on the earnings of these unfortunate women you will strike a death-blow at the taproot of the now flourishing tree of evil.

One worthy chief-inspector remarked to me " that at present it is a mighty hard job to convict a man who is really known to live well, dress well, attend race-meetings, theatres, and the like—on the wages of sin. Convictions are difficult, excepting in the very rare cases where the unfortunate woman will give voluntary evidence against the "pimp." Under the law as it now exists the police must actually have the woman's evidence or must see money passed from her to him, or have definite evidence to that effect.

"I have known quite a young girl," a police officer told me, " to take her nightly earnings home to her 'bludger,' and often get a good hiding for not bringing more; still the woman would not give the wretch away. I begged of her to let me 'put him inside': the poor creature shook her head and remarked that if she did he would kill her when he came 'out.' Sometimes jealousy will prompt an 'unfortunate' to give her brutal master away, but not frequently. I have in my mind one brutal 'bludger,' well known to the police, who actually follows his 'missus' around Leicester Square and takes her earnings from her as she, poor fallen creature, earns them. This brute has been known to bite his wife in the street in his struggle to get from her hand the few pieces of silver she had just earned."

Still, we are powerless under the law to punish such a monster. The power the police want and should have is the power to arrest any known "pimp" who is living on the earnings of unfortunate women, and let the onus of proof that he is not so living rest with the man so detained. That is what is done under our game laws. If a man is seen coming off the grounds of some lordly manor, under suspicious circumstances, he is liable to be arrested and convicted—and frequently is so arrested and convicted—even though no feather, fur, or flesh be found upon him. Under the Prevention of Poaching Act, 1862, it is not necessary to prove or even suggest that a "suspect" has actually committed an act of poaching, and in certain cases suspected persons may be searched by police officers without a warrant, and any supposed incriminating articles in the possession of the suspected persons may be seized.

If the protection of game on great estates is worthy of attention, surely the fearful subject now under review is a thousand times more important in the public interest. The very fact of an idle vagabond being known to live with a public harlot should be sufficient evidence that he is living with the woman for gain, and not for love or for sentiment. And if he could be severely handled by the law for openly living in a house of ill-fame, or living at all with one of the "unfortunates of the pavement"—whether she be his wife or not— a bold and heavy stroke would be aimed at the taproot of the whole trouble. Is that where we should commence? Yes.

That is the first power the police want, and no reasonably-minded man can refuse it. Out of the population of more than seven millions of people in Greater London only one hundred and fifty-one men were convicted last year of living on the earnings of immoral women. Their sentences varied from two weeks to three months —less than half the sentences inflicted on mothers and daughters, respectable women, for breaking windows in the suffragettes' raids.

In Australia the brutal "pimp" who lives on women is dealt with very summarily, and although the whole population is not so

great by a couple of millions as London, the
number of convictions is ten times as great
and the sentence ten times heavier. It is
estimated that fully twenty-five thousand
" pimps " and " bludgers " live on unfortunate
women's earnings in London alone; yet the
number of convictions last year rose only to
the total of a hundred and fifty-one. Surely
it is time women had votes or our law-makers
had sense, and made up their minds to exclaim
with Voltaire, *Écrasez l'infâme !*

The late Lord Brampton—then Mr. Justice
Hawkins—stopped garotting on the Thames
Embankment by an application of the "cat "
on the graduated scale principle as the
offences increased. I would not advocate this
extreme penalty against " pimps " unless a
ruffian were convicted three times—then anything would be good enough, or bad enough,
for such a devil.

In dealing with the white slave traffic the
Government should establish a special-service
brigade composed of trusted officers, none of
whom should rank lower than a detective-
sergeant. We have special-service brigades
to deal with anarchists, illicit stills, illicit
coining, smugglers, etc., but when the white
slave traffic is dealt with it seems to be everybody's business not to lend a hand—and so
little or nothing is done.

The direct dealing with the traffic comes
under a Commissioner at Scotland Yard, a
right worthy gentleman, who is encouraged in

his work by a vote from Parliament. But he has no special officers under him except the general police, and no law to give effect to his work except that law which renders him almost powerless. Had he a special service, composed of men whose ability and judgment could be trusted—none, as I say, below the rank of a detective-sergeant—the results of dealing with this traffic would not be so bad and startling. I admit it would be an unwise policy to give every policeman authority to arrest, on suspicion, persons going abroad with girls. The cure would be worse than the disease. But I do urge that the suppression of the traffic should be placed in the hands of a special-service brigade of experienced and trusted officers, who should have power to ascertain where certain traffickers are landing their victims; to cable to the police in the country of debarkation to place such suspicious persons under surveillance, and, if proved to be trafficking in the white slave iniquity, to arrest them red-handed, take evidence against them abroad, and deport them under escort back to this country. This is done now in cases where men forge cheques, steal watches, etc. Surely it might be tried as a means of protecting the mothers and daughters of the nation !

Arresting on suspicion at the port of embarkation should only be resorted to when trusted officers are fairly sure of their ground. Here is a case in point. Detective-sergeant Wright and Detective-sergeant Dessent, both of Leman Street Station, Whitechapel, some little time back visited an outgoing boat. They saw on board the boat a known and noted " pimp " with two young girls—comely, well-set Jewesses. When the " pimp " saw the detectives, he quickly separated from the girls. Being convinced that something was wrong, the officers secreted themselves. When the " pimp " thought they had departed, he approached the girls and began to exchange papers with them. The officers approached and questioned the girls, who denied all knowledge of the " pimp," although they had just secreted papers he had given them. If the officers had had the adequate powers to detain the three on suspicion, the papers would have probably convicted the " pimp " and saved the girls. But the officers had no authority to interfere unless the girls themselves complained.

This case is only typical of hundreds and hundreds of cases that come under the notice of honourable officials who, however, are powerless to act. How long shall they remain powerless? Parliament must answer that question quickly.

It would be unjust to close these notes on the horrors of Whitechapel without giving a well-deserved meed of praise to the great efforts and splendid results of the work of the Jewish Association for the Protection of Women and Girls among the daughters of the poor and helpless, and in some cases homeless, girl-children of Whitechapel. The police—

usually meagre with words of praise—are eloquent on behalf of this society, whose headquarters are in Baker Street, whose president, Lady Rothschild, is ever zealous, and whose secretary, Mr. S. Cohen, is never idle. Of all the societies brought under my notice the best net results are credited to the Jewish Association alluded to. Surely it is the duty of the rich Jews all over the world to help the workers among the poor women and girls of Whitechapel.

A Last Word by Mrs. Mackirdy

We have finished our task in placing before the public and Parliament, and before the pulpits and the Press, the nauseating details of this horrible traffic in white women. The task has been painful, but the duty to the mothers and daughters of the nation demanded that some one with accurate knowledge should speak. We have done our task. Will the great instructors of the people, the great leaders of, or protectors of, the poor, now do their part? Will Parliament pass a law to protect the women of the nation? Will the Press use its mighty power for the protection of the daughters of the nation? Will the voices of God's ministers sound a note of warning and alarm throughout the country and demand, with the authoritative voice of their high office, that legal protection shall be given to women and girls?

The personal experience of the Eastern

19

slave traffic, and the investigations, are Mr Willis's. It is obvious that a woman could not have personally got this information; but I have been compelled, in my work among women and girls, to know and face agonising things that have happened in our very midst, and now I have done what in me lies to write the facts in this book as modestly and decently as possible, but without disguising them or falsifying them. I have put Mr. Willis's own stories into language less strong than he employed, and now that the work is done I hope I may never have to write so sad and terrible a book again. May it go out with power and blessing, and may God consecrate all this bitter knowledge to the service of humanity, that out of it may rise Wisdom, and Justice, and Mercy.

FINIS

Printed by Hazell, Watson & Viney, Ld., London and Aylesbury.

Telephone—
6659 GERRARD

Telegraphic Address—
"GUCIEN, LONDON"

31 ESSEX STREET S.I.I

LONDON, ENGLAND

October, 1912

STANLEY PAUL & CO.'S
ANNOUNCEMENTS

*** PREVIOUS LISTS CANCELLED.

Napoleon in Exile at Elba, 1814-1815. By NORWOOD
YOUNG, Author of "The Growth of Napoleon," "The Story of
Rome," etc., with a chapter on the Iconography of Napoleon at
Elba by A. M. BROADLEY, Author of "Napoleon in Caricature,"
"The Royal Miracle," etc., with coloured frontispiece and fifty
illustrations from the collection of A. M. Broadley. In one volume,
demy 8vo, cloth gilt, price 21s. net.

This work will be a record of the residence of Napoleon in the Isle
of Elba during the exile which followed his abdication at Fontainebleau
on April the 11th, 1814, and which continued from May the 3rd following until February the 26th, 1815. It will be published on the 31st of
March, 1914, the centenary of the entry of the allies into Paris.

Napoleon in Exile at St. Helena 1815-1821. By
NORWOOD YOUNG, with a chapter on the Iconography of Napoleon
at St. Helena by A. M. BROADLEY, Author of "Napoleon in Caricature," "The Royal Miracle," etc., with two coloured frontispieces and one hundred illustrations from the collection of A. M.
Broadley. Two vols., demy 8vo, cloth gilt, price 32s. net.

This work will give the history of the exile of Napoleon on the island
of St. Helena after the defeat of Waterloo, which terminated the
hundred days revival of his power on June 18th, 1815—from the 16th of
October following until his death on the 5th of May, 1821. Both
writers are authorities upon the subject of which they treat, and the
whole of Mr. Broadley's unrivalled collection of Napoleonic MSS. and
illustrative lore has been generously placed at the disposal of Mr.
Norwood Young for the purposes of this work. Mr. Young has also had
access to many hitherto unexplored sources of information both in
England and abroad. No pains will be spared to make these two
works the final word on a supremely interesting subject.

Intimate Memoirs of Napoleon III. : Personal

Reminiscences of the Man and the Emperor by the late BARON D'AMBES; translated by A. R. Allinson. In two volumes, demy 8vo, fully illustrated, 24s. net the set.

This book is the private diary of a life-long and intimate friend of Louis Napoleon, whose identity is here thinly veiled under a somewhat obvious pseudonym. The Baron first made the acquaintance of the future Emperor when scarcely more than a boy at Arenaberg, the Swiss home where he and his mother Queen Hortense of Holland were living in exile. Deeply affected from the beginning by the personality of Louis Napoleon, the Baron gradually became impressed with the idea that his friend was a son of Napoleon I., and in his diary he alleges some startling evidence in favour of his theory. From his earliest association with Louis he began jotting down incidents, conversations, and reflections as they occurred, and to these he added evidence from every source, letters, documents, newspaper cuttings, which, after the death of Louis Napoleon and within a few years of his own, he prepared for publication. The book therefore supplies a large quantity of first hand material, for the first time in English, for a survey and study of the life and character of one of the most enigmatic figures in modern history. The Baron follows his hero from boyhood through the years of exile and adventure, as a conspirator in Italy, as a refugee in London, as President of the Republic of '48, finally as Emperor, down to the disasters of 1870, the fatal day at Sedan, and the death at Chislehurst. In every phase of that chequered career this unique diary throws illuminating sidelights on a number of interesting and hitherto imperfectly understood episodes.

The Royal Miracle : A Collection of Rare Tracts,

Broadsides, Letters, Prints, and Ballads concerning the wanderings of Charles II. after the Battle of Worcester (September 3— October 15, 1651), with a Preface, Historical Introduction, Appendix and Bibliography by A. M. BROADLEY, Author of "Dr. Johnson and Mrs. Thrale," "Chats on Autographs," "Napoleon in Caricature," etc., etc. In crown 4to, handsome cloth gilt, fully illustrated with portraits, maps, etc., etc., from rare originals, 16s. net.

These reprints include a Broadside History of His Sacred Majesty's most Wonderful Preservation (1660). "White-Ladies, or His Sacred Majesty's most Miraculous Preservation" (1660); "The Royal Oake, etc.," by john Danverd; "Miraculum Basilicon, or the Royal Miracle" (1664); "Claustrum Regale Resevatum, or the King's Concealment at Trent," by A. W. (1667); and the letter of William Ellesdon of Charmouth to the Earl of Clarendon concerning the adventures of Charles II., transcribed from the original letter in the Bodleian Library, Oxford. Many other interesting items are included, and the work is produced in the best possible style.

Bookman says: "A contribution to history so conscientiously and exhaustively written that it is never likely to be superseded. The book is as supremely interesting as it is exact and reliable."

Guardian.—"This book is a storehouse of curious matter. It is a thorough and valuable piece of historical work which says almost the last word upon a subject of fascinating interest."

Outlook.—"Much that is new and interesting is contained in the handsome volume to which the title of 'The Royal Miracle' has been very appropriately given."

Our Future Existence; or, the Death-Surviving Consciousness of Man. By FRED G. SHAW, F.G.S., Assoc. M. Inst. C.E., M.M.S., etc. Author of: "Comets and their Tails, and the Gegenschein Light," etc. In large Crown 8vo, cloth gilt, and full gilt edges, 10s. 6d. net.

Written in an exceptionally lucid and convincing style, this important work, by the most searching and able reasoning, and substantiated by the most extensive armoury of facts, establishes a platform for which mankind has for long been groping. That faith, in the reality of a death-surviving consciousness and an after-existence, which appears to have haunted the mind of man from the earliest dawn of history, has, by Mr. Shaw's most admirable philosophy, found a material and substantial platform on which to rest. Much of the doubt and uncertainty which have been so unfortunately created by the arguments of the Agnostic, the Materialist and the Atheist, will disappear as the suggestive data and the compelling arguments of this most interesting work are perused, for the reader will realise that he has within his own cosmos sufficient evidence of a death-surviving consciousness to assure him that life on earth is but a test, and his body but the casket in which is moulded for good or for evil that transcendental gift from the Architect of the Universe, the soul of man. The volume contains 500 pages of matter printed in a most readable type, on extremely light paper, elegantly bound, gilt edged, and clearly and elaborately indexed. The preface is most valuable, and the evidence by which the author proves his thesis direct and convincing.

The First Signs of Insanity; Their Prevention and Treatment. By BERNARD HOLLANDER, M.D. Author of d "The Mental Functions of the Brain," "Scientific Phrenology," "Hypnotism and Suggestion," "Mental Symptoms of Brain Disease," etc. Demy 8vo, 10s. 6d. net.

This book is not merely a treatise on the causes, prevention and successful treatment of the various forms of insanity, but deals with the numerous problems of mental inefficiency and derangement as they affect the individual and the community, and is intended to be of practical value not only to the general practitioner, but to lawyers, psychologists, and statesmen, as well as to the general student. Whereas most books on insanity deal with the *advanced* stages of the disease, as they are seen in asylums, Dr. Bernard Hollander gives a systematic description of the *earliest* manifestations of mental disorder, as may be witnessed in private practice and observation wards, and analyses these signs and symptoms in such a manner as to make his book easy for reference in doubtful cases. He discusses the methods to be adopted in order to prevent mental breakdown in individuals in whose families there is a neurotic taint and the various measures which are intended to limit the propagation of the unfit, such as restriction of marriage and segregation. Other problems dealt with are: When is a person insane? drink and insanity, insanity and crime, insanity of suicides, testamentary capacity, education of the feeble-minded, private treatment of the insane, surgical treatment of insanity; etc. The book is written in a lucid and easily apprehended style, and deals with a subject of so far-reaching importance that it should appeal to a wide circle of readers.

The Physiology of Faith and Fear; or, the Mind in Health and Disease. By WILLIAM S. SADLER, M.D. Author of "The Science of Living;" or the Art of Keeping Well," "The Cause and Cure of Colds," etc. With an Appendix and Index. Large Cr. 8vo, 580 pp., with 44 full page illustrations, cloth gilt, 6s. net.

Practically every system of modern mental healing is based on some creed or craft and dependent upon the acceptance of some particular moral teaching or religious doctrine. The author of this work approaches the subject from the standpoint of the physiologist and separates its study from association, not with religion as a state of mind, but with any and all particular systems, sects, or forms of religious belief. His desire is not only to call attention to the power of the mind over the body, but also to point out the vast influence of the body over the mind, more particularly the influence of the diseased or disordered physical body on the mental state and the moral tendencies. The argument of the work is pursued in simple language divested of all scientific technicalities and laboratory terminology so that an intelligent schoolboy may fully understand the narrative and comprehend the conclusions. The scientific value of a sunny aspect to a sick room has its natural corollary in the physical value of a cheerful spirit on a Jaded body, and the influence of faith and hope in the maintenance of health and the struggle with disease. This work shows the harmful influence of fear and the wholesome effect of faith and belief.

The Insanity of Genius: and the general inequality of human faculty physiologically considered. By J. F. NISBET. Author of "The Human Machine," etc. Sixth and new edition, with an Introduction by DR. BERNARD HOLLANDER. Crown 8vo, 5s. net.

For over two thousand years some subtle relationship has been thought to exist between genius and insanity. Aristotle noted how often eminent men displayed morbid symptons of mind, and Plato distinguished two kinds of delirium—one being ordinary insanity and the other the spiritual exaltation which produces poets, inventors, or prophets and which he regarded not as an evil, but as a gift of the gods. The *furor poeticus* and the *amabilis insania* of the Romans had reference to the same phenomenon. On the other hand there has always been a strong body of opinion, philosophical and scientific, against the supposed connection of genius with insanity. Locke ascribed all intellectual superiority to education, and Dr. Johnson maintained that genius resulted from a mind of large general powers being turned in a particular direction, while Goethe held that a man of genius sums up in his own person the best qualities of the family or the race to which he belongs. The author enters upon the discussion of the subject in the light of later discoveries and more modern methods of investigation and with a knowledge of the localisation of the functions of the brain and the establishment of kinship between an extensive group of brain and nerve disorders which leads him to the conclusion that, apparently at the opposite poles of human intellect, genius and insanity are, in reality, but different phases of a morbid susceptibility of, or want of balance in, the cerebro-spinal system.

The Human Machine. An Inquiry into the Diversity

of Human Faculty in its Bearings upon Social Life, Religion, Education, and Politics. By J. F. NISBET. Fifth and new edition. Cr. 8vo, 3s. 6d. net.

The *Times* says:—"All, we feel sure, will share our own regret that the author was not spared to do fuller justice to his genuine interest in the higher problems of mental philosophy."

The *Spectator* says:—" An undoubtedly clever and suggestive book. . . . We have rarely met with anything so sound as the author's common-sense criticism of popular Socialism, or the vigorous handling of the much-discussed modern ' sex ' problems."

Literature says:—". . . It leaves an impression deeper and more durable than that produced by works much more ambitious."

Woman Adrift: The Menace of Suffragism. By

HAROLD OWEN. Second edition. Crown 8vo, cloth gilt, 6s.

The *Times*.—"A timely, well-reasoned and comprehensive statement of the case against female suffrage, which should be widely studied."

The *Spectator*.—"This book covers most ably practically the whole ground of argument—political, biological, social—against granting the Parliamentary Franchise to women. It is written in the right spirit, and says nothing in dispraise of women."

The *Pall Mall Gazette*.—"The most patient, the most deliberate, and the most exhaustive answer that has been yet penned to the demand for Woman Suffrage. As a dialectical effort it is indeed remarkable, for it pursues the argument into every byway and recess where the Suffragist is likely to seek refuge, and insists upon bringing her contentions to the issue."

Ancient, Curious and Famous Wills. By VIRGIL

M. HARRIS. 485 pp. 8vo, cloth gilt, 10s. 6d. net.

The author of this work is a well-known lecturer on the subject at St. Louis University. His work deals with about 500 wills obtained from various parts of the world, beginning with the earliest times and coming down to the present day. These wills range from Plato, Aristotle, Virgil and Augustus Cæsar to Mary Stuart, Shakespeare, Voltaire, Wellington, Washington, Whittier, Longfellow, Barnum and Brigham Young. The book teems with anecdotes and reading of the most entertaining kind.

The History of Gravesend and its Surround-

ings, from pre-historic times to the beginning of the Twentieth Century. By ALEX. J. PHILIP. Author of "Gravesend, the Water-gate of London," etc., etc. In four volumes, 12s. 6d. net each.

This history of Gravesend will be issued to subscribers only, the edition being limited to 365 copies of each volume, the first volume to be ready about November, 1912. Subscription forms, with full particulars, on application to the publisher. The work is one of much more than local interest, the position of Gravesend giving it a place in history from ancient times, and its situation on the Thames linking it up with the story of the British navy. The author has had special facilities for collecting materials, and is animated by an enthusiasm which, together with his experience in research work and knowledge of books, qualifies him to produce *the* history of the town he serves as Borough librarian.

Every Man's El-dorado—British South America.

By EDITH A. BROWNE. Author of "Peeps at Greece and Spain," etc. In one volume, demy 8vo, cloth gilt, fully illustrated, 12s. 6d. net.

This is a very welcome and informative work dealing with British Guiana—the "Magnificent Province," as it is styled, and the only British Colony in South America. The author visited the Colony in 1910, and again in 1912, for the purpose of studying the country as a commercial centre and as a holiday resort, and the result is much valuable first-hand information from both points of view. Miss Browne sets forth clearly and concisely what has been done, from an industrial point of view, to develop British Guiana in the past, and discusses the future of the Colony in relation to its natural resources, and the possibilities and prospects of the further development of the country. To the tourist in search of a novel playground, the "Magnificent Province." should prove an ideal country. The travelling facilities are such as will enable him to indulge his inclination to explore unbeaten tracts without discomfort, and also enable him to enjoy to the full the fascination of new and unique surroundings.

A Tour through South America. By A. S.

FORREST. Author of "A Tour through Old Provence," etc. Demy 8vo, cloth gilt, profusely illustrated, 10s. 6d. net.

Mr. A. S. Forrest, the well-known artist and literateur, is now travelling in South America executing commissions for several influential syndicates, and traversing the whole of the country surrounding the Panama Canal. The author's credentials give him unique facilities of exploration, and much that will be written and illustrated in his book, will come before the public for the first time. The book will, therefore, be of first importance to those wishing for accurate knowledge, and a picturesque presentation of the characteristic features of this fascinating country.

The Ridge of the White Waters : Impressions of a

Visit to Johannesburg, with some Notes on Durban, Delagoa Bay and the Low Country. By WILLIAM CHARLES SCULLY. Author of "Between Sun and Sands," "The White Helacourt," etc. In one vol., cloth gilt, with illustrations, 6s. net.

The author of the present most opportune and interesting volume, a well-known resident in South Africa, is no mere surface-seeing globetrotter. As a wanderer, worker, hunter and magistrate, he has been afforded unique opportunities of which he has taken full advantage, for the study of almost every side of life in the colony, and these "impressions," the outcome of, to quote his own words, "a kind of Rip Van Winkle pilgrimage to scenes where I sojourned eight-and-thirty years ago, and where the bones of many of my friends have ever since mouldered in the hot, red sand ; to the Delagoa hinterland— known then as ' The Low Country '—through which I helped to cut the first road from the Transvaal in 1874, and to Johannesburg, that Golden Calf which Anglo-Israel worships, and on the site of which I once hunted blesbucks," give much interesting information regarding South Africa as it is to-day.

In the Footsteps of Richard Cœur de Lion.

By MAUDE M. HOLBACH. Author of "Bosnia and Herzegovina," "Dalmatia," etc. In demy 8vo, fully illustrated, 16s. net.

Born of a warrior race of princes, yet with troubadore blood in his veins, Richard Cœur de Lion united in himself the qualities of soldier and poet. His faults were many, but most of them were those of the age in which he lived. This book aims to sketch truly this almost mythical king, and to bring one of the most interesting characters in history from the land of shadows into the broad light of day, tracing his footsteps through mediæval France and England to Cyprus and the Holy Land, and back along the Adriatic shores to the place of his captivity on the Danube, and finally to his tragic death in the land of his boyhood. The author has a personal acquaintance with the scenes of many of Cœur de Lion's wanderings which gives life to her narrative, and the historical bent which enables her to do justice to the subject.

Princess and Queen: The Life and Times of Mary II.

By MARY F. SANDARS. Author of "Balzac, his Life and Writings." Demy 8vo, illustrated, 16s. net.

The only English biography of Mary II is the one written by Agnes Strickland in her "Lives of the Queens of England," but since then much fresh information has come to light. In 1880, Countess Bentinck published part of Queen Mary's private diary, and in 1886 Dr. Doebner produced other portions of it. These two books give a unique opportunity for an appraisement of the Queen, who confided her most secret thoughts to her precious Memoirs, which she carried on her person in times of danger. Moreover, the writer has visited the Hague, and received valuable assistance from Dr. Kramer, author of a Dutch Life of Queen Mary. The Duke of Portland also has given her access to the unpublished letters at Welbeck, and Lord Bathurst to a number of others written by the Queen to her most intimate friends.

Godoy, the Queen's Favourite. By EDMUND B.

D'AUVERGNE. Author of "The Coburgs," "A Queen at Bay," "Lola Montez," etc. Demy 8vo, illustrated, 16s. net.

A romance of the old Spanish Court. Godoy, the son of a poor country gentleman, had no fortune but his handsome face. This was enough to captivate Maria Luisa, the wife of King Charles IV., a woman comparable in some respects with Catherine II. of Russia. Strange to say, her lover secured an empire over her husband; which lasted till his dying day. Entrusted with the government, Godoy was called upon to contend against no less a foe than Napoleon himself, and for twenty years he held France at bay. Overthrown at last by the odious heir-apparent, afterwards Ferdinand VII., the fallen favourite became a prisoner in the hands of the French at Bayonne. He followed his master and mistress into exile, and died poor and neglected forty years after. His career was one of the most romantic that history affords. The book is largely based on unpublished official documents.

7

The Romance of Sandro Botticelli. A. J. ANDERSON.

Author of "The Romance of Fra Filippo Lippi," etc. Demy 8vo, cloth gilt, with photogravure frontispiece and 16 full-page illustrations on art paper, 10s. 6d. net.

A delightful story of Florence during the Renaissance, with the poets, philosophers, and ladies of the Medici circle as a background, and including the most intimate study of Botticelli's life and art that has yet been written. Commencing with Sandro's life at Prato and telling of the influence that Lucrezia exercised over his character, and Fra Filippo Lippi over his painting, the author depicts his struggles and triumphs with a sure touch, ending with the wave of piagnone mysticism which clouded the last years of his career. When Mr. Anderson loves his characters, he loves them whole-heartedly, and he compels his readers to sympathise with Botticelli as much as they sympathise with Filippo Lippi and the nun Lucrezia.

Famous Artists and their Models. By ANGELO S.

RAPPOPORT, Ph.D. Author of "The Love Affairs of the Vatican," etc. Demy 8vo, 32 full page illustrations, 16s. net.

Those who look upon a work of art with delight seldom fail in their appreciation of the artist's handiwork, but do not always recognise how much they owe to the inspiration of the artist's model. History shows that the greatest triumphs of art have been achieved when enthusiastic devotion to art has been shared by artist and model alike. It is the purpose of Dr. Rappoport's book to trace the effect of the perfect sympathy between artist and model which has produced the masterpieces which are the delight "not of an age, but of all time." The ladies of ancient Rhodes, Corinth and Sicyon were proud to co-operate with Apelles and Zeuxis in the production of such works. Lais of Corinth became one of the favourite models of Apelles, and Phryne, whom he saw bathing at Elusis, sat for his picture of Aphrodite rising from the sea. Alexander the Great, it is said, allowed his favourite Campaspe to sit to the same artist, and when Zeuxis painted his famous picture of Helen he had five of the most beautiful women of Croton as his models. In the days of the Renaissance Roman grandees sat for Raphael, and the models who sat for Titian were not poor professionals working for remuneration, but great ladies of the aristocracy of ducal rank and even royal blood. Dr. Rappoport has made a special study of the history and psychology of the model, and the results are given in the present work.

Duchess Derelict: A Study of the Life and Times of

Charlotte d'Albret, Duchess of Valentinois (wife of Cesare Borgia). E. L. MIRON. Demy 8vo, fully illustrated, 16s. net.

The *Dundee Advertiser* refers to this book as "One of the finest historical monographs of recent times."

The *Globe* says of it:—"No one can read the 'Duchess Derelict,' a particularly apt title, and fail to be touched with the poignant tragedy of one of the saddest stories in history. We can promise the reader who follows this 'Princess of Pity' through the mazes of her faintly outlined story, an absorbing 'hour or two's' entertainment."

The Life of Cesare Borgia. (Third Edition.)

By RAFAEL SABATINI, Author of "The Lion's Skin," "The Justice of the Duke," etc. In demy 8vo, cloth gilt, with coloured frontispiece and other illustrations printed on art paper, 16s. net.

The *Standard* speaks of this work as "a clever and even a brilliant book. It certainly says all that can be said in mitigation of the sweeping censure which has passed almost unchallenged down the ages."

The *Scotsman* says: "This is a readable and well-studied work. It gives a picturesque account both of the House of Borgia and of its most famous scion without falling into romantical exaggerations either way. It cannot fail to interest English students of Italian history."

The *Daily Telegraph* says:—"Mr. Sabatini has a lively and vigorous style, which imparts a freshness to his narrative, and the story of Cesare Borgia's short but varied and remarkable career as here fully and carefully set forward proves as entertaining as it is informative."

Rodrigo Borgia. The Life and Times of Pope Alexander VI. (Father of Cesare Borgia). By the Most Rev. ARNOLD H. MATHEW, D.D. Fully illustrated, demy 8vo, 16s. net.

"Dr. Mathew sets on his title-page a quotation from Leo. XIII.: 'Let writers of history remember never to dare to tell a lie, nor to fear to tell the truth.' This motto the author faithfully follows, with the result of a terrible story of immorality, debauchery, and corruption. The record of those times is truly amazing. The Papacy of the fifteenth century was a bestial resort of immorality, and treachery, and venality, and assassination. One would imagine that it would, like the Roman Empire, have perished in its own vices. Those were the days of the terrible Galeazzo Sforza. . . . This period of Italian history is probably unmatched in the chronicles of at least the more modern world for its cruelty and wantonness and licentiousness. Dr. Mathew's book is a very readable and a very accurate one. He is an impartial historian with a great gift of glozing over nothing for partisan purposes. He has gone to first authorities, and has amassed and arranged his facts well."—H. B. MARRIOTT WATSON, in the *Pall Mall Gazette.*

In Jesuit Land: The Jesuit Missions at Paraguay.

By W. H. KOEBEL. Author of "In the Maoriland Bush," "Madeira, Old and New," "Portugal, Past and Present," etc. Demy 8vo, illustrated, 12s. 6d. net.

The story of the Jesuit missions of Paraguay as told here, forms one of the most fascinating chapters in the complex history of the River Plate Provinces. Mr. Koebel has traced the work of the missions from their inception in the early days of Spanish South American colonisation and discovery, down to the final expulsion of the Jesuits by Bucareli in the middle of the eighteenth century. It is a story of deep interest, often of breathless excitement, and is, at the same time, a close and intimate study of the devoted men, who gave all, even to life itself, to their work; through the story runs a vein of political intrigue which heightens its fascination.

Polly Peachum. The story of Lavinia Fenton, Duchess of Bolton and " The Beggar's Opera." By CHARLES E. PEARCE. Author of " The Amazing Duchess," " The Beloved Princess," " Love Besieged," etc. Demy 8vo, illustrated, 16s. net.

The history of the stage can show no more remarkable a career than that of fascinating and lovable " Polly Peachum, " otherwise Lavinia Fenton, Duchess of Bolton. Described as "nobody's daughter," Polly leaped at a bound into fame, and her star blazed with undimmed lustre during the brief time she was the idol of the public. " Polly Peachum " will be for ever identified with Gay's " Beggar's Opera," a work which occupies a unique place in theatrical annals, not only because it was the first—and best—of English ballad operas, but because for nearly a century and a half it maintained its attractiveness with never fading freshness. A vast amount of material—lampoons, verse, anecdotes, scandal, controversy, bearing upon "The Beggar's Opera " and its heroine, exists in contemporary records, and this material has for the first time been brought together in a connected form. Eighteenth Century stage life is notable for a full blooded vitality peculiar to itself, and the aim of the author has been to draw a picture of the times. The volume will contain numerous illustrations from Hogarth, and from the unrivalled collection of Mr. A. M. Broadley, whose generous help has been accorded.

Reflections of a Sporting Artist. By FINCH MASON (" Uncle Toby "). Demy 8vo, cloth gilt, with 100 illustrations, 16s. net.

Mr. Finch Mason, who is more popularly known as " Uncle Toby," the famous sporting author and. artist, has prepared a volume which will make an irresistible appeal to a very wide circle of readers. It includes reminiscences of Twyford School, under the present Dean of Durham, of life at Eton in the sixties, and the masters and schoolfellows of that period, including Lord Randolph Churchill, William Beresford, V.C.; and others, who have since become famous. In connection with these numerous anecdotes are told, and some well-known characters, from " Spankie " to " Silly Billy," are hit off with an adroit fidelity which only an artist author can compass. A year in business, and another year as a student of architecture under Edward Barry, R.A., pass under review, also the author's experiences on the turf, in the hunting field, and out shooting, which together with recollections of London life by night and day, make up a bright and fascinating volume.

Cameos of Indian Crime. Studies of native criminality in India. By H. J. A. HERVEY (Indian Telegraphs, retired). Demy 8vo, cloth gilt, illustrated, 12s. 6d. net.

Mr. Hervey, who has spent many years in India, has collected a large fund of information concerning native crime, which he deals with in a series of fascinating chapters on Murder, Poisoning, Infanticide, Burglary, Highway Robbery, Forgery, Procuring, Prostitution, Mendacity, Fanaticism, Extortion, Railway Robbery, Tampering with Railways, Beggar Faking, Trumped-up Evidence, Getting at Examination Papers, Drink, Opium Eating, etc.

Evening Standard says: " As good as reading Kipling "; and the *Daily Chronicle,* " one of the best books on Indian Crime of recent years."

Guerilla Leaders of the World. With a preface

by the Earl of Dundonald. By PERCY CROSS STANDING, Author of "The Marshals of Napoleon," and part author of "Our Naval Heroes," "Sea Kings and Sea Fights,"etc. Cr. 8vo,illustrated,6s.net.

Mr. Cross Standing, who was special correspondent for Reuter during the war between France and Siam, has been able to secure much valuable first-hand information concerning notable Guerilla leaders, including Osman Digna and Colonel John S. Mosby, the Confederate raider. Special notes by the Sirdar (Lieut. General Sir F. R. Wingate) have been placed at his disposal.

The European in India. By H. J. A. HERVEY. Author

of "Cameos of Indian Crime." Demy 8vo, illustrated, 12s. 6d. net.

This work, written by a European many years resident in India, sheds a flood of light on the life of the European man and woman in that wonderful country. All sorts and conditions of men and women are dealt with : the military man, the sailor, the civilian—covenanted and uncovenanted—the medical man, the merchant, the press man, the planter, the banker, the railway man, the tradesman, the pensioner, the loafer, the crank, the globe trotter, the married woman—fast and staid—the "miss"—attached and unattached—the grass-widow, the "scorpion," the belle—reigning and pasée—the goody-goody woman, the nostalgic woman, the lady doctor, the midwife, the "slavey," the soldier's wife, "Perdita," and many others. The third part of the book deals with life at the hill stations, the coast stations, and the up-country stations, station clubs, dinner parties, concerts, dances, picnics, weddings, christenings, funerals, etc., etc., etc. This book gives a very clear and interesting insight of European life in India.

The White Slave Market. By MRS. ARCHIBALD

MACKIRDY (Olive Christian Malvery), Author of "The Soul Market," etc., and W. N. WILLIS, Author of "What Germany Wants," etc. Crown 8vo, cloth gilt, 5s. net. Eighth edition.

This is an authoritative book of vital interest upon a subject of great public concern at the present time. It contains life stories, so strange, so pathetic and so dreadful that it must make an instant appeal to the reader's sympathy and sense of justice. No such indictment has ever yet been made, for the whole question is treated of, and all the ramifications of the trade at Home and Abroad are laid bare. Ministers, Members of Parliament, Philanthropic workers and the general public will find here strange " human documents "—stories of actual lives (some actually now being lived)—that will touch them to tears and rouse them to demand for the White Slaves—inarticulate— helpless and unknown, pity and justice. Both the authors are prominent workers in Social Service—Mrs. Archibald Mackirdy is well-known in connection with active rescue work. Mr. W. N. Willis, who is responsible for the facts of the present volume, was for sixteen years a member of the Australian Parliament, and was largely influential in suppressing the Trade in Australia. He has travelled widely, and has spared no effort to obtain and verify his information regarding the Traffic in the East. The work is written in a straight-forward style to give the plain, bare facts of the Trade as it really is.

August Strindberg: The Spirit of Revolt. Studies
and Impressions by L. LIND-AF-HAGEBY. Crown 8vo, illustrated,
6s. net.

Strindberg, the Swedish dramatist and novelist who, on the Continent, ranks with Ibsen, has written seventy plays, psychological, satirical, historical and mystic, and novels, stories and essays, which place him in the forefront of modern writers as an observer of life. The Author gives a vivid picture of the struggles and difficulties of his career. The critical analysis of Strindberg's writings will be opportune in view of the growing interest in his work and personality. He died May 14th, 1912.

The Life of James Hinton. By MRS. HAVELOCK
ELLIS. Author of "Three Modern Seers," "My Cornish Neighbours," "Kit's Woman," etc. Illustrated, 10s. 6d. net.

Mrs. Havelock Ellis is preparing this biography under very favour-able circumstances. Access to private papers, and the assistance of intimate friends, together with her own knowledge and experience, qualify her to treat the subject with greater fullness than was possible to those who preceded her. The book will aim at presenting the man as his friends knew him, a noble, serious student struggling to bring truth into the open.

Granville Barker. A Critical Study. By HAROLD
WESTON. In crown 8vo, cloth gilt, with Portrait, 6s. net.

The most significant movement in the British Theatre of to-day is the rapid development of the repertory idea, especially in the provinces, and no name associated with this movement has more importance than that of Granville Barker. He is not only one of our leading modern dramatists, but it is through his efforts as a producer, and his enthusiasm for what has been called the "Higher Drama," that the repertory movement is what it is to-day. In this book Mr. Harold Weston deals with the life and personality of Granville Barker, with his plays, and with his work as a producer. And in a clever analysis of Granville Barker's methods and ideas, he reveals to what a great extent he is affecting the modern stage.

What Germany Wants. By W. N. WILLIS,
Ex-M.P. (Australia). Author of "Western Men and Eastern
Morals." Crown 8vo, cloth, 2s. net.

This book is a forceful exposition of what the Author regards as the German menace in Europe. The book touches a new key in Imperial affairs, and includes a chapter which unfolds a workable plan for bringing the empire and its great dependencies into union for the defence of the trade arteries of the Mediterranean. The Author deals from inside knowledge. The book goes out to tell civilisation *What Germany Wants*. Every Briton should read it and understand its seriousness.

A Garland of Verse for Young People. Edited
by ALFRED H. MILES. Handsome cloth gilt, 2s. 6d. net.

This is a collection of verse for children, made to satisfy the require-ments of school and home. Never before has an attempt been made to cover in one volume such a wide range of pieces at so small a price. It should be one of the most popular children's books this year.

Samphire. By Lady Sybil Grant

Crown 8vo, cloth gilt, 3s. 6d. net.

A *pot-pourri* of original and humorous inconsequences or essayettes on such subjects as gardening, shops, personal relations, etc., etc., including fanciful skits called "shadows"—analogues, the sources of which it is not difficult to trace, and which the reader is in no danger of taking too seriously from the pen of one who apparently refuses to take anything for granted or to subscribe to any accepted or conventional point of view. Piquant and amusing without any trace of trying to be funny.

Western Men and Eastern Morals. By W. N.

WILLIS. With a preface by R. A. BENNETT, Editor of *Truth.* Crown 8vo, cloth gilt, 5s. net.

The relationship between the white man and the coloured woman in countries under the dominion of the white races presents a problem which increasingly demands attention. The author describes from personal observation the white man's life in the East, the licensed immorality of the Straits Settlement and Japan, and the irregular alliances of the rubber planter, of the Anglo-Burman and the tea planter of Ceylon, and points out the difficulties likely to arise in the near future in dealing with the parti-coloured offspring of these associations. A special preface by the Editor of *Truth* bears corroborative testimony.

Nineteenth Century English Ceramic Art. By

J. F. BLACKER. With about 96 pages of half-tone illustrations, printed on art paper, and 150 line drawings, 10s. 6d. net.

"One of the cheapest art manuals that has appeared in the present generation. For half-a-guinea the reader may obtain over 500 closely printed pages, full of the liveliest and most erudite information, together with some 1,200 beautifully reproduced examples of the best products of English Ceramic Art in the nineteenth century. Invaluable to all lovers of historic ware," says the *Daily Telegraph.*

The Motor: An Interesting Practical Work of Original

Information and Reference for Owners and Makers of Motor Cars. By JOHN ARMSTRONG. Demy 8vo, cloth gilt, with 160 special illustrations, 10s. 6d. net.

This volume is written in non-technical language, mathematical formulæ having been rigidly excluded. New light is thrown on a great variety of constructional features, and the main points in the design and manufacture of the modern motor engine are discussed. A host. of subjects such as clutches, carburation, changed speed mechanism, live axle construction, etc., are fully treated. Hot-air, rotary, and turbine gas motors, six-wheel vehicles, the past, present and future of the motor omnibus and motor cab, are also dealt with in this exhaustive volume.

Paul's Simplicode. By M. Levy

Crown 8vo, cloth, 1s. net.

A simple and thoroughly practical and efficient code for the use of Travellers, Tourists, Business Men, Department Stores, Shopping by Post, Colonial Emigrants, Lawyers, and the general public. Everyone should use this, the cheapest code book published in English. A sentence in a word.

Fourteen Years of Diplomatic Life in Japan.

Stray leaves from the Diary of Baroness Albert d'Anethan, with an introduction by His Excellency Baron Kato, the Japanese Ambassador to St. James's. Fully illustrated with photogravure and half-tone illustrations on art paper. 18s. net. Second edition.

The *Globe* says:—"It abounds 'in intimate touches and acute remarks on the condition of japan, and is quite evidently the work of a clever woman whose eyes were as observant as her intuition was keen."

David Garrick and His French Friends. By

DR. F. A. HEDGCOCK. Demy 8vo, cloth gilt, illustrated. 7s. 6d. net.

The *Athenæum* says:—"Dr. Hedgcock contributes a welcome, because really scholarly, addition to the biography of England's greatest actor."

A Winter Holiday in Portugal. By CAPTAIN GRAN-

VILLE BAKER. With coloured frontispiece and 32 original drawings by the author. Demy 8vo, cloth gilt, 12s. 6d. net.

Bookman:—"Captain Granville Baker writes lightly and pleasantly. He saw a good deal that was charming, not a little that was quaint, and a certain mixture of mediævalism and modernity."

The Beloved Princess. Princess Charlotte of Wales.

By CHARLES E. PEARCE. Author of "The Amazing Duchess," "Polly Peachum," etc. Demy 8vo, cloth gilt, illustrated, 16s. net.

Globe :—"Mr. Pearce, as usual, contrives to make his story interesting by his vivacious style, and a clever use of the materials at his command."

A Great Russian Realist : The Romance and

Reality of Dostoieffsky. By J. A. T. LLOYD. Author of "Two Russian Reformers," etc., etc. Demy 8vo, cloth gilt and gilt top, with illustrations, 10s. 6d. net.

Pall Mall Gazette.—"The most valuable contribution to our knowledge of Russian Literature that an Englishman has produced. Dostoieffsky comes to us with a great, vague human sincerity that, Russian in its expression, is world-wide in its appeal."

The Librarian, an Independent Professional Journal,

for the professional man and all interested in literature. Monthly, 6d., or 6s. 6d. per annum, post free.

"The Librarian" is an invaluable mine of information concerning libraries, from the first stone laid in the structure of the building to the last book placed upon its shelves. It is indispensable to the librarian, the publisher, the bookseller, the book buyer and the book reader alike.

The Commentator. The most out-spoken paper in

England. A sixpenny review for One Penny Weekly.

"The Commentator" is a paper which has the courage of its convictions, and speaks with no uncertain sound. Whatever doubts and fears may paralyse *blasé* politicians, "The Commentator" is free from all ambiguity and vacillation. Published every Wednesday.

Canada To-day, 1912. Its progress, prosperity and

opportunities pictured by pen and camera, including upwards of 300 pictures reproduced from photographs, maps and plans; 240 pp., 13½ × 9½, 1s. net; a limited number in cloth, 2s. net.

This annual is the best repository of absolutely up-to-date information concerning Canada, available for use in Great Britain. It is intended to portray something of what Canada offers in the extent and variety of its resources to the emigrant and the investor.

ALFRED H. MILES'
NEW SERIES FOR BOYS AND GIRLS

Large crown 8vo, 384 pages, fully illustrated, handsome cloth gilt, full gilt edges, **5s. each.**

Christian World :—"Mr. Alfred H. Miles is the Homer of modern Ajaxes and Hectors. He seems to have heard of more brave deeds than any man living."

In the Lion's Mouth : Fierce Fights with Wild Men, Wild Animals and Wild Nature. By Clive Fenn, Theodore Roosevelt, Frank R. Stockton, Ena Fitzgerald, F. W. Calkins, Rowland Thomas, Albert W. Tolman, Fisher Ames. Edited by ALFRED H. MILES. Large crown 8vo, handsome cloth gilt, burnished edges, with coloured illustrations.

Where Duty Calls or Danger : Records of Courage and Adventure for Girls. By Evelyn Everett-Green, Grace Stebbing, Margaret E. Sangster, Ena Fitzgerald, E. W. Tomson, F. W. Calkins and other writers. Edited by ALFRED H. MILES. Large crown 8vo, handsome cloth gilt, burnished edges, with coloured illustrations.

'Twixt Life and Death on Sea and Shore. A Book for Boys. Edited by ALFRED H. MILES.

Daily Chronicle :—"Mr. Miles is always a safe guide where boys' reading is concerned. Here he gives you plenty of stirring things, and the best of it is they are all from real life—true stories that is."

Heroines of the Home and the World of Duty. A Book for Girls. Edited by ALFRED H. MILES.

Lady's Pictorial :—"Each story is of a high standard, and has the healthy atmosphere which characterises all the books of Alfred H. Miles."

A Book of Brave Boys All the World Over. Edited by ALFRED H. MILES.

Truth :—"What could be more fascinating to the boy than the stories of brave deeds contained in 'A Book of Brave Boys'?"

A Book of Brave Girls At Home and Abroad. Edited by ALFRED H. MILES.

Morning Leader :—"It provides numerous and thrilling examples of heroism in all parts of the globe, and ought to prove very inspiring."

In the Teeth of Adventure Up and Down the World. Edited by ALFRED H. MILES.

Manchester Courier :—"A gloriously exciting book for boys."

The Sweep of the Sword. From Marathon to Mafeking. Being a Battle Book for Boys. By ALFRED H. MILES. Dedicated by special permission to Field-Marshal Earl Roberts, V.C. In large crown 8vo. (over 600 pages), with a photogravure frontispiece, 16 full-page illustrations of world-famous battle pictures, printed on art paper, and nearly 150 illustrations in the text, handsomely bound in cloth gilt, with special design, 6s.

Truth :—"Never before has Mr. Miles gathered such a harvest as this in a single volume. It is truly a stupendous volume, and there is quality as well as quantity to recommend it."

Pall Mall Gazette :—"It is a tremendously attractive and manly volume for boys. It is not a book in praise of war, but it celebrates in a fitting way those virtues which war brings out."

United Service Magazine :—"Mr. Miles has compiled an extremely valuable volume from which not only boys but also a great many men will not only gain pleasurable excitement but much useful instruction of real historical value."

THE A B C SERIES

Each in large crown 8vo, fully illustrated, **5s.** net.

A B C of Collecting Old Continental Pottery

By J. F. BLACKER. Author of Nineteenth Century English Ceramic Art, and other works particularised on this page, etc., etc. Illustrated with about 100 line and 50 half-tone illustrations, 5s. net.

"In this new volume of the series Mr. J. F. Blacker provides information and illustrations of wares never previously presented in an inexpensive form to the great army of collectors. Persian, Syrian, Anatolian and Rhodian wares with the lustred Hispano Moresque and Siculo Moresque pottery will take their place side by side with the Majolica of Italy, the faience of France, the Delft of Holland, and the Stoneware of Germany."

The A B C of Japanese Art. By J. F. BLACKER.

460 pages, profusely illustrated with 150 line and 100 half-tone illustrations, printed on art paper, 5s. net.

"An exceedingly useful and timely book. It will guide, assist, and interest the collector in the Art of Old Japan. Those who desire to collect with profit will hardly discover any object so suitable, whilst for home decoration the quaint beauty of Japanese Art is unequalled in its peculiar attractiveness. Technical processes are explained, and the marks, signatures and sale prices are given. *The book would be cheap at double the price.*"—The Court Journal.

The A B C about Collecting (Second Edition).

By SIR JAMES YOXALL, M.P. The subjects include, among others, China, Clocks, Prints, Books, Pictures, Furniture and Violins. With numerous illustrations, 5s. net.

"A beginner cannot well have a better guide "—*Outlook.* "The amateur collector advised by us will certainly possess himself of this volume."—*Academy.*

A B C of Collecting Old English China. By J. F.

BLACKER. With numerous line and 64 pages of half-tone illustrations, printed on art paper, 5s. net.

"To the beginner there could be no surer guide."—*Pall Mall Gazette.* "Mr. Blacker shows what to look for, how to know it, and what to avoid."—*Daily Express.*

A B C of Collecting Old English Pottery. By

J. F. BLACKER. With about 400 line and 32 pages of half-tone illustrations, 5s. net.

"Practically every known variety of old English pottery is dealt with, and facsimiles of the various marks, and the prices realised by good examples at auction are given."—*Observer.* "In this book salt glaze, lustre, slipware, puzzle jugs, Fulham, Astbury, Lambeth, Leeds, Yarmouth, and numerous other wares all receive careful attention. Mr. Blacker speaks with authority, and his pages are full of knowledge."—*Bookman.*

The A B C Guide to Mythology. By HELEN A.

CLARKE. Cr. 8vo, cloth gilt, 400 pp., illustrated, 5s. net.

The gifted author of this book has written and lectured on mythology for many years, and is, from study and research, well qualified to produce a work on the subject well calculated to supply the general need. In this book she traces the rise and development of the various native myths through their Greek, Norse and Oriental phases, with the result that the book may be used either as an authoritative guide to the subject or as an interesting and entertaining work for occasional and recreative reading. The great interest felt at the present time in myths makes the appearance of the volume opportune, and the knowledge and skill of the author give it great value as an educational work of high literary merit.

The A B C Guide to Music. By D. Gregory Mason.

Crown 8vo, cloth gilt, with 12 illustrations, 5s. net.

In this work Mr. Mason discusses the theory of music in a simple and entertaining manner, and then treats in turn piano, orchestral and vocal music, dealing with the master musicians and their work with sure insight and brief, significant analysis. He has avoided technical expressions as far as possible, and his book may be recommended not only to young readers, but also to adult lovers of music who wish to increase their knowledge of musical art.

The A B C Guide to Pictures. By Charles H.

Caffin. Author of "How to Study Pictures." Cloth gilt, 256 pp., fully illustrated, 5s. net.

Mr. Caffin is a well-known author of books on Art. His power of adapting his style to the outlook and point of view of youth makes him especially apt as a guide for the young on the subjects of which he treats, and enables him to point out with a clearness and precision which cannot be mistaken the qualities which make for greatness in pictorial art. He analyses these qualities from well-known examples, and his instructive criticism will be found of great value to parents and teachers wishing to encourage the intelligent appreciation of pictures in the young people of their charge. The author's object is not so much to tell the reader what pictures to admire as to inculcate the principles which will enable him to judge for himself what is most worthy of admiration in art.

The A B C Guide to American History. By

H. W. Elson. Crown 8vo, cloth gilt, with 16 illustrations, 5s. net.

There are few subjects of more profound interest than that of history, and no histories are more important to us than the histories of our own times and of the modern times which led up to them. The rise of the Western world from the discovery of the great American continent by Christopher Columbus to the consummation of the "United States" is full of fascinating romance and inspiring incident, teeming with instructive suggestions regarding the development of nations and the art of government. Mr. Elson traverses the whole ground from the landing of Columbus to the close of the war with Spain and the construction of the Panama Canal. His style is crisp and picturesque.

The above four volumes were originally published in " The Guide Series."

The A B C of Artistic Photography. By A. J.

Anderson. With photogravure plates and half-tone illustrations in black and sepia, etc. Large Crown 8vo, 5s. net.

The Amateur Photographer says it is " A most delightful book, full of pleasant reading and surprises. It is beautifully illustrated with many photogravure and half-tone reproductions of pictures by leading workers. Every amateur photographer with an interest in pictorial work should get it."

Originally published under the title of "The Artistic Side of Photography," at 12s. 6d. net, a cheap edition of this work has long been in demand, and the opportunity has now been taken of placing it in this series of cheap and high class manuals.

TECHNICAL LIBRARY MANUALS

By ALEX. J. PHILIP, Borough Librarian, Gravesend.

1. **The Production of the Printed Catalogue.**
A practical handbook for everyone concerned with printing, 5s. net.
This work deals with the preparation, printing, and publication of catalogues of Libraries, Museums, and Art Galleries, publishers', booksellers' and business houses, with an appendix of type faces.

2. **The Business of Bookbinding** from the point of view of the binder, the publisher, the librarian, and the general reader, crown 8vo, 6s. net; half bound in sealskin, 7s. 9d. net.
This work contains chapters on the manufacture of binders' leather and cloth, and a description of a working bindery with samples of cloth and leather, specially displayed for colour, grain, and material. Photo-micrographs of paper fibres, by Clayton Beadle, illustrate the chapter dealing with book papers. The chapter on leather and its preparation is by Professor Proctor. The glossary of terms has been compiled with the assistance of J. Drew Appleby, and others.

3. **The Library Encyclopædia,** by the foremost authorities, edited by ALEX. J. PHILIP, 30s. net.; after 1912 the price will be raised to 40s. net.
THE LIBRARY ENCYCLOPÆDIA will deal comprehensively with Library Administration, Book Purchasing, Library History, Library Plans and Buildings, Classification, Cataloguing, Office Work and Routine, Mechanical Aids, Advertising, Heating, Lighting, Ventilating, and the various contributory branches of knowledge, Binding, Paper, the Preservation of Records, Museum Work, Practical Printing, Bibliography, Estimating, Specification Work, and all the numerous subjects either directly or indirectly connected with work in public, proprietary, and private libraries and museums.

LIBRARIAN SERIES OF REPRINTS

Reprinted from "The Librarian."

1. **Suggestions towards a Constructional Revision of the Dewey Classification.** By ARTHUR JOHN HAWKES. Price Sixpence net.
A valuable contribution to the knowledge of cataloguing in general and the Dewey system 800 and 900 in particular. Essential to every user of the Decimal system, and to every student.

2. **Library Assistants' Association : an outline of its development and work.** By W. BENSON THORNE. Price Sixpence net.
For the first time the complete history of this most Progressive Association is told in a handy form.

3. **Cinematograph Films : Their National value and preservation.** By ALEX. J. PHILIP. Sixpence net.
Cinematographs and the Public Library ; how each can help the other.

Introduction to Elementary Bibliography. By R. W. PARSONS. Sixpence net. A useful first guide to practical bibliography, one of the most difficult subjects in the Library Association's Examinations.

The Diner's-Out Vade Mecum. A Pocket "What's What" on the Manners and Customs of Society Functions, etc., etc. By ALFRED H. MILES. Author of "The New Standard Elocutionist." In fcap. 8vo (6⅛ by 3⅞), cloth bound, round corners, 1s. 6d. net   Leather, 2s. net.

This handy book is intended to help the diffident and inexperienced to the reasonable enjoyment of the social pleasures of society by an elementary introduction to the rules which govern its functions, public and private, at Dinners, Breakfasts, Luncheons, Teas, At Homes, Receptions, Balls and Suppers, with hints on Etiquette, Deportment, Dress, Conduct, After-Dinner Speaking, Entertainment, Story-Telling, Toasts and Sentiments, etc., etc.

Diners à Deux. By S. BEACH CHESTER, Author of "Anomalies of English Law," etc.   Crown 8vo, 5s. net.

Diners à Deux is a delightful piece of work with a perfect atmosphere, and is written by a man of the world who has studied life from an exceptionally advantageous point of view in different parts of the continent during several decades, and who is full of good stories drawn from very wide experience. The titles of some of these will convey a good idea of the contents, "The Incident' of the Hôtel Splendide," "The Pearls of Mme. La Baronne," "Natalia . . of New York."

Cakes and Ales. A memory of many meals, the whole interspersed with various Recipes, more or less original, the Anecdotes, mainly veracious.   By EDWARD SPENCER ('Nathaniel Gubbins').   Crown 8vo, 4th edition, 2s. 6d. net.

Saturday Review :—"A book from which every restaurant keeper can, if he will, get ideas enough to make a fortune. Sportsmen, stockbrokers, and others with large appetites, robust yet sensitive palates, and ample means, will find it invaluable when they are ordering the next little dinner for a select party of male friends."

The Everyday Pudding Book. By F. K. A tasty recipe for every day in the year, including February 29th. In crown 8vo, strongly bound, 1s. net.

Scotsman :—"Housewives will extend a hearty welcome to the 'Everyday Pudding Book.' It contains a recipe for every day in the year, yet there are not two exactly alike, either in flavour or appearance." *Referee :*—" If you want a tasty recipe for every day in the year you can do nothing better than purchase a copy of the 'Everyday Pudding Book.'"

The Everyday Savoury Book. A tasty for every day in the year. By MARIE WORTH. 1s. net.

The great success of the "Everyday Pudding Book" has suggested the publication of a similar book dealing with savouries in the same inexpensive and practical manner. The two books will be found invaluable for daily household use. With these two books the housewife will indeed be well set up for the economic use of the larder.

Cole's Fun Doctor, one of the two funniest books in the world. By E. W. COLE. 384 pp., cr. 8vo, cloth, 2s. 6d.

The mission of mirth is well understood, "Laugh and Grow Fat" is a common proverb, and the healthiness of humour goes without saying.

Cole's Fun Doctor (2nd series), the other of the two funniest books in the world. By E. W. COLE. 440 pp., crown 8vo, cloth, 2s. 6d.

Dr. Blues had an extensive practice until the Fun Doctor set up in opposition, but now Fun Doctors are in requisition everywhere.

NEW TWO SHILLING (Net) NOVELS

*COUNTESS DAPHNE. "RITA"

THE WHITE OWL. (2nd ed.) KATE HORN

RUFFLES. (2nd ed.) L. T. MEADE

THE LOVELOCKS OF DIANA. (2nd ed.) KATE HORN

THE DOLL. (3rd ed.) VIOLET HUNT

THE ACTIVITIES OF LAVIE JUTT. (2nd ed.)
MARGUERITE and ARMIGER BARCLAY

LOVE'S OLD SWEET SONG. (2nd ed.) CLIFTON BINGHAM

DUCKWORTH'S DIAMONDS. (2nd ed.) E. EVERETT-GREEN

THE CHILDREN OF ALSACE. (2nd ed.) RENÉ BAZIN

THE ARTISTIC TEMPERAMENT. (3rd ed.) JANE WARDLE

"The most brilliant piece of satire that has been published this century."—*Truth*.

For other titles see pp. 44 and 45.

NEW SHILLING (Net) NOVELS

* New revised edition—almost rewritten—and reset from new type.

*DR. PHILLIPS: A Maida-Vale Idyll. FRANK DANBY

TROPICAL TALES (7th edition). DOLF WYLLARDE

THE PERFIDIOUS WELSHMAN (10th ed). "DRAIG GLAS"

THE GARDEN OF LIFE (2nd edition). KATE HORN

No. 5 JOHN STREET (20th edition). RICHARD WHITEING

For other titles see pp. 45 and 46.

NEW SIX SHILLING NOVELS

Captain Hawks, Master Mariner. OSWALD KENDALL

Admirers of the novels of W. W. Jacobs should read this. It is a story of three men who cannot and will not abide dullness. Though separated superficially by discipline and convention, Captain Hawks, Grummet and "Cert'nly" Wilfred are brothers "under their skins," and are controlled by the same insatiable desire for variety. Their thirst for the unexpected is amply satisfied in the search for an illusive cargo of sealskins, purchased without having been seen by Captain Hawks, and though much of the story takes place at sea, all technicalities have been carefully omitted. That the crew are nearly drowned, nearly frozen, nearly starved, and nearly smothered proves that they succeeded in a search for a life where things happen. Their success is also financial, and the story leaves them with a hint of further adventures to follow. A capital yarn.

The Irresistible Mrs. Ferrers. ARABELLA KENEALY
Author of "Nerissa," "The Making of Anthea," "Dr. Janet of Harley Street," "The Woman-Hunter," etc.

The irresistible Mrs. Ferrers is a fashionable beauty, the loveliest, wittiest, best-dressed and most fascinating woman of her century. She is the idol of London society. Hostesses fight and plot to get her to their parties. The men of her world vie with one another for the privilege of driving her to Hurlingham. And yet no breath of scandal touches her. For her ambition is to be known to history as the most beautiful and brilliant woman of her day who charmed all men and succumbed to none. But Lord Lygon comes, a clever and attractive man, estranged from his wife. He lays siege to her, and the story turns upon the rivalry and struggle of the two women; of the wife who devotedly loves him, and of the other who, though fond of him, is loth to sacrifice her dazzling impeccability and to forego her unique position for his sake. A young doctor complicates matters, and there is a scene between Mrs. Ferrers and a homicidal maniac in which she needs all her wits for self-defence. There are some charming children in the book and some original views on the woman question.

The Three Anarchists. MAUD STEPNEY RAWSON
Author of "A Lady of the Regency," "The Stairway of Honour," "The Enchanted Garden," "The Easy-Go-Luckies," etc.

There are fine and beautiful things in this novel. There is true delicate psychology and clean bold handling of subjects which in feebler hands might easily have been unpleasant, if not offensive. There is true pathos and a fine perception of the importance of the tiny incidents and minor happenings of daily life as affecting the human drama. Janet is the unsatisfied, soul-starved young wife of an elderly, weak, cruel and penurious man, and the other principal character is a human stepson at inevitable enmity with so opposite a father, both craving for the fullness of life, the woman a real woman all through, with a fine perception of what is right, intensely desirous of founding a real home and making real happiness; and the young man of warm flesh and blood responding to her pure woman's love and care with more than mere affection. And yet there is not a false note in all the narrative which after a tragic happening ends finely.

A Grey Life: A Romance of Modern Bath. "RITA"
Author of "Peg the Rake," "My Lord Conceit," "Countess Daphne," "Grim Justice," etc.

"Rita" has chosen Bath as a setting for her new novel. She has disdained the "powder and patches" period, and given her characters the more modern interests of Bath's transition stage in the seventies and eighties. Her book deals with the struggles of an impoverished Irish family of three sisters—who establish themselves in Bath—to whom comes an orphaned niece with the romantic name of Rosaleen Le Suir. She is only a child of fourteen when she arrives, but it is her pen that weaves the story and its fascinating mystery of the Grey Lady in the attics. The history and sad tragedies of this recluse give the story its title, though fuller interest is woven into the brilliant and erratic personality of a certain Chevalier Theophrastus O'Shaughnessey, at once the most charming and original sketch of the Irish adventurer ever penned by a modern writer. In fact, one might safely say that the Chevalier is the male prototype of "Rita's" wonderful and immortal "Peg the Rake."

The Three Destinies. J. A. T. LLOYD

Author of "The Lady of Kensington Gardens," "A Great Russian Realist," etc.

The scene of this novel opens in the Elgin Room of the British Museum, where its *dramatis personae* are grouped by chance in front of the familiar statue of the "Three Fates." Among them are three young girls and a boy of eighteen, all quite at the beginning of things and vaguely interested in the mysterious future before them. The fact that they have grouped themselves in front of this particular statue attracts the attention of an old professor, who determines to bring them together again, and experiment with their young lives with the same curiosity that a chemist experiments with chemicals. The scene shifts from the Elgin Room to Ireland, and then to Paris and Brittany, Vienna and Dalmatia, but the hero is always under the spell of that first chance meeting in front of the statue. One person after the other plays with his life, and again and again he and the others report themselves on New Year's Day to the old professor, who reads half mockingly the jumble of lives that he himself has produced. In the end the hero realises that these young girls have become to him in turn modern interpreters of the three ancient Destinies.

The King's Master.

OLIVE LETHBRIDGE and JOHN DE STOURTON

A novel dealing with the troubulous times of Henry VIII., in which the political situation, Court intrigues and religious discussions of the period are treated in a masterly manner. A strong love element is introduced, and the characters of Anne Boleyn and Thomas Cromwell are presented in an entirely new light, while plot and counter-plot, hair-breadth escapes, love, hate, revenge, and triumph all go to form the theme.

Maggie of Margate. A Romance of the Idle Rich.

GABRIELLE WODNIL

, "Maggie of Margate," a beautiful girl with an unobtrusive style which attracted nine men out of ten, was in reality an exclusive lady of title, bored because she sighed for realism and romance, and was affianced to a prospective peer. How she contrived a dual individuality is the pith of the story, which is in no way high flown. Maggie is a delightful creation, and her very erring frailty and duplicity makes us pity her the more. She cannot break away finally from her social status, but to retain it she nearly breaks her heart. The man of her fancy, *Michael Blair*, is the most striking figure in the whole story, which teems with varied characters, all of which hold us intently from the first page to the last. All the world loves a lover, and, therefore, every one will love Michael Blair.

The Celebrity's Daughter. VIOLET HUNT

Author of "The Doll," "White Rose of Weary Leaf," etc.

Life-like portraits, a tangled plot, only fully unravelled in the last chapter, go to the making of Miss Violet Hunt's stories. "The Celebrity's Daughter" has the humour, smart dialogue, the tingling life of this clever writer's earlier novels. It is the autobiography of the daughter of a celebrity who has fallen on evil days. Told in the author's inimitable style.

Paul Burdon. SIR WILLIAM MAGNAY

Author of "The Fruits of Indiscretion," "The Long Hand," etc.

This is a strong story full of exciting incidents. The hero is a farmer crippled for want of capital, which he finds quite unexpectedly. A thunderstorm and an irate husband cause a young banker to seek refuge at the farm, from which a loud knocking causes further retreat to a big family tomb, which becomes his own when the lightning brings some old ruins down and buries both. The banker's bag of gold falls into the hands of the farmer, who profits by its use. Other characters play important parts, and love interest adds its softening charm.

Cheerful Craft.   R. ANDOM

Author of "We Three and Troddles," "Neighbours of Mine."
With 60 original illustrations.

There is nothing sombre or introspective about "Cheerful Craft," and those who agree with Mr. Balfour's view of the need of lighter and brighter books will find here something to please them. Broad humour and rollicking adventure characterise this story. A city clerk rises from obscurity and attains to a position of wealth and dignity, and carries us with him all the way, condoning his rascality for the sake of his ready humour and cheery optimism. After all he is a merry rogue, and he works no great harm to anyone, and much good to himself, and incidentally to most of those with whom he comes in contact. We hardly know in which form to like him most, as Hilary Ford, ex-clerk, lounger and tramp, or Havelock Rose, the son of a wealthy ship-owner, whose place he usurps under circumstances which do credit to the writer's ingenuity without putting too great a strain on the credulity of the reader.

Love's Cross Roads.   L. T. MEADE

Author of "Desborough's Wife," "Ruffles," etc.

This is the story of a good and honourable man who in a moment of sudden temptation fell. How his sin found him out—what he suffered from remorse; how, with all his strivings, he was nearly circumvented, and how, just when he thought all would be well, he nearly lost what was far above gold to him is ably described. The story is highly exciting, and from the first page to the last it would be difficult to put the book down. The account of the villain who sought to ruin Paul Colthurst, and to cause the death of either young Peter or Pamala, is full of terrible interest. But perhaps the most truly life-like character in the whole book is Silas Luke, the poor miserable tramp, who though bribed, tempted, tortured, yet could not bring himself to do the evil thing suggested, and who was saved by the sweet girl who was meant to be his victim. The repentance of the tramp leads to the greater repentance of Paul Colthurst. The story ends happily.

The Swelling of Jordan.   CORALIE STANTON AND

HEATH HOSKIN. Authors of "Plumage," "The Muzzled Ox," etc.

Canon Oriel, an earnest worker in the East End, loved and respected, had years before the story commences, while climbing with his friend Digby Cavan in Switzerland, found in the pocket of his friend's coat, which he had accidentally put on instead of his own, evidence that his friend had robbed his, the canon's, brother and been the cause of his committing suicide. Oriel, in a struggle which took place between the two men, hurled his friend from the precipice. Now the glacier gives up Cavan's rucksack, and any day it may yield up his body. To reveal subsequent developments would spoil the reader's enjoyment of a thrilling plot.

Opal of October.   JOY SHIRLEY

For those born in the month of October, the opal is said to be a lucky stone, and this novel is based upon the assumption that it is so. It is a story of the times of the soothsayers and the witches, when people were all more or less trying to discover the philosopher's stone which turns everything to gold. The witch in this case is a young girl of great beauty, who narrowly escapes the stake

Galbraith of Wynyates.   E. EVERETT-GREEN

Author of "Duckworth's Diamonds," "Clive Lorimer's Marriage," etc., etc.

This is a story of the ill consequence following upon the making of an unwise will. Joyce is the only daughter of the real owner of Wynyates who has let the property to a relative who is the next-of-kin after his daughter. Warned of the uncertainty of his own life he wills the property to his daughter in trust during her minority, and appoints the relative who holds the property as tenant, trustee. Overhearing a conversation between the family lawyer and her uncle, who discuss the unwisdom of placing her in the charge of one who is directly interested in her death, she imagines all kinds of evil intentions on the part of her guardian, and looks with suspicion upon all his counsels for her welfare. Love interests lead to complications, but the unfaithfulness of her lover leaves her free and she finally marries the guardian of whom she had stood so long in fear. It is a very readable book written in the author's best style.

The Ban. LESTER LURGAN

Author of " The Mill-owner," " Bohemian Blood," etc., etc.

This is a story of mystery involving the Ban of Blood. Brenda is a pretty, charming, and very feminine girl of good English family who marries one who adores her, but who has, unknown to himself, Red-Indian blood in his veins. This is revealed to him by an old nurse on her death-bed, and is demonstrated on his return to his wife by the birth of a son who bears unmistakable signs of the terrible inheritance. An old mystery is explained, and new tragedies follow. The child is placed under the care of the grandmother's tribe but soon succumbs, nor does the father long survive the awful experience. After his death Brenda marries her childhood's playmate and first love.

Bright Shame. KEIGHLEY SNOWDEN

Author of " The Free Marriage," " The Plunder Pit," " Hate of Evil," etc.

Stephen Gaunt, an English sculptor famous in Italy, is the father of a son born out of wedlock, whom he has never heard of. In his youth, a light attachment broken in a causeless fit of jealousy drove him abroad, but when the story opens he is a strong and engaging personality. He comes home to execute a commission, and meets his son without knowing him. In doing so, he encounters a couple, childless themselves, who have passed the boy off as their own since infancy, when his mother died. They are an elder half-brother, who has always hated Stephen, and his sensitive, tender and simple wife, who loves the boy with all her heart, fears to lose him, and who is yet tormented by her secret. A romantic friendship springs up between son and father; and the chain of accidents and proofs by which he learns the truth, his struggle for control of the boy, who has genius, and the effect of these events on the boy and his foster mother make a fascinating plot.

A Star of the East : A Story of Delhi. CHARLES

E. PEARCE. Author of " The Amazing Duchess," " The Beloved Princess," " Love Besieged," " Red Revenge," etc.

"East is East and West is West, and never the twain shall meet." This is the theme of Mr. Pearce's new novel of life in India. The scene is laid in Delhi, the city of all others where for the past hundred years the traditions of ancient dynasties and the barbaric splendours of the past have been slowly retreating before the ever-advancing influence of the West. The conflict of passions between Nara, the dancing girl, in whose veins runs the blood of Shah jehan, the most famous of the Kings of Delhi, and Clare Stanhope, born and bred in English conventionality, never so pronounced as in the Fifties, is typical of the differences between the East and the West. The rivalry of love threads its way through a series of exciting incidents, culminating in the massacre and the memorable siege of Delhi. This book completes the trilogy of Mr. Pearce's novels of the Indian Mutiny, of which " Love Besieged " and " Red Revenge " were the first and second.

The Destiny of Claude. MAY WYNNE

Author of " Henri of Navarre," " The Red Fleur de Lys," " Honour's Fetters," etc.

Claude de Marbeille to escape a convent life joins her friend Margot de Ladrennes in Touraine. Jacques Comte de Ladrennes, a hunchback, falls in love with her, and when the two girls go to Paris to enter the suite of the fifteen year old Mary Queen of Scots, he follows and takes service with the Duke of Guise. Claude, however, falls in love with Archie Cameron, an officer of the Scottish Guard, who by accident discovers how Queen Mary has been tricked by her Uncles of Guise into signing papers bequeathing Scotland to France in the event of her dying childless. Cameron is imprisoned, but escapes in time to warn the Scots Commissioners on their way home of this act of treachery. Cameron is followed by a spy of the Guises, and the four Commissioners die by poison. Cameron recovers, and returns to Paris to find that Claude has been sent to some unknown Convent. The rest of the tale relates Cameron's search for his sweetheart, the self-sacrifice of the Comte de Ladrennes, and the repentance and atonement of Margot de Ladrennes, who through jealousy betrays her friend.

Susan and the Duke.   KATE HORN

Author of. "Edward and I and Mrs. Honeybun," "The White Owl," "The Lovelocks of Diana," etc.

Lord Christopher Fitzarden, younger brother of the Duke of Cheadle, is the most delightful of young men. He adopts the old family servants destined for the almshouses by the cynical Duke, who bestows upon him the family house in Mayfair. Nanny, his old nurse, keeps him in order. Susan Ringsford, the heroine, is an early visitor. She is in love with Kit, but he falls madly in love with Rosalind Pilkington, the heiress of a rich manufacturer. The contrast between the two girls is strongly drawn. Susan, sweet and refined—a strong character but of insignificant appearance, and Rosalind radiantly beautiful—ambitious and coarse of nature. The whole party go caravanning with Lady Barchester and an affected little poet, and many love scenes are woven into the tour in the New Forest. Susan and the Duke of Cheadle have a conversation—the Duke loves her in silence, and sees that she loves his brother. He gets up a flirtation with Rosalind, who, anxious to be a duchess, throws over Kit immediately. The Duke disillusions her. Meanwhile Susan and Kit have come together, and the book ends with wedding bells.

Lonesome Land.   B. M. BOWER

A strong, human story in which Valeria Peyson, an Eastern girl, goes out to a desolate Montana town to marry the lover who has preceded her three years before. Unfortunately the lover has not had the moral fibre to stand the unconventionality of Western life, and has greatly deteriorated. However, they marry and live on his ranch, where Valeria finds that the country and her husband are by no means what she thought them. She does her best to make the life endurable and is aided by the kindness of her husband's closest friend, a rough diamond with an honest heart. Out of this situation is unfolded a strong tale of character development and overmastering love that finds a dramatic outcome in happiness for those most deserving it.

Confessions of Perpetua.   ALICE M. DIEHL

Author of "A Mysterious Lover," "The Marriage of Lenore," etc.

Perpetua is the youngest of three daughters of a baronet, all of whom make wealthy marriages, a duke, a viscount and a colonel sharing the baronet's family. The story opens when Perpetua emerges from the care of her governess and enters society under the auspices of the duchess. She marries against the warnings of the countess and divorces the colonel within three months of their union; and yet all proceeds in a perfectly natural and straightforward manner. The process of disillusion from love's enchantment is well described, and other Perpetuas may well learn a lesson from the heroine's experience. The characters are well drawn and distinct, and the narrative develops dramatic incidents from time to time.

A Modern Ahab.   THEODORA WILSON WILSON

Author of "Bess of Hardendale," "Moll o' the Toll-Bar," etc.

This is a very readable novel in the author's best manner. Rachael Despenser, a successful artist, spends a summer holiday in a Westmoreland village, living at an old farm-house, and making friends of the people. Grimstone, a local baronet, is grabbing the land to make a deer run, and Rachael comes into collision with him, but is adored by his delicate little son. Right-of-way troubles ensue, and violence disturbs the peace. Grimstone's elder son and heir returns from Canada, where he has imbibed Radical notions. He sympathises with the villagers, and is attracted towards Rachael, whom he marries. The baronet determines to oust the farmer whom Rachael had championed, when the tragic death of his delicate little son leads him to relinquish the management of the estate to his heir.

The Annals of Augustine.   RAFAEL SABATINI

Author of "Bardelys the Magnificent," "The Lion's Skin," etc.

Mr. Sabatini lays before his readers in "The Annals of Augustine" a startling and poignant human document of the Italian Renaissance. It is the autobiographical memoir of Augustine, Lord of Mondolfo, one of the lesser tyrants of Æmilia, a man pre-natally vowed to the cloister by his over-devout mother. With merciless self-analysis does Augustine in these memoirs reveal his distaste for the life to which he was foredoomed, and his early efforts to break away from the repellant path along which he is being forced. The Lord of Mondolfo's times are the times of the Farnese Pope (Paul III.), whose terrible son, Pier Luigi Farnese, first Duke of Parma, lives again, sinister and ruthless, in these pages. As a mirror of the Cinquecento, "The Annals of Augustine" deserves to take an important place, whilst for swiftness of action and intensity of romantic interest it stands alone.

Dagobert's Children. L. J. BEESTON

"Mr. Beeston's spirited work is already well known to a large circle of readers, but this book is the most powerful he has yet written, and for plot, dramatic incident, and intensity of emotion reaches a very high level. The successive chapters are alive with all the breath and passion of war, and are written with a vividness and power which holds the reader's interest to the last word."

The Redeemer. RENÉ BAZIN

Author of "The Children of Alsace," "The Nun," "Redemption," etc.

This is a romance of village life in the Loire country, with love complications which awaken sympathy and absorb interest. Davideé is a junior mistress in the village school, and the story mainly concerns her love attraction and moral restraint. She is drawn towards Maievel jacquet, a worker in the slate quarries near by, with whom Phrosine, a beautiful young woman who has left her husband, is living. Davideé befriends them, but on the death of their child Maievel goes away, and Phrosine, who dislikes Davideé because of her superior morality, goes in search of her son by her husband. Both return to the village, and Phrosine seeks reunion with Maievel, who refuses her, telling her that their dead son bars the way. Phrosine attributes this to the interposition of Davideé, and ultimately leaves with another lover. There is now no longer any barrier between Maievel and Davideé, who can hence follow her attraction without violating her scruples.

The She-Wolf. MAXIME FORMONT

Author of "A Child of Chance," etc. Translated from the French by Elsie F. Buckley.

This is a powerful novel of the life and times of Cæsar Borgia, in which history and romance are mingled with a strong hand. The author holds Cæsar guilty of the murder of his brother, and shows a strong motive for the crime. The story of the abduction of Alva Colonna on the eve of her marriage with Proslero Sarelli, when she is carried off to his palace at Rome and becomes his slave-mistress, is related. The subsequent events, more or less following history or tradition, include the intro-duction of the dark woman of gipsy extraction, who enamours Cæsar, and poisons the wine by which the Colonna and her old lover Sarelli die. Cæsar is shown strong, brutal, unscrupulous and triumphant. The story closes with a description of his last days and death. This novel has been highly popular in France.

Her Majesty the Flapper. A. E. JAMES

With a picture wrapper of "Her Majesty" in colours.

There is a fresh, natural touch about these episodes in the development of a Flapper which make them breezy and refreshing reading, involving no little amuse-ment. Her Majesty the Flapper is a lady-flapper, of course, neither a bounder nor a cad, but just a flapper. Accessories, willing or unwilling, are her cousins Victoria and Bobbie, a male person over thirty, who tells most of the story, though the Flapper is as irrepressible in the telling of the story as in acting it. Of course, Bobbie is victimised, and the story ends with the coming out of the Flapper, and the final victimisation takes the form of an engagement. Readers will sympathise with Bobbie, and some will envy him.

Chaff and the Wind. G. VILLIERS STUART

Chaff and the Wind is a novel showing the working of the unseen hand, and telling the story of a man who shirked his destiny, and who was forced to watch the career of another who rose to heights of national fame, while he himself drifted like chaff before the wind. It is a novel of incident illustrating a theory, and is therefore more dramatic than psychological. The action of life and destiny on character is more indicated than the action of character on life.

26

The Marble Aphrodite. ANTHONY KIRBY GILL

An imaginative story of a young sculptor who, inspired by Venus, produces an Aphrodite of amazing loveliness and nobility. Carroll, the chief character, is an idealist, a devotee of art, and a worshipper of beauty, and the main theme of the novel is centred in and about his creation of this statue. Other characters include a painter who encourages his young friend's idealism, a wealthy aristocrat of a cynical bent of mind, a beautiful and accomplished actress, a poet, and a society lady married to a man of evil reputation. The conflicting interests of these people, the effects of their actions, tragic and otherwise, the scenes in the studios and the society, theatrical, and Bohemian scenes, including the glimpse given of the night side of London life, form a realistic background or setting for the principal motive, which, though closely interwoven with it, is of a purely imaginative and idealistic character. Psychological analysis enters largely into the author's treatment, and the story reflects here and there certain mental movements of the day.

The Poodle-Woman. ANNESLEY KENEALY
Author of "Thus Saith Mrs. Grundy."

Miss Annesley Kenealy's new novel deals with the feminine side of the great unrest of our time, and she sets herself to answer the questions " What do Women Want? " and "What is the cause of their great unrest ? " It is a charming love story, dealing mainly with two women, a man, and a mannikin. It presents femininism from an entirely fresh standpoint, but polemics are entirely absent. In a series of living moving pictures it shows how the games of life and matrimony are played under rules which put all the best cards of the pack into men's hands. The heroine is an emotional Irish girl, with the reckless romance of the Celt and the chivalry of a woman, who keeps sweet through very bitter experiences. Possessing no world craft she is slave to her heart, and gives and forgives unto seventy times seven. The book is epigrammatic and full of humour.

The Romance of Bayard. LT.-COL. ANDREW C. P.
HAGGARD, D.S.O. Author of "The France of Joan of Arc," " Two Worlds," etc.

"The Romance of Bayard" is one of perennial interest, as a "life," as a "thing of beauty," is a joy for ever. The story of the chevalier, who was "without fear and without reproach " cannot too often be told. The story opens on the " Field of the Cloth of Gold," and its personelle includes Henry of England, Francis of France, the French Queen-mother, the Princess Marguerita, who loved Bayard with intense devotion, and Anne Boleyn, a young French maid of honour. It ends with Bayard's death during the fatal expedition into Italy in 1524. The romance places Marguerita and Anne Boleyn at his side at the last. Col. Haggard's historical romances are all well known and highly popular at the libraries and with the general public, and this one is not likely to fall short of high appreciation.

A Durbar Bride. CHARLOTTE CAMERON
Author of "A Passion in Morocco," "A Woman's Winter in South America," etc.

This is a wonderfully interesting novel, conducting one through labyrinths of exciting scenes and chapters with not a dull moment in the entire production. It is written in Charlotte Cameron's most brilliant style. In the first chapters the author depicts the misery of a young bride whose husband became hopelessly insane during their honeymoon. The pathetic story graphically narrated of Muriel's unsatisfactory life, neither maid, wife, nor widow, and the injustice of the law which binds a woman until death to a mad man is admirably portrayed. Mrs. Cameron is the only writer who has as yet given us from an eye-witness point of view a romance on the Imperial Durbar at Delhi ; where, as the representative of several papers, she had the opportunity of attending the entire ceremonials. The life at the Government Camps, the sweet love story of the hero and heroine, the simple marriage ceremony in Skinner's historic church at Delhi will prove a keen enjoyment to the readers. Their Majesties the Queen, and Queen Alexandra have graciously accepted copies of this novel.

The Career of Beauty Darling. DOLF WYLLARDE

Author of " The Riding Master," " The Unofficial Honeymoon."

" The Career of Beauty Darling" is a story of the musical comedy stage, and endeavours to set forth both the vices and virtues of the life without prejudice. If the temptations are manifold, the author finds much good also in those who pursue this particular branch of the profession, for she says " there are no kinder hearts in the world, I think, than those that beat under the finery of the chorus girl, no better humanity than that' which may be found behind the paint and powder and the blistered eyes." Miss Wyllarde has made plain statements in this, her latest book, and has not shrunk from the realism of the life; but, as she says, even the general public knows that the dazzle and glitter from the front of the footlights is a very different view to that which may be seen behind the curtain.

The Retrospect. ADA CAMBRIDGE

Author of " Thirty Years in Australia," " A Little Minx," etc.

" There can be little hesitation in asserting that this is one of the most delightful books of the year."—*Aberdeen Free Press*

" Miss Cambridge has such a delightful style, and so much of interest to tell us, that the reader closes the book with the sensation of having bidden a dear friend farewell." —*Bristol Times and Mirror.*

" Written throughout with an engaging literary grace."—*Scotsman.*

Francesca. CECIL ADAIR

Author of " The Qualities of Mercy," " Cantacute Towers," etc.

This author possesses all the qualities which make for popularity and can be relied upon to arrest and maintain interest from first to last. The *Guardian* reviewing " Canticute Towers" said—" In it we seem to see a successor of Rosa N Carey," and those who admire the work of Miss Carey cannot do better than take the hint. A strong human interest always appeals to the reader and satisfies perusal.

The Strength of the Hills. HALLIWELL SUTCLIFFE

Author of " A Benedick in Arcady," " Priscilla of the Good Intent," etc.

In this novel Mr. Halliwell Sutcliffe returns to the Haworth Moorland which was the inspiration of all his earlier work; it deals with the strenuous life of the moors sixty years ago and will rank with his strongest and best works. Those who remember our author's " Man of the Moors," " An' Episode in Arcady," " A Bachelor in Arcady," and " A Benedick in Arcady " will not hesitate to follow him anywhere across the moorlands in the direction of Arcadia

Officer 666. BARTON W. CURRIE and AUGUSTIN McHUGH

An uproarious piece of American wit fresh from the Gaiety Theatre, New York, which will be produced on the London boards and in France some time this autumn. It is from the pen of Mr. Augustin McHugh, who has associated himself with Mr. Barton W. Currie in producing it in novel form. Its dramatic success in America has been phenomenal; and whether as a play or a novel, it will doubtless receive a warm welcome in this country.

Devil's Brew. MICHAEL W. KAYE

Author of " The Cardinal's Past," " A Robin Hood of France," etc.

Jack Armiston, awaking to the fact that life has other meaning than that given it by a fox-hunting squire, becomes acquainted with Henry Hunt, the socialist demagogue, but after many vicissitudes, during which he finds he has sacrificed friends and sweetheart to a worthless propaganda, he becomes instrumental in baulking the Cato Street Conspirators of their plot to murder the members of the Cabinet, and eventually regains his old standing—and Pamela. A spirited story.

The Fruits of Indiscretion. Sir William Magnay

Author of "The Long Hand," "Paul Burdon," etc.

This is a story of murder and mystery, in which the interest is well sustained and the characters are convincing. It is absorbing without being melodramatic, and thrilling without being sensational. There is to be a wedding at a country house on the eve of which the best man is killed in the hunting field. Captain Routham is asked to take his place, but disappears. His body is found on the railway track. Rolt, a famous detective, is put on the scent, and gradually probes the mystery. Routham had had a love affair with the heroine in former years, and had been blackmailing her. There is a rascally lawyer in the case who is killed in a carriage accident, and is so saved criminal consequences. In the end the heroine marries her lover.

The Tragedy of the Nile. Douglas Sladen

Author of "The Unholy Estate," "The Tragedy : of the Pyramids," etc.

A military novel dealing with the fate and re-conquest of Khartum. This is even more military than Mr. Sladen's "Tragedy of the Pyramids" and "The Unholy Estate." Mr. Sladen is at his best when he is describing battles, and the book is full of them; but, like Mr. Sladen's other books, it is also full of romance. The author, never content with an ordinary plain-sailing engagement between two young persons, selects one of the *cruces* which present themselves in real life and love. This time it is the case of a beautiful white woman who, being captured at the fall of Khartum, has to enter the harem of Wad-el-Nejumi, the bravest of all the generals of the Mahdi. When she is rescued on the fatal field of Toski, the question arises, Can a white man marry her? There are great figures standing forth in Mr. Sladen's pages—above all, the heroic Gordon in his last great moments at Khartum, and Wad-el-Nejumi, who stormed Khartum and died so grandly at Toski.

The Memoirs of Mimosa. Edited by Anne Elliot

This is a book calculated to make as great a sensation as the famous *Journal* of Marie Bashkirtseff, which electrified a whole continent some years ago; or *The Diary of a Lost One*, which set Germany ringing more recently. It is the intimate and unflinching confession of a brilliant, erotic, and undisciplined woman, who resolves to "live every moment of her life," and succeeds in so doing at the cost of much suffering to herself and others. Her mixture of worldliness, sentiment, fancy, passion, and extraordinary *joie de vivre* make her a fascinating study of a type somewhat rare. At her death she bequeathed these Memoirs to the woman friend who edits them and presents them to the world. We get the woman's point of view in all matters—poetry, politics, sport, music, the stage, and, dominating all, the great problems of sex.

The Return of Pierre. Donal Hamilton Haines

With a frontispiece from a painting by Edouard Detaille.

This is not a novel about the Franco-Prussian War, but the very human story of Pierre, with some of the scenes of the heroic struggle as a background Pierre, a country lad, is the central figure. Other prominent figures are the woman Pierre loves, her father—a fine old Colonel of Dragoons—and a German spy, not without attractive qualities, whose fate becomes strangely entangled with theirs. The book abounds in striking situations, including the discovery and escape of the spy—the departure of the Dragoons for the war—the remorse of a French General who feels personally responsible for the men he has lost—night in a hospital-tent—the last flicker of the defence of Paris and the entry of the German troops.

The Incorrigible Dukane. George C. Shedd

This is a vigorous and inspiriting story of Western life. Jimmy Dukane, son of a cement king, who, disgusted with his son's extravagances, gives him a limited sum, and orders him to go and inspect a dam in course of construction in Nevada, or by way of a pleasant alternative—starve. Jimmy goes and passes through numerous adventures. Has his outfit stolen on his arrival at the nearest station, is knocked about, bullied and impounded by one of the dam men, and has to work as a navvy. Showing grit, he works his way up, and discovers that the manager is defrauding the company, and constructing a fatally faulty dam. Taking command, he saves the Company's reputation for sound workmanship. There is a love story in it, and Enid, the fair, fearless daughter of the superintendent, enables all to end well.

The Thread of Proof.   HEADON HILL
Author of "Troubled Waters," etc.

The principal theme of this volume is the abnormal astuteness of the conductor of a railway restaurant-car, whose power of observation and deduction enables him to solve the many absorbing "mysteries" that come under his ken, and which, as a preventer and detector of crime, put him on a par with any of the great puzzle-readers of fiction. Mr. Headon Hill goes direct to the point, and carries the reader rapidly along from the first page to the last.

A Robin Hood of France.   MICHAEL W. KAYE
Author of "The Duke's Vengeance," etc., etc.

Hated at court and falsely accused of murder, the young Sieur de Pontenac flees to the Forest of Fontainebleau, and becomes the leader of a band of robbers (King Mandrin), beloved of the oppressed canaille, but hated of the nobles, whom he defies and robs. Claire d'Orgiuel, the only child of the Comte d'Orgiuel, having lost heavily at cards, wagers the winner—who has her in his power, and who hopes to force her to marry him—that she will lure "King Mandrin" into the power of his enemies; but, arriving in the Forest of Fontainebleau, ends in falling in love with the "Robin Hood of France."

Neighbours of Mine.   R. ANDOM
Author of "We Three and Troddles," "In Fear of a Throne," etc
With 70 original illustrations by L. GUNNIS.

This broadly farcical story of types and incidents of suburban life will afford as much amusement as the famous "Troddles" books which have in volume form successfully appealed to something like 200,000 readers of all classes, and should prove as popular with those who like a rollicking story. Now and again the author conveys a moral, discreetly, but generally he is content to be extravagantly amusing in depicting adventures, which are sufficiently out of the ordinary to be termed "singular." The book is cleverly and amusingly illustrated throughout the text by a popular artist, who has admirably succeeded in catching the drollery of the narrative

The Loves of Stella.   MRS. SHIERS-MASON
Author of "Hubert Sherbrook, Priest."

Stella O'Donovan, a very poor but also very beautiful and quite unsophisticated Irish girl, lives in an old castle on a lovely but lonely Bay on the Irish coast. She has Spanish blood in her veins, and much of the impulsive and fascinating temperament of the Andalusians. Becoming heiress to a million of money, she decides to go to London and enter Society. Before her departure, a young Norwegian sculptor, Olaf Johansen, of striking appearance, comes to reside in the village. He at once falls in love with Stella, who returns his affection, but who, doubtful of herself, flees to London. Here she appears to meet Olaf again, but it is his twin brother impersonating him. Stella at once succumbs to his love-making, and many highly dramatic scenes follow.

Damosel Croft.   MURRAY GILCHRIST

World says—"As good as taking a holiday to read this tranquil tale of Peakland and its people. . . . The book is redolent of peace and rural beauty and restfulness." *Standard* says—". . . delicious interiors, glimpses of country shining with happiness, old customs and traditions, leaving us at the last with a sense of rest and tranquility, worth, for its refreshment, a thousand plots, a thousand popular romances."

A Babe in Bohemia. FRANK DANBY

Author of " The Heart of a Child," " Dr. Phillips," etc.

This author is not a prolific writer, and, therefore, every work from her pen is awaited with much interest. She stands alone among the best modern writers for originality and freshness in style. This full length novel has been out of print for many years and has now been practically rewritten by the author. Although the thread of the story remains every page has been extensively revised, and will be found to be as good as anything recently done by this popular writer.

The Consort. MRS. EVERARD COTES (SARA JEANNETTE

DUNCAN). Author of " The Burnt Offering," " Cousin Cinderella," " The Path of a Star," etc.

The story of a little man married to a great woman, of their relations and interactions, their battles and despairs, written round the strong and familiar interests of passion and power. The story moves at a gallop, and it is for the reader to meditate and moralise when the book is laid aside.

The Villa Mystery. HERBERT FLOWERDEW

Author of " The Second Elopement," " The Third Wife," etc.

Woven in with the mystery of a crime as baffling as anything imagined by Gaboriau, the pretty love story of Esmond Hare and Elsa Armandy engages the reader's sympathy from the moment of their first meeting. This is in a lonely country road, at midnight, where Elsa is on her knees picking up handfuls of sovereigns that do not exactly belong to her, and the atmosphere of mingled mystery and romance continues to surround their moving and unconventional love story up to the moment of its happy ending.

Prince and Priest. BERYL SYMONS

Author of " A Lady of France."

A romance of mediæval France, which contains atmosphere, colour, life and movement. 1207 is the date when the story opens. Count Bertrand de Crein falls in love with the beautiful Lady Rosamund, whom he is escorting to the Lord of Gervandan in Toulouse, whose wife she is to be. In the meantime the Count of Toulouse is threatened with Rome's curse and an armed crusade to put down heresy. In the subsequent siege and sack of Beziers, Rosamund's husband is killed, and the love of Rosamund and de Crein culminates in marriage. The book is full of excitement, adventure, thrilling escapes, and heart-stirring romance.

Brass Faces. CHARLES McEVOY

An exciting modern story of grip and power, some of the most startling episodes of which concern the kidnapping of a girl who has been turned out of house and home by her father and imprisoned in a house in Kensington. She is rescued by a bachelor, who in turn finds himself in a delicate position. An American female detective plots his arrest and ruin. The story rushes on in a whirl of excitement through a maze of plots and counterplots to a dramatic *dénouement*.

The Meteoric Benson. VINCENT MILLS-MALET

A decidedly new note has been struck in this most readable and interesting novel. As the name indicates it is an aeroplane story, and one of those rare books which must be read at a sitting; incident follows incident in ever-increasing interest, until the reader, breathless from excitement, learns from the last page " what really did happen."

Between Two Stools (Fifth Edition). By RHODA

BROUGHTON. Author of "Red as a Rose is She," "Cometh up as a Flower," etc.

The *Times* says:—"In point of plot, 'Between Two Stools' belongs to the category of Mr. Maxwell's 'Guarded Flame.' ... Few readers, we imagine, would fail to fall in love with so fresh and delightful a heroine as Arethusa. The scene at the end reveals Miss Broughton at her very best."

The Justice of the Duke. (3rd ed.) By RAFAEL

SABATINI. Author of "The Shame of Motley," "The Trampling of the Lilies," "Cesare Borgia," "The Lion's Skin," etc.

The *Globe* says:—"What Mr. Sabatini does not know about the life and times of Cesare Borgia is not worth considering ... excellent."

Exotic Martha (Third Edition). By DOROTHEA

GERARD. Author of "The City of Enticement," etc.

Truth says:—"The story is full of incident, and is told in a lively and humorous fashion."
The *Globe* says:—"The plot is worked out with much ingenuity, and its interest enhanced by the picture of life in the Dutch Colony at Java."

The Unholy Estate; or, the Sins of the Fathers

(Fifth Edition). By DOUGLAS SLADEN. Author of "A Japanese Marriage," "The Admiral," "The Tragedy of the Pyramids," etc.

The *Times* says:—"A vivacious and resourceful novel."
The *World* says:—"An exciting and delightful story filled with marvellously vivid pictures of life in Cairo. One which has not a dull line in it, and will certainly entertain men as much as it will interest and move women."

The Woman-Hunter (Fourth Edition). By ARABELLA

KENEALY. Author of "The Irresistible Mrs. Ferrers," etc.

The *Pall Mall Gazette* says:—"A strong story, admirably told, full of life and passion, and quite the best novel this gifted authoress has written."
The *World* says:—"Clever all through, and those who like psychological novels will readily admit that Miss Kenealy has most skilfully dealt with emotions which are not easily conveyed in cold print."

The Consort (Third Edition). By MRS. EVERARD COTES

(Sara Jeannette Duncan)

The *Daily News* says:—"This is a very clever novel."
The *Daily Telegraph* describes it as "a subtly told story, one which needs a psychological interest on the part of those who peruse it if they are to extract the full flavour."

The Watch Night. A Story of the Times of John

Wesley. By HENRY BETT.

The *Times* describes this book as "a capital picture of the times."
The *Westminster Gazette* calls it "a capital historical novel. ... It is curiously effective in suggesting a bygone day—and this without any of the stock archaisms.
... Vivian may or not be a fictional personality, but he and his fellow-sojourners in these pages are most skilfully presented, and we offer our congratulations to the author."

The Second Woman (Second Edition). By NORMA

LORIMER.

The *Daily Chronicle* calls this book "an interesting story of many emotions."
Literary World says:—"The story is sympathetic and well-written. The pictures of Italy and Italian life are delightful, and make a charming background for a really good tale."

Messrs. Stanley Paul's Publications

Arranged in order of price, from 3d. upwards

⁂ PREVIOUS LISTS CANCELLED

32/- NET

Napoleon in Exile. St. Helena 1815-1821. By NORWOOD YOUNG, with a chapter on the Iconography of Napoleon at St. Helena. By A. M. BROADLEY. Two coloured plates and about 100 illustrations from the collection of A. M. Broadley. Two vols., demy 8vo, 32/- net the set (*see also under 21/-*).

30/- NET

The Library Encyclopædia. By the Foremost Authorities. Edited by ALEX. J. PHILIP. To be issued by Subscription.

28/- NET

The Life and Letters of Laurence Sterne. LEWIS MELVILLE. Two vols., demy 8vo, with coloured frontispiece and other illustrations.

24/- NET

Intimate Society Letters of the 18th Century. By HIS GRACE THE DUKE OF ARGYLL, K.T. In two volumes, demy 8vo, cloth gilt and gilt top. With two photogravure frontispieces and 56 other full-page illustrations, printed on art paper, of original letters, autographs, and other interesting matter.

An Imperial Victim: MARIE LOUISE, ARCHDUCHESS OF AUSTRIA, EMPRESS OF THE FRENCH AND DUCHESS OF PARMA. EDITH E. CUTHELL, F.R.H.S. Illustrated. Two vols., demy 8vo.

The Amazing Duchess: The Romantic History of Elizabeth Chudleigh, Maid of Honour—Duchess of Kingston—Countess of Bristol. CHARLES E. PEARCE. In two volumes, demy 8vo, cloth gilt, with numerous illustrations. Third Ed.

Intimate Memoirs of Napoleon III.: Personal Reminiscences of the Man and the Emperor by the late BARON D'AMBES; translated by A. R. Allinson. In two volumes, demy 8vo, fully illustrated.

Four Ennobled Actresses: The Adventures of the Duchess of Bolton, Countess of Derby, Countess of Essex, Countess of Harrington on and off the Stage, by CHARLES E. PEARCE. Two vols., demy 8vo, with two photogravure frontispieces and 32 half-tone illustrations.

21/- NET

Napoleon in Exile. Elba 1814-1815. By NORWOOD YOUNG, with a chapter on the Iconography of Napoleon and Elba by A. M. BROADLEY. Coloured frontispiece and about 50 illustrations from the collection of A. M. Broadley. Demy 8vo, cloth gilt. For further volumes on St. Helena, to complete the work, see under 32/- net.

18/- NET

Fourteen Years of Diplomatic Life in Japan. Stray leaves from the Diary of BARONESS ALBERT D'ANETHAN, with an introduction by His Excellency the Japanese Ambassador to the Court of St. James (Baron Kato), who was twice Minister of Foreign Affairs during Baron d'Anethan's term in Tokio. Illustrated with photogravure and half-tone illustrations printed on art paper.

16/- NET

A Woman of the Revolution: THÉROIGNE DE MERICOURT. FRANK HAMEL. Demy 8vo. With photogravure frontispiece, illustrated.

Princess and Queen: The Life and Times of Mary II. MARY F. SANDARS. Demy 8vo, illustrated.

Godoy, the Queen's Favourite. EDMUND B. D'AUVERGNE. Demy 8vo, illustrated.

The Life and Times of Rodrigo Borgia. Pope Alexander VI. By THE MOST REV. ARNOLD H. MATHEW, D.D. Very fully illustrated. Demy 8vo.

The Life of Cesare Borgia. RAFAEL SABATINI In demy 8vo, cloth gilt, with coloured frontispiece and other illustrations printed on art paper. Third edition.

Duchess Derelict: A Study of the Life and Times of Charlotte d'Albret, Duchess of Valentinois (the wife of Cesare Borgia). E. L. MIRON. Demy 8vo, fully illustrated.

The France of Joan of Arc. LIEUT.-COLONEL ANDREW C. P. HAGGARD, D.S.O. Demy 8vo, cloth gilt, with photogravure frontispiece and 16 illustrations on art paper.

34

In the Footsteps of Richard Cœur de Lion.
MAUD M. HOLBACH. In demy 8vo, fully illustrated.

The Royal Miracle : A Garland of unpublished or
very Rare Tracts, Broadsides, Letters, Prints and other Rariora
concerning the Wanderings of Charles II. after the Battle of
Worcester (September 3—October 15, 1651), with an Historical
Introduction and Bibliography, together with some account of the
Commemorative Pilgrimage of September 3—9, 1911. By A. M.
BROADLEY. Author of " Dr. Johnson and Mrs. Thrale," " Chats
on Autographs," " Napoleon in Caricature," etc. In demy 8vo,
cloth gilt, fully illustrated, with portraits, maps, etc., from rare
originals.

Jean de la Fontaine : The Poet and the Man.
FRANK HAMEL. In demy 8vo, cloth gilt, illustrated.

The Coburgs : The Story of the Rise of a great Royal
House. EDMUND B. D'AUVERGNE. Photogravure frontispiece and
other full-page illustrations on art paper. Demy 8vo, cloth gilt.

The Beloved Princess. Princess Charlotte of Wales.
By CHARLES E. PEARCE. Demy 8vo, cloth gilt, fully illustrated.

Famous Artists and their Models. ANGELO S.
RAPPOPORT, Ph.D. Demy 8vo, 32 full page illustrations.

12/6 NET

In Jesuit Land : The Jesuit Missions at Paraguay
W. H. KOEBEL. Demy 8vo, fully illustrated.

A Winter Holiday in Portugal. CAPTAIN GRAN-
VILLE BAKER. With coloured frontispiece and 32 original drawings
by the author. Demy 8vo, cloth gilt.

Spain Revisited : A Summer Holiday in Galicia.
C. GASQUOINE HARTLEY. In demy 8vo, cloth gilt. With coloured
frontispiece and numerous illustrations, printed on art paper.

In the Maoriland Bush. W. H. KOEBEL
Demy 8vo, fully illustrated.

Sicily in Shadow and in Sun. MAUD HOWE
With a map and 100 illustrations from photographs, and drawings
by John Elliott. Demy 8vo, cloth gilt.

The Gay King. Charles II., his Court and Times.
DOROTHY SENIOR. Demy 8vo, illustrated.

Every Man's El Dorado (British South America).
By EDITH A. BROWNE. Demy 8vo, illustrated.

Cameos of Indian Crime. Studies of native crimi-
nality in India. H. J. A. HERVEY (Indian Telegraphs, retired).
Demy 8vo, cloth gilt, illustrated.

The Artistic Side of Photography. In Theory and Practice. A. J. ANDERSON. With 12 photogravure plates and other illustrations. Demy 8vo.

The Amateur Photographer says:—" A most delightful book, full of pleasant reading and surprises. It is beautifully illustrated with many photogravure and half-tone reproductions of pictures by leading workers. Every amateur photographer with an interest in pictorial work should get it."

Police and Crime in India. SIR EDMUND C. COX, Bart. Demy 8vo, cloth gilt, illustrated.

" An interesting and timely book. . . . Sir Edmund Cox tells many remarkable stories, which will probably astound readers to whom the ways of the East are unknown."—*Times.*

" In perusing the many extraordinary details in which this book abounds, the reader feels as if he had opened the Arabian Nights of Criminality."—*Evening Standard.*

10/6 NET

Nineteenth Century English Engravings. W. G. MENZIES. About 96 full pages of half-tone illustrations.

Nineteenth Century English Ceramic Art. J. F. BLACKER. ' With 1,200 illustrations.

A Tour through South America. A. S. FORREST Demy 8vo, cloth gilt, profusely illustrated.

David Garrick and his French Friends. Dr. F. A. HEDGCOCK. Demy 8vo, cloth gilt, fully illustrated.

The Motor. A complete work on the History, Construction, and Development of the Motor. JOHN ARMSTRONG. Illustrated by 100 drawings and photographs.

The Romance of Sandro Botticelli. A. J. ANDERSON Demy 8vo, cloth gilt, with photogravure frontispiece and 16 full-page illustrations on art paper.

The Life of James Hinton. MRS. HAVELOCK ELLIS Illustrated.

A Great Russian Realist : (Dostoieffsky.) J. A. T. LLOYD. Demy 8vo, cloth gilt and gilt top, with illustrations.

In the Land of the Pharaohs : A Short History of Egypt from the fall of Ismael to the Assassination of Boutros Pasha. DUSE MOHAMED. Demy 8vo, illustrated.

The Argentine Republic. Its History, Physical Features, Natural History, Government, Productions, etc. A. STUART PENNINGTON. Demy 8vo, cloth gilt, illustrated.

Two Russian Reformers (IVAN TURGENEV AND LEO TOLSTOY). J. A. T. LLOYD. Demy 8vo, cloth gilt, illustrated.

The Romance of Fra Filippo Lippi. A. J. ANDERSON. Second Edition. With a photogravure frontispiece and 16 full-page illustrations, on art paper, demy 8vo.

Our Future Existence; or, The Death Surviving Consciousness of Man. By FRED G. SHAW, F.G.S. Large crown 8vo, cloth, gilt edges.

Ancient, Curious, and Famous Wills. By VIRGIL M. HARRIS. Demy 8vo.

The First Signs of Insanity. Their Prevention and Treatment. By BERNARD HOLLANDER, M.D. Demy 8vo.

7/6 NET

An Actor's Note Books. Being a record of some Memories, Friendships, Criticisms and experiences of FRANK ARCHER. Demy 8vo, 32 half-tone illustrations.

Home Life under the Stuarts, 1603-1649. ELIZABETH GODFREY. 19 photogravure and half-tone illustrations. Demy 8vo.

The Quantities of a Detached Residence; TAKEN-OFF, MEASURED AND BILLED. With drawings to scale in pocket of cover. By GEORGE STEPHENSON. Demy 8vo, cloth gilt.

"We can honestly and heartily recommend it."—*Building News.*

"The student who conscientiously follows this work through will have a thorough grounding in the art of quantity surveying which subsequent practice with other examples will soon develop."—*Surveyor.*

Wall Paper Decoration. By ARTHUR SEYMOUR JENNINGS.

STANLEY PAUL'S 6/- NOVELS

Cantacute Towers.	CECIL ADAIR
Francesca.	CECIL ADAIR
The Qualities of Mercy.	CECIL ADAIR
A Man with a Past.	A. ST. JOHN ADCOCK
Cheerful Craft.	R. ANDOM
Neighbours of Mine 60 Illustrations.	R. ANDOM
A Week at the Sea.	HAROLD AVERY
Every Dog His Day	HAROLD AVERY
The Activities of Lavie Jutt.	MARGUERITE and ARMIGER BARCLAY
The Baron of Ill Fame.	HESTER BARTON
The Children of Alsace.	RENÉ BAZIN
The Redeemer.	RENÉ BAZIN
His Will and Her Way.	H. LOUISA BEDFORD
Maids in Many Moods.	H. LOUISA BEDFORD
Dagobert's Children.	J. L. BEESTON
The Watch Night.	HENRY BETT
Loves Old Sweet Song.	CLIFTON BINGHAM
Lonesome Land.	B. M. BOWER
Between Two Stools.	RHODA BROUGHTON
The New Wood Nymph.	DOROTHEA BUSSELL
The Retrospect.	ADA CAMBRIDGE
A Durbar Bride.	CHARLOTTE CAMERON
A Passion in Morocco.	CHARLOTTE CAMERON
Suffragette Sally.	G. COLMORE
Because of a Kiss.	LADY CONSTANCE
The Broken Butterfly.	RALPH DEAKIN

Stanley Paul's Six Shilling Novels—continued.

A Mysterious Lover.	ALICE M. DIEHL
Confessions of Perpetua.	ALICE M. DIEHL
The Marriage of Lenore.	ALICE M. DIEHL
Their Wedded Wife.	ALICE M. DIEHL
The Justice of the King.	HAMILTON DRUMMOND
The Three Envelopes.	HAMILTON DRUMMOND
Married when Suited.	MRS. HENRY DUDENEY
The Consort.	MRS. EVERARD COTES (SARA JEANNETTE DUNCAN)
The Imperishable Wing.	MRS. HAVELOCK ELLIS
The Promoter's Pilgrimage.	C. REGINALD ENOCK, F.R.G.S.
The Third Wife.	HERBERT FLOWERDEW
The Villa Mystery.	HERBERT FLOWERDEW
The She-Wolf.	MAXIME FORMONT
Exotic Martha.	DOROTHEA GERARD
The City of Enticement	DOROTHEA GERARD
Damosel Croft.	R. MURRAY GILCHRIST
The Marble Aphrodite.	ANTHONY KIRBY GILL
Madge Carrington and her Welsh Neighbours.	"DRAIG GLAS"
Clive Lorimer's Marriage.	E. EVERETT-GREEN
Duckworth's Diamonds.	E. EVERETT-GREEN
Galbraith of Wynyates.	E. EVERETT-GREEN
The Romance of Bayard.	LIEUT.-COL. ANDREW C. P. HAGGARD
Two Worlds: A Romance.	LIEUT.-COL. ANDREW C. P. HAGGARD
The Return of Pierre.	DONAL HAMILTON HAINES
A Lady of the Garter.	FRANK HAMEL
God Disposes.	PELLEW HAWKER
The Thread of Proof.	HEADON HILL
The Bride of Love.	KATE HORN
The Lovelocks of Diana.	KATE HORN
The Mulberries of Daphne.	KATE HORN
The White Owl.	KATE HORN
Susan and the Duke.	KATE HORN
Swelling of Jordan.	CORALIE STANTON AND HEATH HOSKEN
The Muzzled Ox.	CORALIE STANTON AND HEATH HOSKEN
The Celebrity's Daughter.	VIOLET HUNT
The Doll.	VIOLET HUNT
Her Majesty the Flapper.	A. E. JAMES
A Robin Hood of France.	MICHAEL W. KAYE
Captain Hawks, Master Mariner.	OSWALD KENDALL
The Poodle-Woman.	ANNESLEY KENEALY
The Irresistible Mrs. Ferrers.	ARABELLA KENEALY
The Woman-Hunter.	ARABELLA KENEALY
Hodson's Voyage.	W. H. KOEBEL
Veeni the Master.	R. FIFIELD LAMPORT
The Three Destinies.	J. A. T. LLOYD
The Second Woman.	NORMA LORIMER
The Ban.	LESTER LURGAN
Paul Burdon.	SIR WILLIAM MAGNAY, BART.
The Fruits of Indiscretion.	SIR WILLIAM MAGNAY, BART.
The Long Hand.	SIR WILLIAM MAGNAY, BART.
The Meteoric Benson.	VINCENT MILLS-MALET
The Mystery of Redmarsh Farm.	ARCHIBALD H. MARSHALL
The Love's of Stella.	MRS. SHIERS-MASON
Brass Faces.	CHARLES McEVOY
Love's Cross Roads.	L. T. MEADE
Ruffles.	L. T. MEADE
When we are Rich.	WARD MUIR
The Amazing Mutes.	WARD MUIR
Fear.	E. NESBIT
A Star of the East: A Story of Delhi.	CHARLES E. PEARCE
Red Revenge: A Story of Cawnpore.	CHARLES E. PEARCE
The Three Anarchists.	MAUD STEPNEY RAWSON
A Woman with a Purpose.	ANNA CHAPIN RAY
A Grey Life.	"RITA"
The Justice of the Duke.	RAFAEL SABATINI
The Desire of Life	MATILDE SERAO

The Incorrigible Dukane.	GEORGE C. SHEDD
Two Girls and a Mannikin.	WILKINSON SHERREN
Opal of October.	JOY SHIRLEY
The Unholy Estate.	DOUGLAS SLADEN
Bright Shame.	KEIGHLEY SNOWDEN
The Free Marriage.	KEIGHLEY SNOWDEN
Love in Armour.	PHILIP L. STEVENSON
Across the Gulf.	NEWTON V. STEWART
The Cardinal.	NEWTON V. STEWART
The Ascent of the Bostocks.	HAROLD STOREY
The King's Master.	OLIVE LETHBRIDGE and JOHN DE STOURTON
The Unseen Hand.	G. VILLIERS STUART
Prince and Priest.	BERYL SYMONS
The Lotus Lantern.	MARY IMLAY TAYLOR
Our Guests.	ST. JOHN TREVOR
A Prisoner in Paradise.	H. L. VAHEY
Camilla Forgetting Herself.	H. L. VAHEY
Where Truth Lies.	JANE WARDLE
An Empress in Love.	FRED WHISHAW
A Modern Ahab.	THEODORA WILSON WILSON
Maggie of Margate.	GABRIELLE WODNIL
The Destiny of Claude.	MAY WYNNE
The Red Fleur De Lys.	MAY WYNNE

6/- NET

A Tour through Old Provence. A. S. FORREST
Large Crown 8vo, profusely illustrated, cloth gilt.

A Motor Tour through England and France.
ELIZABETH YARDLEY. Crown 8vo, illustrated.

Guerilla Leaders of the World. By PERCY CROSS
STANDING. With a preface by the Earl of Dundonald. Crown 8vo, illustrated.

Old Clifford's Inn. PERCIVAL J. S. PERCEVAL
A history of the earliest of the old Inns at Chancery. Illustrated with nearly 50 drawings by the author. Large crown 8vo, cloth gilt.

Our Fighting Sea Men. LIONEL YEXLEY
Large crown 8vo, cloth.

A Woman's Winter in South America.
CHARLOTTE CAMERON. Crown 8vo, illustrated.

Joy of Tyrol. Edited by J. M. BLAKE
Illustrated with over 100 original drawings in the text by the Author. In crown 8vo, cloth gilt.
"The book is a triumph."—*Evening Standard.*

The Physiology of Faith and Fear ; or, the Mind
in Health and Disease. By WILLIAM S. SADLER, M.D.

The Ridge of the White Waters. Impressions of
a visit to Johannesburg, with some notes on Durban, Delagoa Bay, and the Low Country. By WILLIAM C. SCULLY. Illustrated, Crown 8vo.

The Retrospect.   ADA CAMBRIDGE
Crown 8vo, cloth gilt.

Woman Adrift. The Menace of Suffragism. HAROLD
OWEN. Crown 8vo. Second edition.

The Sweep of the Sword. From Marathon to Mafe-
king (A Complete Battle Book). ALFRED H. MILES. Dedicated
by special permission to Field-Marshal Earl Roberts, V.C. In
large crown 8vo. (over 600 pages), with a photogravure frontispiece,
16 full-page illustrations of world-famous battle pictu.es, printed
on art paper, and nearly 150 illustrations in the text, handsomely
bound in cloth gilt, with special design.

Our National Songs.   ALFRED H. MILES
With Pianoforte Accompaniments. Full music Size. Cloth, gilt
edges.

5/- NET

The White Slave Market. By MRS. ARCHIBALD
MACKIRDY (Olive Christian Malvery). Author of "The Soul
Market," etc. And W. N. Willis, 16 years Member of Parliament
of Australia. Crown 8vo, cloth.

French Music in the Nineteenth Century.
ARTHUR HERVEY. Crown 8vo, with Portraits.

Sea and Coast Fishing (with special reference to
Calm Water Fishing in Inlets and Estuaries. F. G. AFLALO.
With over 50 illustrations, from drawings and photographs, printed
throughout on art paper. Crown 8vo.

Diners à Deux.   S. BEACH CHESTER
Crown 8vo.

Love Letters of a Japanese. Being the corre-
spondence of a Japanese man with his English betrothed. G. N.
MORTLAKE. Second ed., with an Introduction by Dr. MARIE
C. STOPES. Large crown 8vo, white cloth gilt, chaste design.

The History of Garrards, Crown Jewellers, 1721—
1911. Printed throughout on art paper, in two colours, with
nearly 40 whole-page illustrations. Cr. 8vo, cloth gilt.

The A B C about Collecting (second edition). SIR
JAMES YOXALL, M.P. Large cr. 8vo, profusely illustrated with
numerous line and 32 pages of half-tone illustrations. The subjects
include, among others, China, Clocks, Prints, Books, Pictures,
Furniture and Violins.

A B C of Collecting Old English China. J. F.
BLACKER. Large cr. 8vo, profusely illustrated with numerous line
and 64 pages of half-tone illustrations, printed on art paper.

The A B C of Japanese Art.   J. F. BLACKER
Profusely illustrated with 150 line and 100 half-tone illustrations, printed on art paper. In large crown 8vo.

A B C of Collecting Old English Pottery.   J. F. BLACKER. Large cr. 8vo, illustrated with about 400 line and 32 pages of half-tone illustrations.

The A B C of Collecting Old Continental Pottery. J. F. BLACKER. Large cr. 8vo, fully illustrated with line and half-tone illustrations.

The Production of the Printed Catalogue. The Preparation, Printing, and Publication of Catalogues of Libraries, Museums, Art Galleries, Publishers, Booksellers and Business Houses, with a Chapter on the Monotype Machine, and an Appendix of Type Faces, by ALEX. J. PHILIP. Cr. 8vo, illustrated.

A B C Guide to Mythology.   HELEN A. CLARKE
5s. net.

A B C Guide to Music.   DANIEL GREGORY MASON
5s. net.

A B C Guide to Pictures.   CHARLES H. CAFFIN
5s. net.

A B C Guide to United States History. HENRY W. ELSON. 5s. net.

Standard Concert Repertory, and other Concert Pieces. GEORGE P. UPTON. Fully illustrated with portraits. In cr. 8vo, cloth gilt.

Anomalies of the English Law. "The Law in the Dock." S. BEACH CHESTER. Crown 8vo, cloth.

5/-

ALFRED H. MILES' NEW SERIES

For Boys and Girls. Large crown 8vo, 384 pages, fully illustrated.

In the Lion's Mouth. Fierce Fights with Wild Men, Wild Animals, and Wild Nature. By THEODORE ROOSEVELT, CLIVE FENN, etc. With coloured plates. A Book for Boys.

Where Duty Calls; or Danger Stories of courage and adventure. By EVELYN EVERETT-GREEN, GRACE STEBBING, etc. With coloured plates. A Book for Girls.

'Twixt Life and Death on Sea and Shore. A Book for Boys.

Heroines of the Home and the World of Duty. A Book for Girls.

A Book of Brave Boys All the World Over.

A Book of Brave Girls At Home and Abroad.

In the Teeth of Adventure Up and Down the World.

The Case for Protection. ERNEST EDWIN WILLIAMS, F.R.S.S. Large cr. 8vo.

The Boy's Book of Sports, Pastimes, Hobbies and Amusements. E. KEBLE CHATTERTON. Cloth gilt.

The Library of Elocution. Edited by ALFRED H. MILES.

4/- NET

Coloured Designs for Wall and Ceiling Decoration. Edited by ARTHUR SEYMOUR JENNINGS. Port folio.

3/6 NET

Woman in Music. GEORGE P. UPTON With an Appendix and Index. In small crown 8vo, cloth gilt, 3s. 6d. net. Persian yapp, gilt (boxed), 5s. net.

The Practical Art of Graining and Marbling. JAMES PETRIE. In 14 parts, 3s. 6d. net each.

The Human Machine. An Inquiry into the Diversity of Human Faculty in its Bearings upon Social Life, Religion, Education, and Politics. J. F. NISBET. Fifth and new edition. Crown 8vo.

Original Poems. By ALFRED H. MILES. Crown 8vo, cloth gilt, with photogravure portrait frontispiece.

"The poems cover a wide range of thought and emotion. Many of the lyrics are full of tenderness and charm. The ballads have colour, warmth and movement, and at times a touch of that fine enthusiasm that stirs the blood like the sound of a trumpet. Mr. Miles is a poet of the people."—*The Bookman.*

The Aldine Reciter. Modern Poetry for the Platform, the Home, and the School. *With Hints on Public Speaking, Elocution, Action, Articulation, Pitch, Modulation, etc.* By ALFRED H. MILES. Crown 4to, 676 pages, cloth gilt.

Three Modern Seers (JAMES HINTON, F. NIETZSCHE AND EDWARD CARPENTER). MRS. HAVELOCK ELLIS. Illustrated with 4 photogravure plates, crown 8vo, cloth gilt.

3/- NET

Practical Gilding, Bronzing and Lacquering. FREDK. SCOTT-MITCHELL. 175 pages, crown 8vo.

Practical Stencil Work. FREDK. SCOTT-MITCHELL

Practical Church Decoration. ARTHUR LOUIS
DUTHIE. 176 pages, crown 8vo.

Decorators' Symbols, Emblems and Devices.
GUY CADOGAN ROTHERY! 119 original designs, crown 8vo.

The Painters' and Builders' Pocket Book. (New
Edition.) PETER-MATTHEWS.

Scumbling and Colour Glazing.

2/6 NET

Marriage Making and Breaking. CHARLES TIBBITS
With Foreword by A. C. Plowden, Esq., Chief Magistrate at
Marylebone Police Court. In cr. 8vo, cloth.

The Beau. Illustrated with photogravures and line drawings. Nos. 1 and 2 now ready. 2/6 net each.

The Welshman's Reputation. "AN ENGLISHMAN"
In crown 8vo, cloth.

A Garland of Verse for Young People. Edited
by ALFRED H. MILES. Handsome cloth gilt. ;

The Lord of Creation. T. W. H. CROSLAND

The Egregious English. ANGUS McNEILL
Crown 8vo.

Monte Carlo. Facts and Fallacies. SIR HIRAM S.
MAXIM. With illustrations by George A. Stevens. Crown 8vo.

The Flowing Bowl. A Treatise on Drinks of all
kinds and of all periods, interspersed with sundry anecdotes and
reminiscences. EDWARD SPENCER ('Nathaniel Gubbins'). Crown
8vo.

Cakes and Ales. A memory of many meals, the whole
interspersed with various Recipes, more or less original, the Anecdotes, mainly veracious. EDWARD SPENCER ('Nathaniel Gubbins').
Crown 8vo, 4th edition.

Pluto and Proserpine. A Poem. JOHN SUMMERS.
In crown 8vo.

This is my Birthday. ANITA BARTLE. With an
introduction by ISRAEL ZANGWILL. Handsomely bound, gilt and
gilt top, 756 pages, 2s. 6d. net.; paste grain, limp, gilt edges (boxed),
3s. net: paste grain, padded, gilt edges (boxed), 4s. net; velvet
calf, gilt edges (boxed), 5s. net.
A unique birthday-book containing beautiful and characteristic
quotations from the greatest poets, artists, philosophers, statesmen,
warriors, and novelists.

43

Cole's Fun Doctor. First Series. The funniest book in the world. E. W. COLE. 384 pp.; crown 8vo, cloth, 2s. 6d.

Cole's Fun Doctor. Second Series. The funniest book in the world. E. W. COLE. 440 pp , crown 8vo, cloth, 2s. 6d.

A White Australia Impossible. E. W. COLE
Crown 8vo, cloth.

Truth. E. W. COLE
Cloth gilt, crown 8vo.

2/- NET

Cole's Intellect Sharpener. E. W. COLE
Demy 4to, with numerous illustrations.
Containing 2,000 Riddles, and 500 Puzzles and Games.

Federation of the Whole World. Edited by E. W. COLE.
Being fifty prize essays for and against the Federation of the World, illustrated with representive portraits of all nations. Crown 8vo, cloth.

This Funny World. F. RAYMOND COULSON (DEMOCRITUS). Author of "A Jester's Jingles." Crown 8vo, cloth gilt.

A Book of Short Plays. MRS. DE COURCY LAFFAN. Crown 8vo.

Zinc Oxide and its uses. J. CRUICKSHANK SMITH, B.Sc., F.C.S., with a chapter by DR. A. P. LAURIE.

Phases, Mazes and Crazes of Love. Compiled by MINNA T. ANTRIM, with coloured illustrations on each page. 18mo.

Your Health! IDELLE PHELPS. A book of toasts, aphorisms and rhymes. With coloured illustrations by H. A. KNIPE. 18mo.

Home Occupations for Boys and Girls. BERTHA JOHNSTON Small 8vo, cloth.

How to Train Children. EMMA CHURCHMAN HEWITT. Small 8vo, cloth.

"RITA'S" NOVELS. 2/- NET EACH.
Uniform Revised Edition in Cr. 8vo, cloth, coloured wrapper.

The Countess Daphne.	My Lord Conceit.
Corinna.	The Man in Possession.
Asenath of the Ford.	Faustine.
Edelweiss.	The Laird of Cockpen.

"Rita" has a gift for portraying the emotions of the heart which few modern writers have equalled, and this new revised edition of her stories should meet with wide acceptance.

2/-

Sugar Round the Pill. E. W. COLE
A cyclopedia of Fib, Fact and Fiction, containing some 1,500 items of amusing and ingenious Falsehood and Fact, and 1,250 items of Fun. In crown 8vo, cloth.

STANLEY PAUL'S 2/- (net) NOVELS

Cr. 8vo, cloth, pictorial wrapper, 2s. net each.

The Bungalow under the Lake (2nd edition). CHARLES E. PEARCE

Clive Lorimer's Marriage (2nd edition). E. EVERETT-GREEN

Pretty Barbara (2nd edition). ANTHONY DYLLINGTON

Impertinent Reflections (5th edition). COSMO HAMILTON

Lying Lips (2nd edition). WILLIAM LE QUEUX

The Riding Master (6th edition). DOLF WYLLARDE

In Fear of a Throne (2nd edition). 50 illustrations. R. ANDOM

The Lion's Skin (2nd edition). RAFAEL SABATINI

Young Nick and Old Nick (2nd edition). S. R. CROCKETT

Love, the Thief (5th edition). HELEN MATHERS

Tropical Tales (7th edition). DOLF WYLLARDE

The Cheerful Knave (4th edition). E. KEBLE HOWARD

The Trickster (3rd edition). G. B. BURGIN

Love Besieged (3rd edition). CHARLES E. PEARCE

The Artistic Temperament (3rd edition). JANE WARDLE

1/6. NET

The Diners-Out Vade Mecum. A pocket "Who's Who" on the manners and customs of Society Functions, Toasts and Sentiments, Indoor Amusements, etc. ALFRED H. MILES. In fcap. 8vo (6⅛ × 3⅛), cloth bound, round corners, 1s. 6d. net. Leather, 2s. net.

Verses. DOLF WYLLARDE
With Photogravure Frontispiece. Paper, 1s. 6d. net. Cloth, 2s. 6d. net.

STANLEY PAUL'S 1/- (net) NOVELS

Stiff pictorial board covers, **1s. net**; cloth, **2s. net.**

22 **The Garden of Life.** 2nd Edition. KATE HORN

23 **No. 5, John Street.** 19th Edition. RICHARD WHITEING

24 **Dr. Phillips:** A Maida-Vale Idyll. FRANK DANBY

27 **Tropical Tales.** 7th Edition. DOLF WYLLARDE

1 **The Widow**—to say Nothing of the Man. HELEN ROWLAND

2 **Thoroughbred.** FRANCIS DODSWORTH

45

3 **The Spell of the Jungle.**   ALICE PERRIN
4 **The Sins of Society** (Drury Lane Novels).   CECIL RALEIGH
5 **The Marriages of Mayfair** (ditto).   E. KEBLE CHATTERTON
6 **A Ten Pound Penalty.**   H. NOEL WILLIAMS
7 **Priests of Progress.**   G. COLMORE
8 **Gay Lawless.**   HELEN MATHERS
9 **A Professional Rider.**   Mrs. EDWARD KENNARD
10 **The Devil in London.**   GEO. R. SIMS
13 **Fatal Thirteen.**   WILLIAM LE QUEUX
14 **Brother Rogue and Brother Saint.**   TOM GALLON
15 **The Death Gamble.**   GEO. R. SIMS
16 **The Mystery of Roger Bullock.**   TOM GALLON.
17 **Bardelys, the Magnificent.**   RAFAEL SABATINI
19 **The Cabinet Minister's Wife.**   GEO. R. SIMS
20 **The Dream—and the Woman.**   TOM GALLON
21 **The Ghost Pirates.**   W. HOPE HODGSON

THE SATIRICAL SERIES, 1/- NET

25 **The Perfidious Welshman.**   "DRAIG GLAS"
   10th Edition. Containing a reply to his Critics.
26 **America—Through English Eyes.** 2nd Edition.   "RITA"
11 **The Unspeakable Scot.**   T. W. H. CROSLAND
12 **Lovely Woman.**   T. W. H. CROSLAND
18 **Billicks.**   A. ST. JOHN ADCOCK

1/- NET

Arnold's Handbook of House Painting, Decorating, Varnishing, Graining, etc.   HERBERT ARNOLD

Paul's 'Simplicode.' M. LEVY. Crown 8vo.

The Everyday Pudding Book. F. K. A tasty recipe for every day in the year. Crown 8vo, strongly bound.

Everyday Savouries : A Savoury for every day in the year. By MARIE WORTH. Crown 8vo, strongly bound.

Drawing Room Entertainments. New and Original Monologues, Duologues, Dialogues and Playlets for Home and Platform use. Edited by ALFRED H. MILES. In crown 8vo, red limp, 1s. net; cloth gilt, 1s. 6d. net; paste grain, gilt, 3s. net; Persian yapp, gilt, 4s. net.

Ballads of Brave Women. Crown 8vo, red limp, 1s. net; cloth gilt, 1s. 6d. net; paste grain, gilt, 3s. net; Persian yapp, gilt top, 4s. net.

The Shilling Music Series. Edited by ALFRED H. MILES. Each with Pianoforte Accompaniments. Full Music size. 1s. net each.

1 FORTY ENGLISH SONGS	5 FAVOURITE SONGS FOR THE CONTRALTO VOICE
2 FIFTY SCOTCH SONGS	
3 THIRTY-SIX ENGLISH SONGS AND BALLADS	6 SONGS OF THE QUEEN'S NAVEE
4 FIFTY IRISH AND WELSH SONGS	7 FAVOURITE SONGS FOR THE TENOR VOICE

Canada To-day, 1912. Its Progress, Prosperity and Opportunities. 300 illustrations, Maps and Plans, 240 pp. (13½×9½), 1s. net; or half-bound stiff boards, 2s. net.

Divorce in its Ecclesiastical Aspect. Being a rejoinder by 'Viator' to "The Question of Divorce" by the Bishop of Birmingham. Crown 8vo, cloth, 1s. net.

Sidelights on the Court of France. By LIEUT.-COL. ANDREW C. P. HAGGARD, D.S.O. Cloth.

6D. NET

The Librarian and Book World. The Independent Professional Journal for the Professional Man. Published Monthly, 6d. net.

Ideal Cookery. (10th Edition.) LILIAN CLARKE. 8vo, boards, 6d. net.

Punctuation Simplified. (*22nd Thousand.*) T. BRIDGES. Medium 8vo, 6d. net.

The Burden of 1909. ELDON LEE. In crown 8vo, paper cover, 6d. net.

The Coming Dominion of Rome in Britain. By the author of 'The Great Pyramid.' Crown 8vo, paper, 6d. net.

The Aldine Reciters. Edited by ALFRED H. MILES. In crown 4to, double columns, 128 pages. Price 6d. net each.

THE ENGLISH RECITER	THE SCOTCH RECITER
THE AMERICAN RECITER	THE MODERN RECITER
THE VICTORIAN RECITER	THE SHAKESPEARE RECITER

The New Reciter Series. By various Authors. Edited by ALFRED H. MILES. 96 pages, large 4to, double columns, clear type on good paper, handsome cover design in three colours, 6d. net. (Also in cloth, 1s. net.)

THE FIRST FAVOURITE RECITER | THE UP-TO-DATE RECITER

6D.

The A1 Reciter Series. (Over half-a-million copies already sold.) By various Authors. Edited by ALFRED H. MILES. Each in large folio, paper cover, well printed. Price 6d. each.

1	THE A1 RECITER	4	THE A1 ELOCUTIONIST
2	THE A1 SPEAKER	5	THE A1 READER
3	THE A1 BOOK OF RECITATIONS	6	THE A1 BOOK OF READINGS

3d. NET

The Budget and Socialism of Mr. Lloyd George. J. BUCKINGHAM POPE. In crown 8vo, paper, 3d. net.

French Gardening without Capital. E. KENNEDY ANTON. In medium 8vo, paper, 3d. net; cloth, 9d. net.

1D.

The Commentator. The real Conservative weekly. One Penny. Weekly.

STANLEY PAUL'S "CLEAR TYPE" SIXPENNY NOVELS

NEW TITLES.

Lightning Source UK Ltd.
Milton Keynes UK
UKHW02f2219060918
328454UK00016B/1115/P